廣州美術館藏明清繪畫

Paintings of the Ming and Qing Dynasties from the Guangzhou Art Gallery

廣州美術館・香港中文大學文物館聯合主辦

Jointly presented by the Guangzhou Art Gallery
& the Art Gallery, The Chinese University of Hong Kong

香港中文大學・中國文化研究所・文物館
一九八六年十月十八日至十二月十四日
18th October to 14th December, 1986
The Art Gallery, Institute of Chinese Studies
The Chinese University of Hong Kong

鳴　謝

本展覽專刊承　偉倫基金會有限公司及北山堂基金有限公司贊助印刷經費，謹此致謝。

Acknowledgement

The publication of the exhibition catalogue is made possibile by grants from the Wideland Foundation Limited and the Bei Shan Tang Foundation Limited.

編　輯：高美慶
展品著錄：謝文勇　李航勝　李煥眞
攝　影：葉立中　關子鴻
設　計：麥耀翔　陳國强
翻　譯：黎淑儀　黃莎莉　林漢堅
資料搜集：黎淑儀　黃莎莉　余雪霞　林漢堅

Editor: Mayching Kao
Original entries: Xie Wenyong, Li Hangsheng, Li Huanzhen
Photography: Sidney Yip, Kwan Tze Hung
Design: Philip Mak, Bruce Chan
Translation: Lai Suk Yee, Wong Sar Li, Lam Hon Kin
Research: Lai Suk Yee, Wong Sar Li, Yu Suet Har, Lam Hon Kin

目　錄

Contents

前　言

廣州美術館成立於一九五七年春，由當時的廣州市朱光市長倡議創辦的。館址設在越秀山五層樓東側，是以徵集、收藏、陳列、研究古今中外美術作品爲主要任務的博物館。

廣州美術館建館以來除努力蒐集有關文物外，還蒙各界熱心人士大力支持，葉恭綽先生、蔣光鼐先生、容庚教授、楊銓先生等都曾給本館捐獻珍貴名蹟。藏品中有宋代文同《墨竹圖》、元代李衎《紆竹圖》、黃子久《山水軸》、明代沈周的《吳門十二景册》、林良的《秋樹聚禽圖》、仇英的《停琴聽阮圖》等等，特別是明清以來廣東畫家的作品和當代廣東畫家的作品尤爲我館收藏的重點。建館以來，已出版的藏畫集有《石濤山水册》、《八大山人戲墨册》、《沈周吳門十二景册》、《居廉花卉草蟲册》、《居巢扇面選集》、《廣州美術館藏畫選集》一、二集。此外還經常提供藏畫給有關刋物刋登。

通過藏品展覽以豐富羣衆的文化生活，同時給美術家和學者提供借鑑和研究的方便，建館以來曾陸續舉辦綜合性的藏畫展覽和專題性的展覽，如清代揚州畫派展覽、明清扇面展覽、歷代畫竹展覽、明清人物畫展覽、居巢居廉畫展、嶺南畫派展覽以及當代畫家畫展等等，還結合知名人士對我館贈畫舉辦有關捐獻書畫展覽。爲了加强與各地兄弟館的藏畫交流，先後多次與故宮博物院、上海博物館、吉林省博物館、徐悲鴻紀念館、香港中文大學文物館等合辦藏畫交流展出，1982年我館嶺南畫派部分藏畫前往日本展出，很受歡迎。

現值建館三十周年之際，蒙香港中文大學文物館舉辦《廣州美術館藏明清繪畫展覽》，並編印展品圖錄，供各界喜愛我國繪畫的人士觀賞，及美術界研究參考。圖錄資料拍攝、整理、編輯及英譯工作，除本館有關業務人員參與外，大量工作得香港中文大學文物館高美慶館長和林業强副館長及中文大學文物館同寅共同協力完成，謹此致以衷心感謝，並祝展覽成功。

黃　鶯
廣州美術館館長

前　言

廣州美術館爲紀念建館三十五周年慶典，與香港中文大學文物館合辦《廣州美術館藏明清繪畫》展覽。此次展覽乃廣州美術館與本館繼《明清廣東書法》展覽及《明清廣東繪畫》展覽的成功基礎上的第三次合作。於此謹祝該館業務蒸蒸日上，百尺竿頭更進一步。感謝該館多年來對本館的支持指導，並爲未來穗港兩地文物機構的緊密合作，致以深切的期望。

中國繪畫在明清兩代彬彬大盛，書畫名家巨子的活動中心，雖以江南及中原爲主，而流風所披，廣州以位居南疆要津的優越條件，加以粵人乘遊宦經商之便多方搜求，寖寖然成爲北方書畫名蹟薈萃之區。有清中葉以後，尤其盛極一時。舉其要者，如吳榮光的筠清館、潘正煒的聽颿樓、孔廣陶的嶽雪樓、以至近現代辛耀文、何荔甫、容庚諸氏所藏，都卓然名世。這些私人收藏雖然各擅勝場，然而各守其珍，世人難得一睹。直至現代博物館的出現，致力於文物的廣納精研，公開陳列，然後千百年來之秘寶乃得成爲天下之公物。廣州美術館在匯集舊藏的基礎上更廣收現代名家作品，乃成爲既具歷史傳統亦富地域特色的一方重鎮。

此次展覽定名爲《廣州美術館藏明清繪畫》展覽，要求在展覽場地所限的九十九種卷、軸、册頁之中，全面展示明清兩代五百餘年間的繪畫歷史，是近乎不可能的事。然而觀者可以發現，廣州美術館充分結合其館藏特色，在數以千計的畫作中選出一百零二家，尤其是取其大而不遺其小地展示了兩代畫壇的廣度和百花競放的繽紛盛貌。明初畫壇浙、吳二派雙峯並峙，而吳派則在明代中葉因沈周、文徵明的崛興而獨擅，奠定文人畫風的主流。展品取捨亦以吳派爲重，包括沈周、文徵明及其後繼者如謝時臣、王穀祥、文伯仁、陳淳、陳栝父子。而於浙派則以一山水長卷爲代表。晚明畫壇重鎭由蘇州東移松江，展品包括一代宗師董其昌與其所統攝的華亭派顧正誼、蘇松派趙左與及雲間派沈士充。亦有異軍突起的藍瑛及陳洪綬等人的作品。

至於明末清初，畫壇百彩紛呈，有獨具個性、追求氣韻意趣的明遺民如“四僧”等人，亦有上承玄宰家風、講究端嚴典雅、筆精墨妙的“清初四王”及其後繼者。此外尚有以龔賢爲首的“金陵畫派”及由弘仁代表的“新安畫派”，可謂極一時之盛。及至清代中葉，“揚州八家”遠祧石濤，再放異彩，流風餘韻，及於清末海上名家。此次展出的明清作品，於大家不求其全備，而特宜注意者，一則在兼顧各個發展時期的支流餘裔，例如“四王”的正宗派傳人延續至晚清的戴熙及張之萬，而淮揚畫家則兼及顧符稹、王雲、顏嶧、蔡嘉等，均足以充實我等對正宗派以至淮揚畫壇的認識。二則在展示廣東地方畫家的特色，展出張穆、黎簡、謝蘭生、蘇六朋及蘇仁山的作品。以一館所藏，巨細兼包地顯示明清繪畫的精要，必能擴展觀者的視野。

此次展覽的籌辦，荷蒙中國文化部文物局、廣東省文化廳及廣州市文化局的鼎力支持，廣州美術館黃鶯館長及謝文勇副館長領導該館專家挑選展品及撰寫展品著錄。並蒙謝文勇副館長惠撰專文，介紹重點展品。而本館同寅則負責拍攝展品、設計展場及展覽專刊的編印與英譯工作。此外，荷蒙新華社香港分社惠助聯絡，本校馬臨校長、中國文化研究所前任所長鄭德坤教授及現任所長陳方正博士多方賜教，饒宗頤教授及李潤桓先生指導工作，夏羅莎女士協助修訂英譯。展覽專刊印刷經費承偉倫基金會及北山堂基金惠贈，並此謹致謝忱。

高美慶
香港中文大學文物館館長

Foreword

The Guangzhou Art Gallery was established in the spring of 1957 at the suggestion of Mr. Zhu Guang, the then mayor of Guangzhou. It is located to the east of the five-storey Zhenhai Tower on Yuexiu Hill. The Gallery's main objectives are to collect and store ancient and modern works of art from China and abroad, while serving as a centre for their display and research.

Since its inauguration, the Guangzhou Art Gallery has made strong efforts to build up its permanent collection, enjoying substantial support from the community. The generous donations from Mr. Ye Gongchuo, Mr. Jiang Guangnai, Mr. Yang Quan and Professor Rong Geng have enriched our collection significantly. Some of the more important items in the Gallery include two bamboo paintings by Wen Tong of the Song dynasty and Li Kan of the Yuan dynasty. Landscape of the Yuan dynasty is represented by Huang Gongwang and that of the Ming is seen in an album of twelve views of Suzhou by Shen Zhou and *Listening to Music by the Waterfall* painted by Qiu Ying. The Gallery places special emphasis on works by Guangdong painters dating from the Ming dynasty to the present day, of which *Birds Gathering on Autumnal Trees* is an outstanding example. The Gallery's numerous publications include *Landscape Album of Shitao, An Album by Bada Shanren, Twelve Views of Wumen by Shen Zhou,. An Album of Flowers and Insects by Ju Lian, Selected Fan Paintings of Ju Chao*, and two volumes of *Paintings in the Collection of the Guangzhou Art Gallery*. The collection is also made available to scholarly publicatons from time to time.

To enrich the cultural life of the community, as well as to provide opportunities for research by scholars and artists, exhibitions are organized with selections from our collections. Since our inauguration we have presented general exhibitions based on our own collections and also those devoted to special themes in Chinese art. Examples include bamboo paintings throughout the ages, fan paintings and figure paintings of the Ming and Qing dynasties. Paintings of the Yangzhou school of the Qing dynasty were featured in one exhibition, and the works of Ju Chao and Ju Lian in another. Exhibitions have also been organized from paintings of the Lingnan school and of contemporary artists. In addition, exhibitions of works donated to the Gallery have been presented with the cooperation and support of the donors. To facilitate exchanges with other museums, the Gallery has organized joint exhibitions with the Palace Museum Beijing, the Shanghai Museum, the Jilin Provincial Museum, the Xu Beihong Memorial Museum and the Art Gallery of the Chinese University of Hong Kong. In 1982, paintings of the Lingnan school selected from our collection travelled to Japan in an exhibition that was very well received.

The year 1986 marks the thirtieth anniversary of the Guangzhou Art Gallery. To celebrate this occasion, an exhibition of *Paintings of the Ming and Qing Dynasties from the Guangzhou Art Gallery* is being mounted at the Art Gallery of the Chinese University of Hong Kong. In the preparation of this joint exhibition, we owe a special vote of thanks to the entire staff of the Art Gallery of the Chinese University of Hong Kong, in particular to Dr. Mayching Kao, Curator and Mr. Peter Lam, Assistant Curator. I would like to express my best wishes for the success of this exhibition.

Huang Ying
Curator
The Guangzhou Art Gallery

Foreword

The exhibition of *Paintings of Ming and Qing Dynasties from the Guangzhou Art Gallery*, jointly organized by the Guangzhou Art Gallery and the Art Gallery of the Chinese Univeristy of Hong Kong, is the third co-operative exhibition project between the two musenms. It carries special significance as it is presented in celebration of the thirty-fifth anniversary of the founding of the Guangzhou Art Gallery. We would like to take this opportunity to offer our sincere congratulations and to look forward to closer cooperation between the museums in Guangzhou and Hong Kong in the years to come.

The central stage for Chinese painting in the Ming and Qing period was the Jiangnan region. Yet Guangzhou, as a hub of communication in Southern China, was not untouched by the main currents of artistic development. Collecting activities thrived, spurred by efforts of native people who actively sought for painting and calligraphy while on official posts and commercial missions in various parts of China. Major collections such as those of Wu Yongguang, Pan Zhengwei and Kong Guangtao were formed since the mid-Qing period. Xin Yaowen, He Lifu, Yong Geng and many others continued this tradition in the modern period. These private collections, each with their notable treasures, were, however, not accessible to the general public. Therefore, the founding of museums in the present century is meaningful in that through their collecting, studying and displaying activities treasures of art are now common property of the people. The Guangzhou Art Gallery, building on the foundation of the past centuries and also expanding to include modern works, develops into an important regional museum with strong historical tradition as well as local colour.

Ninety-nine scrolls and albums by one hundred and two artists have been selected for exhibition, covering the period from the mid-Ming to the late Qing dynasty. While making no attempt to organize a comprehensive exhibition to trace all the developments in Chinese painting in the past five centuries, we hope that the breadth of the painting development in the two dynastics, with all its varied richness, can be demonstrated in the present exhibition. The absence of works by some of the important artists of the Ming and Qing period may be compensated by the inclusion of minor masters whose presence would give a more complete picture of a stylistic current or an artistic centre. For example, the development of the Orthodox school can be traced to the late Qing period in the works of Dai Xi and Zhang Zhiwan. Or the complexity of the art scene in Yangzhou is demonstrated by the works of Gu Fuzhen, Wang Yun, Yan Yi and Cai Jia placed alongside those by the more popular Yangzhou Eccentrics. In addition, major artists from Guangdong were also included in the exhibition to highlight regional developments in the period under discussion. In so doing, we hope that the selection from the painting collection of the Guangzhou Art Gallery may broaden our knowledge and understanding of the later development of Chinese painting.

In the course of preparation for this exhibition, we have enjoyed strong support from the Administrative Bureau of Museums Department and Archaeological Data of the Ministry of Culture of China, the Development of Culture of Guangdong Province, the Guangzhou Bureau of Culture and the Hong Kong Branch of Xinhua News Agency, for which we are deeply grateful. Sepcial thanks are due to the staff of the Guangzhou Art Gallery, who under the leadership of Ms. Huang Ying, Curator and Mr. Xie Wenyong, Assistant Curator, made the selection of exhibits and prepare the catalogue entries. Mr. Xie Wenyong has graciously contributed a long essay on the exhibits which will be included in the exhibition catalogue. The Art Gallery staff assumes the responsibility of photographing the exhibits, mounting the exhibition and publishing this catalogue. To Dr. Ma Lin, Vice-Chancellor of the Chinese Unviersity, Professor Cheng Te-k'un, former Director of the Institute of Chinese Studies and Dr. F.C. Chen, the Institute's current Director, we offer our appreciation for their personal concern and guidance. We are indebted to Professor Jao Tsung-i and Mr. Lee Yun-woon who have guided us through this exhibition project, and Mrs. Rosalind Haddon of the Friends of the Art Gallery who has rendered valuable assistance in our English translations. The publication of this catalogue is made possible by the generous grants from the Wideland Foundation and the Bei Shan Tang Foundation. For their continued support we offer our heartfelt appreciaton.

Mayching Kao
Curator, Art Gallery
The Chinese University of Hong Kong

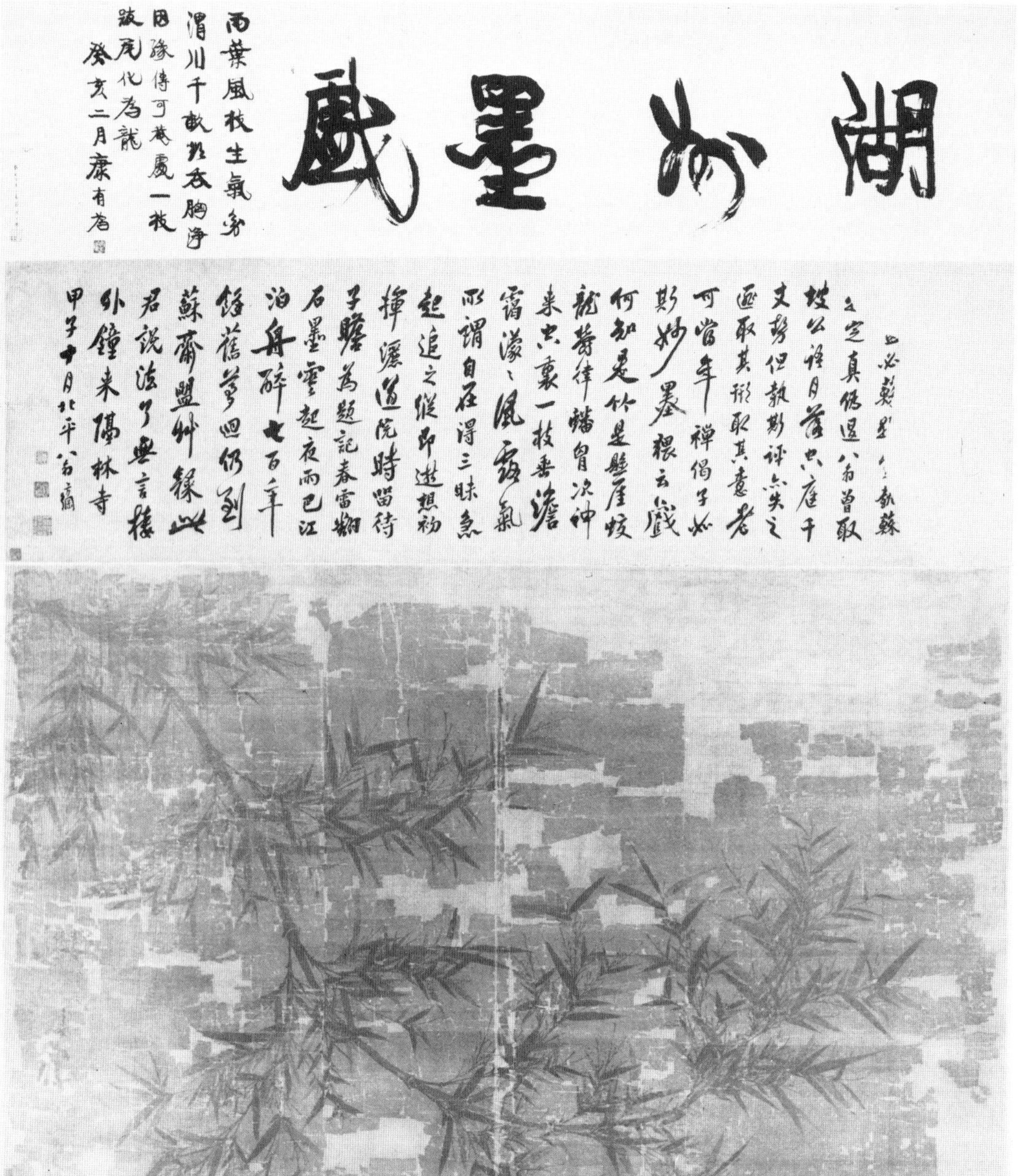

附圖1　Fig.1

讀畫小記

謝文勇

廣州美術館館藏中國古代書畫，以明淸作品居多，亦藏有北宋文同（1018－1079）《墨竹圖》（圖一）和元代李衎（1245－1320）《紆竹圖》（圖二），均爲淸代中期廣東書畫鑑藏家吳榮光（1773－1843）舊藏。吳氏《辛丑銷夏記》卷四記錄了《紆竹圖》，①《墨竹圖》則未見歷代古籍著錄。該畫在吳氏於公元一八〇二年收藏以前，上推算至文同卒年公元一〇七九年，七百多年間的流傳情況未明。近年由莫元瓚先生捐贈我館。入藏後在北京故宮博物院首次展覽，並於本館藏畫選集第一集發表。②國內外有關鑑定家多認爲是文同存世屈指可數眞蹟。關於以上二畫的文章，本館藏畫選集及台灣《故宮文物月刊》均有專文論述。③

《廣州美術館藏明淸繪畫》展覽中的明代山水畫，有浙派、吳派及晚明各派的作品。

浙派作品有明人《山水卷》（展品２）及藍瑛(1585－1664後)《秋山圖》（展品24）等。明人《山水卷》長達二千多厘米，高近十厘米，堪稱山水卷巨作。從筆勢和布局看，顯然受夏珪（十三世紀前期）《溪山淸遠圖卷》影响，但《淸遠卷》則行筆蒼老强勁，而明人長卷墨色淋漓，筆少染多，山石作斧劈皴，用筆棱角方硬，濃淡層次有變化，遠近分明，具馬遠（活躍於1190－1264間）、夏珪一派筆法特色。署有"錢塘戴進"欵。按《明畫錄》稱戴進（1388－1462）"山水源出郭熙（約1010－1090）、李唐（約1070－1150年代）、馬遠、夏珪，而妙處自發之，俗所謂行家兼利家者也。"④《圖繪寶鑑》等書均稱他山水得諸家之妙。此卷爲中山大學容庚教授捐贈。經鑑定：戴欵識不眞，定爲明人作品。從風格看屬浙派一路。明李開先《中麓畫品》後序記述戴氏曾慨嘆稱："吾胸中頗有許多事業，怎奈世無識者，不能發揚。"⑤《明畫錄》也稱他"死後人始推爲絕藝"。⑥可見此卷當作於戴氏去世後，不然他在世畫未爲看重，誰顧化這麼大功力畫此長卷假冒戴進作品呢？此圖布置有緊有鬆，相生相應，一樹一石，都有一局物色，筆在墨先，色依墨態，使筆、墨、色得有機妥貼配合，具大家氣格，非庸庸畫工所能。在流傳的古代書畫中，往往會碰到像此卷一樣，欵識不眞，但作品時代接近，藝術水平極高，如按所署欵識看待當然不合實際。若就此束之高閣，不給面世，也至爲可惜。能先標其時代而展覽或編入圖錄，供大家觀賞研究，會更有好處的。

《秋山圖》爲藍瑛五十歲時所作。藍瑛於畫史多被列作浙派後期之秀，其實這是不很切實的。浙派的畫筆多出自李唐、馬遠、夏珪，而《明畫錄》稱藍氏"畫山水，初年秀潤，摹唐宋元諸家，筆筆入古，而於子久究心尤力。"⑦藍氏曾云："此如書家眞楷，必由此入門，始能各極變化。"⑧可見他不但是推崇黃子久（1269－1354）用筆，並認爲學畫，也要學他筆法入手。從《秋山圖》看，山石於披麻、荷葉皴間，筋筋相屬，有勢有頓，確是來自黃公望的筆法，和馬夏喜用的大小斧劈皴是互不相關的。而且墨線純樸圓渾，簡約蒼潤，設色淡雅淸麗，沒有奇峭、剛勁的筆勢。藍瑛的作品存世較多，有年欵爲各家著錄的便有五十多件，此畫可算是藍畫巨幅大作。

吳派沈周（1427－1509）的作品有《吳門十二景册》（展品１），此册詩畫對題，均出自沈周手筆。董其昌（1555－1636）《畫禪室隨筆》題沈啓南畫册云："寫生與山水，不能兼長，惟黃安叔能之。……我朝則沈啓南一人而巳。此册寫生，更勝山水，間有本色，然皆眞虎也。"⑨董其昌以上所題不是此畫册，但用之對照甚爲恰貼而中肯。按"寫生"當指模擬自然景色而寫，而"山水"則應指自然景象經過畫家主觀情思的熔鑄蹟化而成的創作。顧名思義，《吳門十二景册》，是對吳縣及其附近十二處名蹟勝景的寫生之作，但他不是一般的對景寫生，而是自然景象經過畫家的意境和概括，運用巧妙藝術才能而表現出來的藝術境界。畫面富有詩意的情思熔鑄和意境的開拓。自作對題詩和畫相得益彰，互爲交輝。此册筆法灑脫純熟，繁處不促，簡處氣壯，雄勁凝練，沉著圓潤。用墨濃淡相托相消，淺薄深厚有層有次，遠近空間通透明朗。原作保留明代裝裱，是沈周傳世小品畫册珍品。上海書畫出版社珂羅版按原大印製發行。

學沈周筆法的山水畫以謝時臣（1487－1567後）的《匡廬瀑布圖軸》（展品５）堪稱巨幛，畫心高二二〇厘米，闊一四一厘米。此圖畫江西廬山，巖壑雄健、林木蒼翠，雲氣騰溢，一望無際，落墨厚重，氣魄豪偉，筆力挺拔，筆勢縱橫，人物乘騎結行，瀟灑自如。姜紹書《無聲詩史》稱讚他作畫頗有膽氣，正是這樣。但批評他"氣勢有餘，韶秀不足"，⑩這就有點過於苛求了。倒是《圖繪寶鑑續纂》說他"尤善於水，江潮湖海，種種皆妙。"⑪更爲恰切。此圖下幅的激浪便畫得很生動，極具功力。

明人花鳥畫中，王穀祥（1501－1568）的《花卉卷》（展品8）先後經鑑定家多人鑑定，未有異議。徐邦達先生定爲陳栝（十六世紀中期）代筆，並於《古書畫僞訛考辨》發表三點論據⑫：一是王世貞（1526－1590）《藝苑卮言》中稱王氏“中年絕不肯落筆，凡人間所傳者皆贋本也”；第二該畫葉筋用筆略見尖佻，和陳栝《五色葵花圖》（展品9）筆法一式無二；第三王畫《花卉卷》比陳畫《葵花軸》早九年，二人活動期間差不多。以徐先生目鑑慧眼，和豐富鑑別經驗，他的意見當可定論。但以此畫來說，我認爲有些地方還是值得探討的。一此畫用筆和題識可否是分別爲兩人筆迹，徐先生認爲欵字或爲王氏較早年未成熟時筆，並對其所題內容：

“辛丑之歲（嘉靖二十年，即1541年）春多霪雨，寂坐小齋，避濕喧也。漫閱圖籍，頗覺適意。既而得石田先生所作花卉，自春徂冬，種種不遺。余亦高興，勉寫一過，恐聰明未始能及，見者必笑走也。酉室王穀祥記。”

徐先生認爲不假，但却認爲其自題語內容不足信，叫“不要太信任他們的謊言”⑬。一般來說一位畫家，踏上中年正是創作的旺盛期，怎能夠就絕不肯落筆。該畫卷後紙顧元跋所稱“先生中年後絕不爲人落筆”的說法較合情合理，因爲厭於應酬，不爲人落筆，這是著名畫家多有碰到的常情，但不等於就此不作畫，須知藝術創作是情思靈感衝動而產生的，那能這麼簡單就洗手不幹呢！不少畫家因眼疾，右手病殘還是作畫不停的例子屢見不鮮的。至於說找別人代筆，不外是爲應酬需要，而此畫沒署上欵。《無聲詩史》記王穀祥：“……轉吏部代郎中，司選事。時太宰鋐陰陽倒置，先生堅持法不肯阿，因數與忤，遂忽忽不樂，念母老，乞歸養，而其兄故在，尙書用例格，酉室謫倅眞定。遂歸養母者幾三十年。持身峻潔，不妄交一人，手錄古文籍至數百千卷，咸精好不忍觸手，以詞翰徵者不輒應，杜門却掃，焚香而坐，一室之內，琳琅金薤謐如也。”⑭可見王氏中年後不樂意以文學書畫應酬世俗，而不是自己擱筆就此不幹。以他這麼高潔的性格，那能編此假話自欺欺人。且該畫有萬歷御府印璽數方，顯然作者去世後不久便流入內府，誰願把一幅當代畫家代筆畫呈送入宮，自討苦受。筆法上兩人都是學沈周、文徵明（1470－1559），筆致自有相似的地方。此畫比陳畫筆致淸秀，絕少草率氣習。看來值得研究、商榷處還多。

在吳門四家中，仇英（1494/5－1552）曾學畫於周臣（約1450－1535後），具有院派風貌，《虞初新志》戴文進傳張潮跋有：“其初爲漆工，兼爲人采繪棟宇，後徙而業畫。”⑮《無聲詩史》等書也稱他：“所出微，嘗執事丹青，周臣異而教之……。”⑯“所出微”當指“兼爲人采繪棟宇”的漆工生活而言。仇英後來和文徵明、唐寅（1470－1523）、祝枝山（1460－1526）等善詩書畫的文人交上朋友，更以賣畫過活。還到過項元汴（1525－1590）家裡住過，臨摹項家所藏古畫。仇英的生卒年，胡藝曾收集有關資料⑰推論他約生於明成化十八年（1482），卒於嘉靖三十八年（1559）。並根據《秘殿珠林》卷二十和卷八，所記仇英在明正德二年（1507）臨趙松雪（1254－1322）《松蔭老子圖》（該畫有祝允明題識），及明嘉靖三十五年（1556）作《佛位果應册》（有文徵明題跋），推算出兩畫首尾相距五十年。可知仇英從事繪畫實踐活動不少於五十年，當漆工的時期不會太長。從仇英流傳的作品來看，沒有工匠習氣可証，《停琴聽阮圖》（展品6）便可說明問題。此畫山石用小斧劈皴，行筆靈動剛柔相濟，鈎勒渲染得宜，山石凹凸分明，樹幹用粗筆，葉用雙鈎，高低疏密，穿插得致，賦色淸雅文秀，氣格淸新，筆法嚴密，人物氣格淸曠，一筆不苟，細緻入微，體態自然，神氣生動，確是不凡之作。惲壽平（1633－1690）在《南田畫跋》稱讚他“風華妍雅，又饒古趣，伯駒以後，無與爭能者矣。”⑱便是極爲中肯的評語，就連門戶之見極深的董其昌也在《畫旨》題仇英《臨光武渡河圖》稱讚說：“位置古雅，設色妍麗，爲近代高手第一。”⑲仇英晚年和文徵明過往甚密，爲文氏畫了不少畫。此圖有文鼎（1766－1852）“後山藏於停雲舊築”題簽，當爲文徵明家舊物，淸代鑒藏家李佐賢（1807－1876）《書畫鑒影》著錄，⑳也曾爲田谿書屋主人何荔甫先生收藏過。

董其昌在《畫旨》開卷便說：“畫家六法，一曰氣韻生動。氣韻不可學，此生而知之，自然天授。然亦有學得處，讀萬卷書，行萬里路。胸中脫去塵濁，自然丘壑內營，成立郛郭，隨手寫出，皆爲山水傳神。”㉑可見他把“氣韻”看爲繪畫美學的審美最高標準，畫家要達到這境界，除了天授的才華外，便要“讀萬卷書”，廣博學識吸取前人經驗，“行萬里路”，要體察自然景象，師法自然，方能對氣韻有所作爲。董其昌這一主張原是無可非議的。但在同書中他又說：“文人之畫，自王右丞始，其後董源、巨然、李成、范寬爲嫡子；李龍眠、王晋卿、米南宮及虎兒，皆從董巨得來。直至元四大家，黃子久、王叔明、倪元鎭、吳仲圭，皆其正傳。吾朝文沈，則又遠接衣缽。若馬夏及李唐、劉松年，又是大李將軍之派，非我曹當學也。”㉒董其昌自己以文人畫的正統爲幌子，刮起了一股大倡復古之風，無異是一邊講文人畫，一邊毁文人畫，造成一種把“文人畫”理解爲脫離現實，玩弄筆墨的主觀遊戲。最近蘇東天在《董其昌的“文人之畫”》一文中說董其昌對李思訓一派畫未曾發表貶詞。㉓其實董其昌對仇英及南宋院派個別畫家也有褒獎之詞。但他把這派畫看成“至如刻畫細謹，爲造物役者，乃能損壽，蓋無生機也。”㉔試問畫無生機，還有什麼可說。反過來他對所謂王維（701－761）以來一派却褒獎之詞不絕於口，怎能說他是客觀地看待二派畫藝呢？有人說：“董其昌作畫，雖是學古入手，但他只是‘心存目想’，而不是從刻意臨摹得來的。”董其昌在《畫旨》談到對王維的崇拜時說過：“……且右丞自云：宿世謬詞客，前身應畫師。余未嘗得覩其蹟，但以想心取之，果得與眞肎合，豈前身曾入右丞之室，而親覽其盤礴之致，故結習不昧乃爾耶。”㉕其實我們說董其昌提倡復古，就在於他不重視《畫旨》開卷時自己所說過的話，無視於畫家對自然的感受和作品的情思意境，而是脫離現實，主觀地追求古人的風格和筆墨，較多地以臨摹代替創作，把筆墨技巧放在首位，以致內容與形式的不統一，使作品缺乏新氣息，這次展出的《剪江草堂圖》（展品12）便是大家公認爲董其昌晚年較有代表性作品。再觀賞原濟（1642－1707）的《詩畫册》（展品34），兩畫一比，便令人耳目一新；原濟才是眞正着眼於藝術本身，深入現實，眞正做到“搜盡奇峯打草稿”，謀求畫中之詩，畫中之我。每一畫面都充沛着自己的情思，每畫題識都無不富現實意境，每一筆法都極變化生動之致。令人百看不厭，越看越愛，這才是眞正的“文人畫”，發揚了文人畫的光輝。這樣說不是否定董其昌的筆墨工夫，或否定他對山水畫風格的研究，和對各家評論的貢獻。在繪畫領域中，學習古人要像石濤那樣能“借古以開今”，“我之爲我，自有我在。古之鬚眉，不能生在我之面目；古之肺腑，不能安入我之腹腸。我自發我之肺腑，揭我之鬚眉，縱有時觸著某家，是某家就我也，非我故爲某家也”。㉖這是多麼鮮明而有獨創性。和董其昌拜倒在古人筆下，唯古人筆墨是尊的傾向，眞是天大的不同。石濤的藝術成就，連和他筆法格格不入的王原祁（1642－1715）也稱讚爲“海內丹青家，不能盡識，而大江以南，當推石濤爲第一”。並說：“余與石谷皆有所未逮”。㉗原濟《詩畫册》原爲清代廣東孔氏嶽雪樓舊藏，有張維屏（1780－1859）、陳其琨、熊景星（1791－1856）等廣東咸豐年間名人對題。石濤從小時離開廣西後，先後到過廬山、常熟、嘉興、江寧、宣城、揚州、南京、北京、天津等地，未見到過廣東，但和廣東的屈大均（1630－1696）、梁佩蘭（1629－1705）、程可則（1627－1676）都結爲好友。廣東畫家很佩服石濤的高超藝術水平。謝里甫《常惺惺齋書畫題跋》便讚揚石濤說：“此公一落墨，便有天外奇境飛上筆端。”㉘《詩畫册》有庚午（1690）、癸酉（1693）、丁丑（1697）自書年款可知是他四十九至五十六歲前後的作品，這對研究石濤生平和繪畫技法是極爲珍貴的實物。

清初新安派畫家漸江（1610－1664），畫史稱他：“初學一峯，晚法雲林。得其畫足當雲林。”可見他的畫蹟是難得可貴。《始信峯圖》（展品29）作於癸卯年春，是他卒年作品。㉙該畫右邊有王艮題識行書四行稱：“紫雲千堵削秋容，不信人間有此峯。記與老人松畔立，至今眉髮帶烟濃。壬癸間予客芝陽，漸公自黃山來，偕予將往匡廬，留寓且讀齋，爲主人呂君圖此而余題識之，廣𣏾樵王艮。”王艮原名王煒，字不菴、無悶，比漸江年輕十六歲，爲漸江好友，多次偕遊黃山。汪世清、汪改廬編寫的《漸江及其師友活動年表》康熙壬寅，漸江五十三歲條有：“十一月，……時漸江將遊廬山，與許楚、程守、戴本孝、汪度山圖及僧南雲拾殘相聚五日，備臻歡適。諸子賦詩浩往，遂即成行。抵鄱陽，與王煒相會。以雪阻不克入山，即度歲於呂士鶴御青之且讀齋中。”㉚此段記錄和本圖漸江及王艮二題相合可証。

始信峯在黃山北面，與上升峯、石筍峯鼎足而立。山體是堅硬的花崗岩，石間有許多節理裂隙，中有松樹盤根而生，有的平直向上生長，有的依勢屈卧，各顯剛毅挺拔的意態。此畫從筆致來看，清峭曠絕，確有脫胎倪雲林的筆法，但他把花崗岩的峯巒和巨石，簡煉爲挺健的輪廓線條，比倪畫別有特色。在簡括的線條描繪下，堅硬的石質在目，石隙生長的松樹，顯示出挺勁的節操，一股堅貞的靈氣充沛了畫面。此畫不但表現了黃山險峻的奇峯勝景，也體現了漸江的氣格和藝術特色，是其晚年代表作品。

描繪黃山景色的另一畫，是梅淸（1623－1697）的從孫梅翀（十七世紀晚期）的《文殊院觀海圖》（展品50）。文殊院即玉屏樓，樓後爲玉屏峯，是黃山腹心地帶，地勢高昂，鄰近是蓮花、天都等名峯，樓左迎客松，樓右送客松，遇有雲霧可觀黃山前海。此圖畫滾滾雲霧如無邊大海，而高出霧上的山峯却似大海中的島嶼，景象壯觀。全幅用王蒙（1308－1385）蜷曲如蚯蚓的小線條皴筆，特別誇張山頂的筆勢與墨色，使人產生仙山雲海流動感。線條不加修飾和點苔，一股清氣照人，別有氣慨。

清初王時敏（1592－1680）、王鑑（1598－1677）、王翬（1632－1717）、王原祁（1642－1715）四王的山水畫，繼承了元四家和董其昌的筆法，以“古色蒼然”爲好。他們“遇古人眞本，向上研求。視其定意若何？結構若何？出入若何？偏正若何？安放若何？用筆若何？積墨若何？必於我有一出頭地處，久之自與脗合矣。”㉛他們攻擊和自己不同流派不遺餘力。特別是王原祁以畫壇正統自居，氣勢不可一世說：“明末畫中有習氣惡派，以浙派爲最。至吳門雲間，大家如文沈，宗匠如董，贋本溷淆，以訛傳訛，竟成流弊，廣陵白下，其惡習與浙派無異，有志筆墨者，切須戒之。”㉜四王中以王時敏筆力最高，作畫用筆於著力與不著力之間見著力，運腕虛靈，筆致蒼潤秀嫩，恬靜沉古。王鑑筆致渾厚蒼勁，翠轡春嶂，設色尤勝三家。王原祁蒼鬱厚重，霸悍高曠，兀傲自大。唯王翬重視觀察實景，筆勢淸勁秀雅，有生活氣息。"四王"的山水畫，摹古、步履古人，以正統派自居，排斥其他各派，其流弊影響甚廣，但他們在摹古中對古人的筆墨繼承和整理遺產，還是功力甚高和有貢獻的。

從展出的王時敏《秋山圖》（展品26）、王原祁的《仿大痴山水》（展品47）和王翬的《竹窩圖》（展品44）等作品都可領略其筆墨功力。特別王時敏的《秋山圖》更是他晚年的傑作。

正當四王畫風以正統派壟斷了北方畫壇的同時，中原一帶的南京和揚州等地便逐漸地聚集了一批以淸高自許，或藝術創作不願多受約束的畫家。他們以詩酒相娛，志趣相合，賣畫爲生，各擅所長，畫筆豪放自如，詩意淸淡高雅，過着淸貧自樂的文人生活，最爲大家知名的是"金陵八家"和"揚州八怪"。"金陵八家"是龔賢、樊圻、高岑、鄒喆、吳宏、葉欣、謝蓀、胡慥等。八家中畫風不盡一致，除龔賢外，所畫山水人物以淸秀明靜見長。而龔賢却以沉雄深厚，墨色濃渾，氣慨壯偉，獨具風貌，爲八家之首。他的作品以水墨居多，像展出的絹本設色《秋山飛瀑圖》（展品35）便是極爲難得的作品。程正揆（1604－1676）評他的畫筆："如龍馭鳳，似雲行空，隱現變幻，渺乎其不可窮，蓋以韵勝，不以力雄者也。"㉝確是極盡變化，氣韻墨韻各有神采，筆力雄勁寓於含蓄，不露聲色。細看他的畫筆運行輕重，便可理會。

"揚州八怪"作畫，山水、人物、花鳥各有所長，特別是花鳥畫更別開生面，水墨豪放不受約束，顯示出自由奔放的氣勢，有情有理，敢作敢爲，詩書畫相融，面目淸新。他們主張"各有靈苗各自探"，强調作畫要順應各人的個性發展，在文人畫的發展中作出新貢獻。這次展出有金農（1687－1764）、黄愼（1687－1768後）、李鱓（1686－1760後）、汪士愼（1686－約1759）、李方膺（1695－1754）、鄭燮（1693－1765）、羅聘（1733－1799）等人的作品（展品68－69、71－75）。有的水墨淋漓，筆勢縱橫，有的筆致淸雅，意態高潔，有的流暢俊逸，奇趣橫生。在觀賞了"四王"畫後，八怪的作品，令人感到一股淸新的情思感人面目。在此值得一提的是華嵒（1682－1756）的作品。華嵒原籍福建上杭，長時期住在杭州和揚州，一生過着"常共妻孥飲粥糜，登盤瓜豉茹芹葵。貧家自有眞風味，富貴之人那得知。"（華嵒《幽居遣興》詩）㉞ 淸貧高潔的賣畫生活。展出的華嵒《山水花鳥册》（展品66）爲香港楊銓先生捐贈美術館的。此册顯示了華嵒山水、人物、花鳥全能的功力，具有率意、疏宕、空靈的情致。他曾說過："山水有佳趣，雲煙無俗情。澹人懷道樂，森木向春榮。結構循吾法，哦吟倩鳥聲。未論工與拙，且可愜平生。"㉟這幾幅山水小品筆致雋秀娟美，意境空靈淸疏，詩情畫意，極爲融洽。人物畫則表現出閒適、淸淡的意態，仕女畫則流露出幽雅的情調。特別是花鳥畫的造詣最高，他用寫意帶工的畫法，把禽鳥的毛羽畫得那麼有鬆有貼，自然疏朗，神態活躍生動，給人有親切而純樸的美感。細細觀賞這四開花鳥畫，好像身處自然界的花鳥樂園，畫眉恬靜悠然在刷羽，雲雀淸亮地鳴唱，而綬帶鳥枝頭打轉覓食，錦翎親呢相隨追逐。畫家傾注的情思是多麼的親切自然，充溢着自然界生機蓬勃的氣息。在技法上，他不守一家一派，而有自己突破。畫禽鳥的毛羽採用乾筆擦毛，然後用色烘染的手法最巧妙。善於捕捉禽鳥瞬間的動態和神意，是明淸其他花鳥畫家所不及的。

淸代的揚州不單出現了八怪和華嵒這樣傑出的寫意畫家，也出現了李寅（十七世紀晚期至十八世紀前期）、蕭晨（同前）、顏嶧（1666－1749尙在）、袁江（十七世紀晚期至十八世紀前期）、袁耀（十八世紀）等以工筆見長的界畫家。《江樓對奕圖》（展品65）便是顏嶧的傑出作品。用筆工整細緻，但不刻板平滯，山石着墨不多，挺拔超脫，境地寬舒，生活氣息濃郁。

指頭畫的記載，《歷代名畫記》記述有唐代的畢宏見到張璪的作品驚歎說："異其唯用禿筆，或以手摸絹素，因問璪所受？璪曰：'外師造化，中得心源。'畢宏於是擱筆。"㊱張璪在禿筆落墨後用手抹開，雖然有手摸抹，但還是用筆爲主爲先。而高其佩（1672－1734）的指畫（展品56）却是用手指代替筆，利用指甲運墨，斜傾手指在紙上運行，使墨隨指出而成線，顯然這是帶有特別手藝性質，畫成的效果別具意趣，有點現代西洋畫行動派的趣味。此册指畫是高氏較有代表性作品，畫面往往是揮指寥寥數下，便簡煉生動，在漫不經心中充溢着畫家眞切的情思。不矯揉造作，也不華飾點染，意態自然，耐人尋味。高其佩的指畫與其說是發展了用手作畫的技法，更重要的是他重視了張璪關於"外師造化，中得心源"的創作思想。從畫册中自題識便可看到他下筆簡括，但下筆前每幅畫都是經過對現實的感觸而構思創作的。

展出的高鳳翰（1683－約1748）《綠天淸蔭圖》（展品67）也是以指作畫的，但氣格與意態和高其佩迥別，是情意散豁、水墨汎濫，好像使酒狂歌，放誕不羈，氣勢冲冲，他作畫情意充沛，晚年病痺，改用左手作畫，水平不減右手。

竹有高節虛心，傲霜耐寒，勁直淸高，搖風弄影等性狀。歷代詩人、畫家都喜歡以它爲題材吟詩作畫。廣州美術館館藏歷代畫竹作品除了前提及的文同《墨竹圖》和李衎《紆竹圖》外，這次展出的便有戴明說（十七世紀中期）的《墨竹圖》、諸昇（1618－1689後）的《三友圖卷》、李鱓的《竹蕉圖》、鄭燮的《竹石圖》、吳昌碩（1844－1927）的《風竹圖》等（展品41、42、69、73、99）。戴明說的《墨竹圖》（展品42）從形體和氣度來看是繼承了文同墨竹的風貌，顯示着清勁恬靜的格調。諸昇的《三友圖》(展品41)畫的是蘭、竹、石。蘭有秀質幽香，竹有勁直虛心，石有磊落巉岩等性狀，一向都爲詩人雅士列作"三友"，畫家也喜以它爲題作畫。諸昇畫竹比戴明說顯得更有意匠的編排與組合，行筆爽朗清快。李鱓和鄭燮是同期活動於揚州的畫竹名手，兩人都有清廉明潔的氣質，和清新的才思。從畫竹的格調看，鄭氏墨韵明淨，瀟灑清發，而李氏則水墨汎濫，情意奔放，在水墨寫意中意態各相懸殊。吳昌碩的《風竹圖》（展品99），却借一股"飄飄一氣怒呼號"的風力把竹的梢葉吹得蹦跳搖盪不止。表現出竹清勁挺拔的氣質，在筆法上他以書法入畫，筆勢厚重雄渾，富有金石意味。

註　釋

①吳榮光：《辛丑銷夏記》，據北平莊氏洞天山堂藏清光緒乙巳（1905年）刋本影印本，卷四，頁9b－10a。

②即《藝苑掇英》第16期（1982年４月），封面及頁44。

③謝文勇：《介紹二幅宋元名竹》，同註②。又李霖燦：《文同墨竹的雙胞案》，《故宮文物月刋》第一卷第３期（1983年６月），頁76－80。

④徐沁：《明畫錄》，卷二，頁26。載于安瀾編：《畫史叢書》，（上海人民美術出版社，1963）第二册。

⑤李開先：《中麓畫品》，後序，頁2a;載黃賓虹、鄧實編：《美術叢書》，（上海神州國光社，1928），第二集第十輯。

⑥同註④。

⑦同註④，卷五，頁63。

⑧同註④。

⑨董其昌：《畫禪室隨筆》，據民國初年石印本，（上海進步書屋，192-？），卷二頁14b。

⑩姜紹書：《無聲詩史》，卷三，頁44。載于安瀾編：《畫史叢書》第三册。

⑪藍瑛、謝彬：《圖繪寶鑑續纂》，卷一，頁３。載于安瀾編：《畫史叢書》第二册。

⑫徐邦達：《古書畫僞訛考辨》，（南京江蘇古籍出版社，1984），下卷：文字部份，頁142－143。

⑬同註⑫。

⑭同註⑩，卷三，頁37。

⑮《虞初新志．戴文進傳》後張潮跋語，（上海大達圖書供應社，1934），卷八，頁104。

⑯同註⑩，卷三，頁41。

⑰胡藝：《仇英生卒考》，《朵雲》，第五集（1983年５月），頁46。

⑱惲壽平：《南田畫跋》，卷三，頁26b。載黃賓虹，鄧實編：《美術叢書》，第四集第六輯。

⑲董其昌：《畫旨》，載于安瀾編：《畫論叢刋》，（北京人民美術出版社，1962），上卷，頁93－94。

⑳李佐賢：《書畫鑒影》，據北平莊氏洞天堂藏清同治十年（1871）刋本影印本，卷二十一，頁17b-18a。

㉑同註⑲，頁71。

㉒同註⑲，頁76。

㉓蘇東天：《董其昌的文人之畫》，《朵雲》，第八集（1985年12月），頁170。

㉔同註⑨，頁8a。

㉕同註⑲，上卷，頁81。

㉖《苦瓜和尚畫語錄》變化章第三，見于安瀾編：《畫論叢刋》，上卷，頁148。

㉗轉引自鄭拙廬：《石濤研究》，（北京人民美術出版社，1961），頁28。

㉘謝蘭生：《常惺惺齋書畫題跋》，卷上，題清湘山水。據李少泉藏鈔本影印本（澳門文集圖書公司，1974？）。

㉙按汪世清推算弘仁卒於清康熙二年癸卯十二月二十二日，即公元1664年１月19日。參考汪世清：《清初四大畫僧合考》，《香港中文大學中國文化研究所學報》，第十五卷（1984），頁184。

㉚汪世清、汪改廬：《漸江及其師友活動年表》，載汪世清、汪聰編纂：《漸江資料集》，（合肥安徽人民出版社，1984），頁249。

㉛王原祁：《雨窻漫筆》，載黃賓虹、鄧實編：《美術叢書》，初集第二輯，頁2b。

㉜同前註，頁1a。

㉝轉引自王伯敏：《中國繪畫史》，（上海人民美術出版社，1982），頁582。

㉞轉引自王靖憲：《華嵒的藝術思想及其成就》，《朵雲》第二集（1981年11月），頁186。

㉟同前註，頁193。

㊱張彥遠：《歷代名畫記》，俞劍華註，（上海人民美術出版社，1964），頁201。

附圖2 Fig.2

Notes on Paintings in the Guangzhou Art Gallery

Xie Wenyong

The Guangzhou Art Gallery painting collection is primarily from the Ming and Qing periods. The exceptions are the *Bamboo in Ink* (fig. 1) by Wen Tong (1018-1079) of the Northern Song dynasty and *Bomboo in Colour* (fig. 2) by Li Kan (1245-1320) of the Yuan dynasty. Both paintings were formerly in the collection of Wu Rongguang (1773-1843), a major collector in Guangdong in the mid-Qing period. Wu recorded the Yuan painting in the catalogue of his collection, *Xinchou xiaoxia ji*.[1] Curiously, the Song painting was not recorded in any of the ancient texts and there is a gap of more than seven hundred years between Wen Tong's life-time and 1802 when the painting came into the hands of Wu Rongguang. It was donated to this Gallery in recent years, and subsequently exhibited for the first time at the Palace Museum in Beijing. It has been published in *Selected Paintings in the Collection of Guangzhou Art Gallery*.[2] Studies have been done on this painting and experts both in China and abroad generally agree on its authenticity.[3]

In the present exhibition, landscape painting of the Ming dynasty is represented by the Zhe School, the Wu School and the various schools of late Ming period. Paintings belonging to the Zhe School are: the *Landscape Scroll* (cat. no. 2) and *Autumn Mountains* (cat. no. 24) by Lan Ying (1585-after 1664). The *Landscape Scroll*, donated by Professor Rong Geng of Zhongshan University, measuring 50 cm in height and 2,073 cm in length, can be considered a monumental work. In terms of brush technique and composition, it shows an obvious influence of Xia Gui's (fl. first half of the 13th century) work, the *Pure and Remote Views of Streams and Mountains*. But Xia's brushwork is much more vigorous, while the later painting is richer in ink washes. The painting displays the stylistic characteristics of the Ma Yuan-Xia Gui landscape tradition of the Southern Song dynasty. The mountains and rocks, modelled by the "axe-cut" textural strokes, are sharp and angular. The ink gradations are rich and the spatial relationship clear. The painting bears a signature of Dai Jin (1388-1462), an accomplished painter of the early Ming period who was credited with the founding of the Zhe School. However, upon close inspection by scholars this signature has been considered spurious. The painting can still be dated to the Ming dynasty and its style falls well within the sphere of the Zhe School. The exceptional quality of this long scroll, with its vital interplay of solids and voids and the harmonious fusion of ink and colour, shows that it could only have come from the hand of an outstanding artist. For this reason, inspite of its problem in attribution, this painting is included in this exhibition so that it can be made available for further study.

Lan Ying, who painted *Autumn Mountains* (cat. no. 24) at the age of fifty, has often been regarded as the last master of the Zhe School. Such a designation is not quite appropriate, for it is commonly known that the brush methods of the Zhe School evolved from Li Tang, Ma Yuan and Xia Gui. Yet with Lan Ying's painting style, it was mentioned in *Minghua lu* that he imitated the masters of the Tang, Song and Yuan dynasties and that he was particularly devoted to the study of Huang Gongwang.[4] To Lan Ying, the art of Huang Gongwang was as basic and vital as the study of regular script to a calligrapher.[5] Take *Autumn Mountains* as an example, the mountains are modelled by long, undulating strokes called "hemp-fibre" or "lotus leaf" textural strokes. Such brush manner could only have come from Huang Gongwang and bears no resemblance to the "axe-cut" textural strokes favoured by Ma Yuan and Xia Gui. Moreover, this painting is devoid of any bizarre or forceful brushwork. Instead, the brushwork is simple and mellow, the colours light and elegant. A number of Lan Ying's paintings have survived to this day, including over fifty that are dated and recorded. This particular painting can be counted among his larger compositions.

Shen Zhou (1427-1509) of the Wu School is represented in this exhibition by *Twelve Views of Wumen* (cat. no. 1). This is an album of twelve paintings depicting the scenic spots in and around Wuxian, which is present-day Suzhou, Jiangsu province. Shen Zhou, whose talent for sketching from nature and composing imaginary landscapes was held in high esteem by the late Ming master Dong Qichang (1555-1636),[6] fused objective observation and subjective feeling together to create a poetic artistic realm. Each painting is accompanied by a poem on the facing page, composed and written by Shen Zhou himself.

The pictorial and the calligraphic elements complement each other to realize the poetic intent of the artist. As for the paintings, they exemplify the artist's mastery in the manipulaton of the brush, being both vigorous and firm. The ink washes are rich in tonal gradations and the spatial construction is lucid and ordered. The album, preserved until today in its mounting from the Ming dynasty, is a rare work among the small-size paintings by Shen Zhou that have come down to us.

Xie Shichen (1487-after 1567) followed the style of Shen Zhou. His painting the *Waterfall of Mount Lu* (cat. no. 5) can be considered a monumental piece of art. Measuring 220 cm in height and 141 cm in width, the painting portrays Mount Lu in Jiangxi province. It shows the magnificent, towering mountains with lush vegetation surrounded by clouds and mists. His brush manner is bold and energetic, while the ink is heavy and thick. He was equally at ease with the delicate small figures placed in the painting. Jiang Shaoshu, in *Wushengshi shi,* praised his boldness on the one hand and criticized his deficiency in harmony and sensitivity on the other.[7] Jiang might seem over critical in his comments, but that is compensated by *Tuhui baojian xuzuan* which gave him credit for his superb draughtsmanship in depicting water in its myriad manifestations.[8] This skill is well demonstrated by the lively breakers seen in the lower portion of the painting.

Among the paintings of birds and flowers by Ming artists, the handscroll of flowers (cat. no. 8) by Wang Guxiang (1501-1568) has been authenticated by a number of connoisseurs. However, it is appropriate to mention here that Mr. Xu Bangda of the Palace Museum in Beijing attributes this handscroll to Chen Gua (fl. mid-16th century) who was painting on Wang's behalf. He gave his reasons in his monumental work, *Gu shuhua wei'e kaobian.*[9] First of all, he cited the words of Wang Shizhen (1526-1590) in *Yiyuan zhiyan* that Wang Guxiang "in his middle years absolutely refused to paint. All surviving works are without exception forgeries." Second, the lines of the leaf veins in the painting are quite sharp and light, resembling the brush manner found in Chen Gua's *Hollyhock in Five Colours* (cat. no. 9). Third, this handscroll, dated to 1541, was painted only nine years before the *Hollyhock* of Chen Gua, which made the two artists more or less contemporaries. As a renowned connoisseur of Chinese painting, Mr. Xu Bangda's verdict should be considered definitive. However, I think there is still room for further discussion.

One of the issues is the separate authorship of the painting and the inscription. While Mr. Xu attributes the painting to Chen Gua, he considers the inscription as an authentic work by Wang Guxiang in his early years. The inscription reads:

> In the spring of the *xinchou* year (1541) it rained excessively. (I) sat quietly in my studio to avoid the dampness and the bustle. Casually reading books and paintings, I felt quite enjoyable. Then I acquired a flower painting by Shitian Xiansheng (Shen Zhou) which included all flowers from spring to winter without omission. I was so delighted that I strove to paint after it once. I am afraid that my talent cannot begin to compare with (Shen Zhou) and that those who see this painting will walk away laughing. Inscribed by Youshi, Wang Guxiang.

The content of the inscription clearly contradicts the theory of separate authorship as proposed by Mr. Xu, he therefore exhorted us not to be taken by the lies of the artists.[10]

It is difficult to accept that an artist would stop painting entirely in his middle years, a time in life when his creative energy is at its peak. I tend to agree with Gu Yuan, who wrote in the colophon of this painting, that Wang from his middle years onwards refused to paint for others. To be tired of painting for others as a social obligation is a common affliction suffered by renowned masters, but that does not necessarily mean that they would stop painting all together. We know that artistic creation comes from impulses of the heart and the mind, if it can be stopped so easily, why do we still see so many artists continuing to paint even after they have suffered a disability of the eyes or their right hand?

Another issue concerns the matter of having someone do this painting on his behalf (*daibi*). This normally happens when one needs to fulfill a social obligation. Yet the painting under discussion bears no dedication, so that we know that this painting was not intended for some one. Moreover, *Wushengshi shi* recorded events from Wang Guxiang's life showing that he was a person with integrity and lofty ideals.[11] His uncompromising character also kept him from answering social obligations with his literary and artistic accomplishments, but he could still paint for himself. Indeed, it would be difficult to imagine a man like Wang fabricating lies to deceive both himself and others.

The painting has several seals of the Imperial Household in the reign of Wanli (1573-1620), indicating that the painting entered the imperial collection soon after the death of the artist. If the painting was indeed by Wang in name only, who would dare to submit it and suffer the consequence? Stylistically Wang Guxiang and

Chen Gua may resemble each other as they both followed Shen Zhou and Wen Zhengming (1470-1559). In comparison, the bursh manner in the painting by Wang is more refined and elegant than Chen's and is less careless. Further research and discussion will add to our understanding of this painting.

Among the Four Masters of the Wu School, Qiu Ying (1494/5-1552) had studied painting under Zhou Chen (ca. 1450-after 1535) and his style bears a resemblance to that of the painting academy. Qiu Ying came from a humble and uneducated background. He possibly worked as a lacquer artisan before turning into a professional painter.[12] He became acquainted with the literati circle of Wen Zhengming, Tang Yin (1470-1523) and Zhu Zhishan (1460-1526) and enjoyed the patronage of Xiang Yuanbian (1525-1590), having lived in Xiang's home as a "painter in residence" and copied his collection of ancient paintings. As for Qiu Ying's birth and death dates, Hu Yi hypothesized that he jas born in 1482 and died in 1559. His evidence was two paintings dated 1507 and 1556 listed in the catalogue of the imperial collection, *Bidian zhulin*.[13] Being fifty years apart, Qiu Ying's span of artistic activity, therefore, could not be less than that. His early career as a decorative painter must have been brief.

The surviving paintings of Qiu Ying indicate clearly that he had transcended his artisan background; *Listening to Music by the Waterfall* (cat. no. 6) is a good example. The artist uses short "axe-cut" textural strokes to give a three dimensional quality to the rocks and mountains. His vigorous brushwork alternates between firmness and suppleness; his outlines are accurate and his ink washes rich in tonality. Coarse brushstrokes are employed for the tree trunks while fine lines are applied to the foliage, creating an interesting pattern of contrasting density. The figural group is finely painted, capturing their naturally graceful postures. Apart from the disciplined brush manner of the artist, the painting is enhanced by colours that are elegant and refined. This superb painting not only demonstrates the technical mastery of Qiu Ying, its refreshing mood gives testimony to the praises sung to him by such literati artists of the Orthodox school as Dong Qichang (1555-1636)[14] and Yun Shouping (1633-1690)[15].

Qiu Ying was closely associated with Wen Zhengming in his later years and painted a number of works for him. This painting bears a label inscribed by Wen Ding (1766-1852) which reads: "Collected by Houshan at the Tingyun Villa of Former Days." This is a clear indication that the painting belonged to the famliy of Wen Zhengming, since Wen Ding was a descendant and Tingyun as the name of a villa was also associated with Wen Zhengming. The painting has been recorded by Li Zuoxian in *Shuhua jianying*[16] and has been in the collection of He Lifu of The Tianxi Studio.

Dong Qichang, the dominant figure in late Ming art, stressed the importance of *qiyun* (breath-resonance) in his theories. He said on the first page of his collected writing, *Huazhi*:

> An artist has six canons, the first is *qiyun shengdong* (breath-resonance-life-motion). The breath-resonance cannot be acquired by study but is inborn in the painter. It is the gift of Heaven, yet some of it may be learned. If one has studied ten thousand volumes and walked ten thousand miles, then one's mind will be freed from dust and dirt. Mountains and valleys will form within one quite naturally and the outer boundary will become established. Whatever casually produced by the hand will transmit the spirit of the landscape.[17]

It is clear that Dong considered *qiyun* as the highest aesthetic ideal which can be achieved through the dual channel of learning extensively from the past experiences of the ancients and from the observation of nature. While these approaches are beyond criticism, Dong placed greater emphasis on the study of ancients in the same book. He said:

> The painting of the literati began with Wang Wei. Later, Dong Yuan, Li Cheng, and Fan Kuan were his proper issue. Li Gonglin, Wang Shen, Mi Fu and his son Youren all stemmed from Dong and Ju. From there (the succession) goes straight on to the Four Masters of Yuan: Huang Gongwang, Wang Meng, Ni Zan and Wu Zhen. They all belonged to the correct (orthodox) line of transmission. In our dynasty Wen Zhengming and Shen Zhou have also distantly succeeded to the robe and begging bowl (of Bodhidharma, i.e., the symbol of succession in Chan Buddhism). As for Ma Yuan, Xia Gui, Li Tang, and Liu Songnian, they belong to the lineage of Li Shixun; they are nothing that we officials ought to study.[18]

With statements like this Dong hoisted the banner of the orthodoxy of literati painting and stirred up the wind of archaic revival. he was actually doing a disservice to literati painting, removing it from nature and reality and turning it into a subjective game of playful ink and brush.

Modern scholars such as Su Dongtian and Xu

Bangda attempt to interpret Dong's theory in a more favourable light. Su mentioned that Dong never actually condemned the lineage of Li Shixun.[19] In fact, there were times when Dong even praised Qiu Ying and individual artists working in the academic style of the Southern Song dynasty. However, he has described works of this school as "meticulous like a carved painting. (They become) slaves of *zaowu* (nature); (the artists') life span would be cut short as there is no vital force (in these paintings)."[20] How can we say that Dong has been objective in his appraisal of the two schools when he sang praises of the lineage of Wang Wei and called paintings in the other lineage devoid of vitality? As for Xu Bangda, he interpreted the study of ancients as advocated by Dong into a creative spiritual communion, quite distinct from deliberate and slavish imitation. We object to Dong Qichang's archaic revivalism only because he failed to keep his word as recorded on the opening page of *Huazhi*. He ignored the artist's response to nature and the expressive element in artistic creation in his subjective pursuit of the style and brush manner of the ancients, thus draining Chinese painting of its vitality.

The Thatched Cottage of Jianjiang (cat. no. 12) by Dong Qichang, featured in this exhibition, has been widely accepted as a representative work from his late period. Yet if we compare it to the *Album of Paintings and Poems* (cat. no. 34), by Yuanji we are immediately captivated by the refreshing vitality in this album. Yuanji was a true artist who was deeply involved in reality. He searched exhaustively for strange peaks to sketch, at the same time imbued his paintings with a poetic mood and self-expression. Every leaf in this album is expressive of the artist's personal feeling and his involvement with the real world. The brushwork is full of variety and vitality. This is what we consider to be a true literati painting. In so saying we do not mean to minimize Dong Qichang's contribution to the theoretic and stylistic studies of Chinese painting, but Yuanji's attitude to the ancients is indeed refreshing, original and diametrically opposed to Dong Qichang. The following is a famous quotation by Yuanji which reads:

> For the self to be self, there must be a selfhood. The beard and eyebrows of the ancients may not grow on my face, nor could their lungs and bowels be placed in my body. I shall vent my lungs and bowels and display my own beard and eyebrows. Though at times my paintings may come close to someone else's, it is he who comes to accommodate me, and not I who want to imitate his style.[21]

The artistic achievement of Yuanji was recognized by those artists in the Orthodox school, including Wang Yuanqi (1642-1715), who acknowledged that Yuanqi was the foremost painter south of the Yangzi River.[22]

This *Album of Paintings and Poems* by Yuanji was previously owned by Kong Guangtao, a renowned collector in Guangdong in the Qing dynasty, and was appended by colophons of eminent literary and artistic figures in Guangdong in the Xianfeng era. Though Yuanji travelled extensively after leaving his native town in Guangxi province as a child, it was not known whether he ever visited Guangdong. Qu Dajun (1630-1696), Liang Peilan (1679-1705) and Cheng Keze (1627-1676) were amongst his friends, all natives of Guangdong. Moreover, the superb artistic achievements of Yuanji commanded tremendous respect from artists in Guangdong. For example, Xie Lansheng (1760-1831) described Yuanji's painting in *Changxingxingzhai shuhua tiba* in this way: "As soon as this master starts to paint, strange scenery beyond the horizon flies to his brush."[23] The album is dated 1690, 1693 and 1697 on three separate leaves, so that it could have been done when the artist was in his late forties and mid-fifties. This provides valuable material for the study of the artist's life and artistic techniques.

Hongren (1610-1664) of the Xin'an School of the early Qing period studied the art of Huang Gongwang at first, then turned to Ni Zan. His paintings were highly valued; acquiring a painting by Hongren carries the same connotation for refined taste as owning one by Ni Zan. *The Shixin Peak of Mount Huang* (cat. no. 29) featured in this exhibition was painted in the spring of the *guimao* year, the year that he died.[24] On the right-hand margin of the painting is a colophon consisting of four lines of calligraphy in the running script. It was written by Wang Gen who was a good friend of Hongren and the two visited Mount Huang together several times. In the colophon Wang recorded how this painting came about. He said:

> Between the years *Ren* (*yin*, 1662) and *gui* (*mao*, 1663) I was visiting Zhiyang. Reverend Jian (Hongren) came from Mount Huang to accompany me to Mount Lu. He stayed at the Qiedu Studio where he painted this work for his host Mr. Lu and I inscribed it. Guangjie Qiao, Wang Gen.

This meeting between Hongren and Wang Gen was also mentioned by modern scholars Wang Shiqing and Wang Gailu who furnished additional information that the trip to Mount Lu was delayed because of a snowfall. Instead they stayed behind in Poyang and celebrated the new year as the guests of Lu Shihe at Qiedu Studio.[25]

The Shixin Peak is located to the north of Mount Huang, forming a triangular link with Shangsheng Peak and Shisun Peak. It is composed of hard granite with many cracks and joints from which pine trees of different shapes wrought by nature break through with great vitality. The simple and sparse brush techniques in this painting remind us of Ni Zan of the Yuan dynasty. However, Hongren has achieved his individuality by injecting a new vigour and strength into his lines in the depiction of the granite rocks and overlapping mountain peaks. This painting not only captures the magnificent beauty of the precipitous mountain scenery, it is also permeated by a pure and serene mood that could only have come from the lofty character of the artist himself. It justly deserves an honoured palce among the late works of Hongren.

Mount Huang is the subject of another painting in the exhibition, entitled *Sea of Clouds at Wenshuyuan* (cat. no. 50) by Mei Chong, the great-grandson of Mei Qing. Wenshuyuan is another name for Yupinglou. Behind it is the Yuping Peak, which is the main area of Mount Huang. Other high peaks of Mount Huang such as Lianhua Peak and Tiandu Peak are nearby. The Wenshuyuan is flanked by the Beckoning Pine (*Yinke song*) at the left and the Send-you-off Pine (*songke song*) at the right. On a misty day this is the place from which to view the sea of clouds, called the *qianhai* of Mount Huang. The painting by Mei Chong, in depicting this part of Mount Huang, is filled with rolling clouds and mists as boundless as the sea. The towering peaks emerge from this sea of clouds looking like islands. It is indeed a magnificent spectacle. The entire painting is covered by short and curling brushstrokes derived from the style of Wang Meng (1308-1385), the mountain summits are emphasized by forceful brush strokes and the ink colours. In this way, the painting conjures up a floating imagery of fairy mountains in clouds.

Landscape painting of the "Four Wangs" of the early Qing period, namely Wang Shimin (1592-1680), Wang Jian (1598-1677), Wang Hui (1632-1715), and Wang Yuanqi (1642-1715), perpetuated the brush methods of the Four Masters of the Yuan dynasty and Dong Qichang of late Ming. They valued an antique flavour in their paintings and based their own artistic creations on the thorough study of the ancients.[26] Moreover, these artists considered themselves the Orthodox masters, condemning those who deviated from their path. Wang Yuanqi even said openly:

> There were mannered and vulgar schools in late Ming painting, among them the Zhe school was the worst. With great masters of the Wu and the Yunjian schools like Wen (Zhengming), Shen (Zhou) and Dong (Qichang), there were so many forgeries in circulation so that their styles became corrupted as time went on. (The art) in Guangling (Yangzhou) and Baixia (Nanjing) is as vulgar as the Zhe school. Those who aspire to painting must make sure to avoid it.[27]

The Orthodox school and the Four Wangs exerted tremendous influence in the Qing dynasty. It has even been said that their rigid adherence to ancient models and their derogatory attitude to other schools may have caused the decline of Chinese painting. However, their proficiency in brush techniques and their study of the artistic heritage should still be acknowledged.

Of the Four Wangs, Wang Shimin (cat. no. 26) was the most skilful in the manipulation of the brush. He achieved a sense of serenity and vigour with a seemingly effortless brush and a flexible wrist. Wang Jian (cat. no. 27) painted in a heavy and forceful style. His colour sense is the best of the Four Wangs. Wang Yuanqi (cat. no. 47) was a proud and confident artist and his brush manner is also heavy and expressive. Only Wang Hui (cat. no. 44) paid any attention to the observaton of nature, so that his pure and elegant style is enriched by a feeling of life. The paintings by the Four Wangs included in this exhibition are representative of their accomplishments in the handling of the brush and ink, particularly the *Autumn Mountains* by Wang Shimin, which can be considered a masterpiece from his later period.

While the Four Wangs dominated the art scene in the north with their orthodox style, Yangzhou and Nanjing provided the setting for artists who professed to be above worldly ambitions and who engaged in creative work independent of conventional rules. They shared common interests in life and art, amusing themselves with poetry and wine. They earned a meagre but leisurely living from the sale of their paintings. They specialized in various subjects, creating lofty images with an unrestrained brush. The most famous of these artists were the so-called "Eight Masters of Nanjing" and the "Eight Eccentrics of Yangzhou".

The "Eight Masters of Nanjing" refer to the following artists: Gong Xian (1619-1689), Fan Qi (1616-ca. 1695), Gao Cen (second half of 17th century), Zou Zhe (1636-ca. 1708), Wu Hong (?-1668), Ye Xin (mid-17th century), Xie Sun (mid-17th century) and Hu Zao (mid-17th century). Their styles are quite different, yet their paintings generally demonstrate a feeling of lightness and clarity. The exception is Gong Xian, who worked with dark and heavy ink washes to build up monoumental compositions permeated by a sombre mood. Gong Xian was therefore the acknowledged leader of the group. His paintings are mainly in ink, with which he could achieve the greatest variety of lines and tones (cat. no. 36). The *Cascade in Autumn Mountains* (cat. no. 35) featured in this exhibition is a very rare painting of ink and colour on satin.

The Yangzhou Eccentrics found their most outstanding achievement in the painting of flowers and birds, though they were equally at ease in any subject matter. They have created refreshing and innovative styles which are expressive of their bold personalities and spontaneous techniques, incorporating their cultivation in poetry, calligraphy and painting. They stressed the paramount importance of individual character in artistic expression. In so doing, they have made a positive contribution to the development of literati painting in China.

The Yangzhou artists whose works are included in this exhibition are Jin Nong (1687-1764), Huang Shen (1687-after 1768), Li Shan (1686-after 1760), Wang Shishen (1686-ca. 1759), Li Fangying (1695-1754), Zheng Xie (1693-1765) and Luo Pin (1733-1799). Some paintings are characterized by flowing ink washes and spontaneous brushwork, while others are marked by delicacy and loftiness. Some may create novel effects with a fluid brush. The invigorating spirit of the Yangzhou Eccentrics becomes immediately apparent, particularly after viewing the paintings of the Four Wangs.

Hua Yan (1682-1756) is an artist that deserves our special attention. A native of Shanghang, Fujian province, Hua Yan settled in Hangzhou and Yangzhou for long periods. He led an impvoerished but contented life as a professional artist.[28] The *Album of Miscellaneous Subjects* (cat. no. 66) featured in this exhibition has been donated by Mr. Yang Quan of Hong Kong. It is a great display of his versatility as an artist. He once said of his own art:

> Mountains and streams are imbued with fine delights,
> The clouds and mists are free of worldly attachments.
> The lofty gentleman feels contented in embracing the *dao*,
> While woods in the forest thrive with the approach of spring.
> I follow my own methods in constructing (this painting),
> Even before considering my technical competence,
> (Painting) gives me lifelong happiness.[29]

In the landscape scenes in this album the artist succeeded in achieving a perfect harmony between pictorial form and poetic feeling. The brushwork is refined and elegant, the composition spacious. The figures that he painted are leisurely and relaxed, while his ladies always carry themselves gracefully. Hua Yan was best known for his flower-and-bird painting. He has achieved a distinctive style that combines the descriptive power of the detailed manner (*gongbi*) and the expressive simplicity of the free and spontaneous style (*xieyi*). In this way, the feathers of the birds are portrayed naturalistically and the lively spirit of the birds can also be captured. Upon close inspection of the four leaves of birds and flowers in this album, we feel as if we are transported to a natural wonderland. A thrush is brushing its feathers leisurely and a lark is singing loudly and clearly. We see a paradise flycatcher perched on a branch, looking for its prey, and two beautiful birds are chasing one another playfully. These paintings are filled with the thriving vitality of the natural world and the intimate feelings of the artist. Technically Hua Yan did not adhere to any one school or artist. He has created his own artistic language. For example, he used a dry brush to portray the bird feathers, followed by layers of colour washes. His ability to capture the movement and the expression of the birds is without parallel among the artists of the Ming and Qing dynasties.

Yangzhou in the Qing dynasty also produced artists who gained recognition for their detailed architectural paintings. They were Li Yin, Xiao Chen, Yan Yi, Yuan Jiang and Yuan Yao, mainly active from the late seventeenth to eighteenth centuries. *Playing Chess in a Pavilion by the River* (cat. no. 65) by Yan Yi is one of his major works. It is painted by a disciplined hand in a meticulous manner. Yet the brushwork is still vigorous. The composition is spacious and imbued with a sense of real-life.

Finger painting was recorded as early as the Tang dynasty in *Lidai minghua ji*.[30] The artist Zhang Zao applied ink wash on silk with a worn-out brush, then he used his hand to spread out the ink wash to create pictorial images. Unlike Zhang Zao who used both the brush and the hand, Gao Qipei (1672-1734) relied on his fingers entirely to finish a painting, creating novel effects not unlike action painting in modern Western art. *The Album of Finger Painting* (cat. no. 56) can be counted among Gao's representative works. The pictorial surface is masterfully used by a few quickly and casually sketched lines. An animated spirit and feeling of immediacy permeate the paintings, giving them a captivating charm. These paintings demonstrate how Gao advanced the techniques of finger painting, and more importantly, he inherited the creative concept of Zhang Zao, who first formulated the idea that an artist should "externally study after nature and internally reach for the mind's source." When we read the inscriptions of each of these paintings, we will realize that his images may be abbreviated, but they are all inspired by the artist's personal experience in reality.

Another finger painting in this exhibition is *Banana and Rock* (cat. no. 67) by Gao Fenghan (1683-ca. 1748). In sharp contrast to the painting by Gao Qipei in both technique and style, the painting is an outburst of the untrammelled spirit of the artist. Executed as if drunk with wine and song, it seems to overflow with ink washes. Gao was totally committed to art, to the extent that he overcame a disability of his right-hand in his old age and learned to paint no less skilfully with his left-hand.

In Chinese art bamboo is the symbol of integrity, modesty and endurance. It is tall and erect in appearance and graceful in movement. Therefore, it is the favourite theme for poets and artists of successive periods. A total of five paintings of bamboo are displayed in this exhibition. The *Bamboo* (cat. no. 42) in ink by Dai Mingshuo (mid-seventeenth century) follows the tradition of Wen Tong of the Song dynasty emphasizing the vigorous and serene character of the plant. In Zhu Sheng's (1618-after 1689) scroll of *Three Friends* (cat. no. 41), the virtues of integrity and modesty as symbolized by bamboo are complemented by orchids, the symbol of elegance and remote fragrance. Together with rocks, which are associated with the qualities of straight-forwardness and sturdiness, the three have been called the "three friends" by poets and literati. Both Li Shan and Zheng Xie were renowned painters of bamboo active in Yangzhou. They also gained recognition for their uncorrupted and noble character, as well as their original ideas. However, their bamboo paintings are quite different in style. While Zheng was noted for lucidity in ink and elegance in form, Li splashed ink onto the pictorial surface to give vent to his unrestrained feeling. Wu Changshi (1844-1927) is represented by *Bamboo in Wind* (cat. no. 99). He has captured the unyielding spirit of this noble plant under the onslaught of a fierce wind. The bamboo leaves are painted with powerfully heavy strokes that remind us of the calligraphy engraved on bronzes and stones.

Notes

1. Wu Rongguang, *Xinchou xiaoxia ji* (*Zhuangshi dongtiantang* editon, Beiping, 1905), *juan* 4, pp. 9b-10a.
2. The same as vol. 16 of *Yiyuan Duoying* (April, 1982), cover and p.44.
3. Xie Wenyong, "*Jieshao erfu Songyuan mingzhu*" (Introducing two famous bamboo paintings of the Song and Yuan dynasties), *ibid*. See also Li Lincan, "*Wen Tong mozhu di shuangbao an*" (A case of two versions of *Bamboo in Ink* by Wen Tong), *Gugong wenwu yuekan*, vol. 1, no. 3 (June, 1983), pp. 76-80.
4. Xu Qin, *Minghua lu, juan* 5, p.63. Collected in *Huashi congshu*, ed. Yu Anlan (Shanghai, 1963), vol. 2.
5. *Ibid.*
6. Dong Qichang, *Huachanshi suibi* (Shanghai, 192-?), *juan* 2, p.14b.
7. Jiang Shaoshu, *Wushengshi shi, juan* 3, p.44. Collected in *Huashi congshu*, vol. 3.
8. Lan Ying and Xie Bin, eds. *Tuhui baojian xuzuan, juan* 1, p.3. Collected in *Huashi congshu*, vol. 2.
9. Xu Bangda, *Gushuhua wei'e kaobian* (Studies in connoisseurship of ancient calligraphy and painting), (Nanjing, 1984), Vol.II: text, pp. 142-143.
10. *Ibid.*
11. Jiang Shaoshu, *Wushengshi shi, juan* 3, p.37.
12. See commentary by Zhang Chao following the biography of Dai Wenjin in *Yuchu xinzhi* (Shanghai, 1934), *juan* 8, p.104.
13. Hu Yi, "*Qiu Ying shengzu kao*" (An investigation into the birth and death dates of Qiu Ying), *Duoyun*, vol. 5 (May, 1983), p.46.
14. Dong Qichang, *Huazhi*, collected in Hualun congkan, ed. Yu Anlan (Beijing, 1962), vol. 1, pp. 93-94.
15. Yun Shouping, *Nantian huaba, juan* 3, p.26b. Published in *Meishu Congshu*, eds. Huang Binhong and Deng Shi (Shanghai, 1928), vol.4, series 6.
16. Li Zuoxian, *Shuhua jianying* (*Zhuangshi dongtiantang* edition, Beijing, 1871), *juan* 21, pp.17b-18a.
17. Dong Qichang, *Huazhi*, p.71. English translation adapted from Osvald Siren, *Chinese Painting: Leading Masters and Principles* (New York, 1956-58), vol.5, p.16.
18. *Ibid.*, P.76. English translation adapted from James Cahill, *The Distant Mountains: Chinese Painting of the Late Ming Dynasty, 1570-1644* (New York and Tokyo, 1982), p.14.
19. Su Dongtian, "*Dong Qichang di wenren zhi hua*" (Scholar's painting of Dong Qichang), *Duoyun*, vol.8 (December, 1985), p.170.
20. Dong Qichang, *Huachanshi suibi*, p.8a.
21. *Kugua heshang huayulu*, ch.3. Published in *Hualun congkan*, vol.1, p.148. English translation quoted from Ju-hsi Chou "The Evolution of Daoji's Thought on Painting," *New Asia Academic Bulletin*, vol.4 (1983), p.338.
22. Quoted from Zheng Zhuolu, *Shitao yanjiu* (Studies on Shitao), (Beijing, 1961), p.28.
23. Xie Lansheng, *Changxingxingzhai shuhua tiba*, vol.1. 1974 reprint edition of manuscript copy in the collection of Li Shaoquan.
24. According to Wang Shiqing, Hongren passed away on the 22nd day, twelfth month, the *guimao* year. This corresponds to January 19, 1664 in the Western calendar. See Wang Shiqing, "*Qingchu sida huaseng hekao*" (Combined investigation on the four monkpainters of the

early Qing period), *Journal of the Institute of Chinese Studies of the Chinese University of Hong Kong, vol. 15* (1984), p.184.

25. Wang Shiqing and Wang Gailu, "*Jianjiang ji qi shiyou huodong nianbiao*" (Chronology of Jianjiang and his teachers and friends) in *Jianjiang ziliao ji* (Collection of source materials on Jianjiang), (Hefei, 1984), p. 249.

26. Wang Yuanqi, *Yuchuang manbi,* published in *Meishu congshu*, vol.1, series 2, p.2b.

27. *Ibid.*, p.1a.

28. Quoted from Wang Jingxian, "*Hua Yan di yishu sixiang ji qi chengjiu*" (The artistic thought and achievements of Hua Yan), *Duoyun*, vol.2 (November, 1981), p. 186.

29. *Ibid.*, p. 193.

30. Zhang Yanyuan, *Lidai minghua ji*, annotated by Yu Jianhua (Shanghai, 1964), p.201.

年　表
Chronology

明朝 Ming dynasty

洪武	Hongwu	1368 — 1399
建文	Jianwen	1399 — 1403
永樂	Yongle	1403 — 1425
洪熙	Hongxi	1425 — 1426
宣德	Xuande	1426 — 1436
正統	Zhengtong	1436 — 1450
景泰	Jingtai	1450 — 1457
天順	Tianshun	1457 — 1465
成化	Chenghua	1465 — 1488
弘治	Hongzhi	1488 — 1506
正德	Zhengde	1506 — 1522
嘉靖	Jiajing	1522 — 1567
隆慶	Longqing	1567 — 1573
萬曆	Wanli	1573 — 1620
泰昌	Taichang	1620 — 1621
天啟	Tianqi	1621 — 1628
崇禎	Chongzhen	1628 — 1644

清朝 Qing dynasty

順治	Shunzhi	1644 — 1662
康熙	Kangxi	1662 — 1723
雍正	Yongzheng	1723 — 1736
乾隆	Qianlong	1736 — 1796
嘉慶	Jiaqing	1796 — 1821
道光	Daoguang	1821 — 1851
咸豐	Xianfeng	1851 — 1862
同治	Tongzhi	1862 — 1875
光緒	Guangxu	1875 — 1908
宣統	Xuantong	1908 — 1911

畫目

沈周	1. 吳門十二景册
明人	2. 山水長卷
文徵明	3. 扇面册
陳淳	4. 荔枝賦圖卷
謝時臣	5. 匡廬瀑布圖
仇英	6. 停琴聽阮圖
文伯仁	7. 谿山仙館圖
王穀祥	8. 花卉卷
陳栝	9. 五色蜀葵圖
孫克弘	10. 菊竹貓蝶圖
顧正誼	11. 仿黃公望天池石壁圖卷
董其昌	12. 剪江草堂圖
趙左	13. 溪山清遠卷
李流芳	14. 山水册
沈士充	15. 寒林讀書圖
蔣靄	16. 峻壁飛泉圖
劉原起	17. 城闕驟雨圖
魏克	18. 松蔭流泉圖
王中立	19. 花鳥卷
張翀	20. 花鳥草蟲册
惲向	21. 濯泉自潔圖
沈顥	22. 擬南宗各家山水册
葛徵奇	23. 故山尋道圖
藍瑛	24. 秋山圖
陳洪綬	25. 三松圖
王時敏	26. 秋山圖
王鑑	27. 仿各家山水册
程正揆	28. 江山卧遊圖
弘仁	29. 黃山始信峯圖
查士標	30. 寒樹奇峯圖
梅清	31. 山水通景十屏
朱耷	32. 花鳥雜畫册
原濟	33. 愛蓮圖
	34. 詩畫册
龔賢	35. 秋山飛瀑圖
	36. 雲山結樓圖
葉欣	37. 山水册
金陵畫家	38. 山水册
陳舒	39. 芙蓉一甲圖
張穆	40. 春柳三馬圖
諸昇	41. 三友圖卷
戴明說	42. 墨竹圖
章谷	43. 八景册
王翬	44. 竹窩圖
惲壽平 唐宇昭	45. 蘭蓀柏子圖
上睿	46. 採芝圖
王原祁	47. 仿大癡山水圖
文點	48. 山水册
顧符稹	49. 漢中勝覽圖卷
梅翀	50. 文殊院觀海圖
王晉	51. 松濤携琴圖
陳書	52. 花卉册
楊晉	53. 仿李營丘溪山雪霽圖
黃鼎	54. 山水卷
沈宗敬	55. 濃蔭山莊圖
高其佩	56. 指畫雜册
唐岱	57. 仿大癡山水圖
張宗蒼	58. 雪景山水圖
董邦達	59. 仿王紱溪山深秀卷
李世倬	60. 煙雨歸舟圖
鄒一桂	61. 玉堂富貴圖
崔鏏	62. 百雀圖
張經	63. 載鶴圖
王雲	64. 山水册
顏嶧	65. 江樓對奕圖
華喦	66. 山水花鳥册
高鳳翰	67. 指畫綠天清蔭圖

汪士慎	68. 松柏圖
李　鱓	69. 竹蕉圖
蔡　嘉	70. 馮虛閣秋爽圖
金　農	71. 梅花圖
黄　愼	72. 五湖夜雨圖
鄭　燮	73. 竹石圖
李方膺	74. 蒼松怪石圖
羅　聘	75. 水仙圖
閔　貞	76. 調琴圖
王　宸	77. 仿各家山水册
王　宸 閔　貞	78. 青坷坪圖
沈宗騫	79. 城南山色圖
童　鈺	80. 墨梅圖
王學浩	81. 萍跡山水圖
張　崟	82. 桂蔭涼適圖
奚　岡	83. 西湖放舟圖
陳　壿	84. 松亭授讀圖
童　衡	85. 雙鹿圖
上官慧	86. 山水圖
黎　簡	87. 爲虛舟作山水圖
謝蘭生	88. 山水册
改　琦	89. 竹下仕女圖
湯貽汾	90. 臨青藤書屋八景册
戴　熙	91. 海天霞唱圖
張之萬	92. 今雨樓卷
蘇六朋	93. 清平調圖
蘇仁山	94. 香積圖
趙之謙	95. 五色牡丹圖
任　熊	96. 人物册
任　薰	97. 花鳥四屏
任　頤	98. 湔裙仕女圖
吳昌碩	99. 墨竹圖

List of Paintings

Yang Jin	53. Streams and Mountains after Snow after Li Cheng
Huang Ding	54. Landscape
Shen Zongjing	55. Mountain Retreat amid Trees
Gao Qipei	56. Album of Finger Painting
Tang Dai	57. Landscape after Huang Gongwang
Zhang Zongcang	58. Snowy Landscape
Dong Bangda	59. Landscape in the Style of Wang Fu
Li Shizhuo	60. Returning Boat in Rain and Mist
Zuo Yigui	61. Magnolias and Peonies
Cui Sui	62. A Hundred Sparrows
Zhang Jing	63. Boat Carrying Crane
Wang Yun	64. Landscape Album
Yan Yi	65. Playing Chess in a Pavilion by the River
Hua Yan	66. Album of Miscellaneous Subjects
Gao Fenghan	67. Finger Painting of Banana and Rock
Wang Shishen	68. Pine and Cypress
Li Shan	69. Bamboo and Banana
Cai Jia	70. The Fengxuge in Autumn
Jin Nong	71. Prunus Blossoms
Huang Shen	72. Night Rain
Zheng Xie	73. Bamboo and Rock
Li Fangying	74. Pine and Rock
Luo Pin	75. Narcissus
Min Zhen	76. Ladies Playing *Qin*
Wang Chen	77. Landscapes after Various Masters
Wang Chen **Min Zhen**	78. Portrait of Keping
Shen Zongqian	79. Mountains at South of the City
Tong Yu	80. Prunus Blossoms
Wang Xuehao	81. Landscape
Zhang Yin	82. Cooling in the Shade of Cassia Trees
Xi Gang	83. Boating on West Lake
Chen Zun	84. Lecturing in Pavilion among Pine Trees
Tong Heng	85. Two Deer
Shangguan Hui	86. Landscape
Li Jian	87. Landscape Dedicated to Xuzhou
Xie Lansheng	88. Landscape Album
Gai Qi	89. Ladies under Bamboo
Tang Yifeng	90. The Eight Views of Qingteng Studio
Dai Xi	91. Landscape
Zhang Zhiwan	92. Jinyu Lou
Su Liupeng	93. Li Bai Composing the *Qingpingdiao*
Su Renshan	94. The *Xiangji* Story
Zhao Zhiqian	95. Peonies in Five Colours
Ren Xiong	96. Album of Figure Painting
Ren Xun	97. Flowers and Birds
Ren Yi	98. Lady Laundering
Wu Changshi	99. Bamboo in Wind

5

6

7

11

11

20.5

20.11

24

2

28

29

34.2

35

38.6

38.8

77.2

77.12

88.1

88.2

93

95

98

97A

沈　周

明代　1427－1509

字啟南，號白石翁，人稱石田先生。長洲（江蘇蘇州）人。居相城，畫有家學，讀書不仕。善詩文、書法。畫山水、人物、花鳥無一不工。中年畫法謹細，晚年粗簡，自成一家，爲"吳派四大家"之首。

1. 吳門十二景册

紙本水墨册頁十二開　各25.6×22.5厘米

此册山水十二開，寫吳縣名勝，用筆圓厚，景意簡遠，偶設人物小居，生趣盎然。雖無款無印（僅第三開有"容庚祕匧"白文鑑藏印），然每開均有自書詩對題，並署"沈周"款及鈐朱文"啟南"方印。其後有張寰於嘉靖丙午（1546年）春三月跋稱：張爲山治吳郡三年，離職告別，以此册相贈事。還有朱子謙跋及時人吳子玉爲容庚題跋。容庚教授生前捐贈廣州美術館。圖册現保存原明代裝裱。

自書詩對題：

(1) 虎丘山
虎阜山形勝，吳人四季遊。風生鈴語亂，池淨劍光浮。右虎丘山。沈周。

印章：
啟南（朱文方印）
（以下各開所鈐印章同）
鑑藏印章：
容庚祕匧（朱文方印）

(2) 玄墓山
玄墓山中寺，天開圖畫中。憑闌聊極目，心境覺虛空。右玄墓山。沈周。

(3) 虎山橋
天地開奇觀，湖山雪月宵。此時誰領略，人在虎山橋。右虎山橋。沈周。

(4) 南峯
南峯古禪居，萬竹晴更好。日晏始開門，白雲僧自掃。右南峯。沈周。

(5) 橫塘
詰曲橫塘路，微茫有幾家。春風餘二月，花映酒帘斜。右橫塘。沈周。

(6) 光福山
鄧尉山中好，幽尋可杖藜。風光宜五月，處處熟楊梅。右光福山。沈周。

(7) 天池山
天池插天際，石壁翠寒（此句疑脫一字）。仰面看雲出，掀髯欲墮冠。右天池山。沈周。

(8) 賀九嶺
野樹靄晴暉，山光落杯酒。昔日吳王來，于茲賀重九。右賀九嶺。沈周。

(9) 上方山
石徑無塵到，松窗有夢關。遐思清絕處，僧在上方山。右上方山。沈周。

(10) 覺海寺
覺海清幽甚，僧居不可尋。虛堂秋月白，曾此卧雲深。右覺海寺。沈周。

(11) 姑蘇臺
麋鹿荒臺上，春風開野花。只今游衍客，不見舊繁華。右姑蘇臺。沈周。
鑑藏印章：
夢簾香閣（朱文方印）

(12) 蓮花峯
蓮花發奇秀，突兀插天表；披襟凌太清，一覽衆山小。右蓮花峯。沈周。

另附題跋二開：

題跋（一）：
爲山先生張侯治吳郡之三年，將課最入覲，告行於友人石川張子。張子以石田小册貺焉。侯慨然曰：吾明刑茲郡，夙夜在公，不遑寧處。所謂吳門十二景者，信美而未暇一涉焉，盖未嘗不往來予懷。吾茲披圖，湖山之勝，了然在目，不啻履巉嶙而聽潺湲也。古人以澄懷卧游自適，所得不旣多乎。石川子曰：吾侯信多遺愛於吾郡，圖書之外，行李蕭然，一册之貺，聊伴琴鶴耳矣。于是二峯朱子旁觀贊助，爲之憮然曰：二君子授受兩無媿色矣。乃掀髯長嘯而別。嘉靖丙午（1546年）春三月之吉，婁曲張寰書於擬陶軒。

題跋印章：
張允淸氏（朱文方印）
石川世居（朱文方印）
省訓堂（朱文長方印）

題跋（二）：
爲山郡侯，秉憲三載，化令惟肅，而終始一節，冰蘗著聞，迺石川大夫爰繪吳門十二景以獻，庸表侯圖書數卷之蹟。余得快覩，輒綴數語，以見懷賢慕德之私，甘棠之愛，不媿古人，而攀卧之誠，其何能忘云。二峯朱隆禧再拜書。

題跋印章：
都諫之印（白文方印）
朱子謙氏（白文方印）

題跋（三）：

吳子玉題，不錄。

Shen Zhou

Ming dynasty 1427-1509

Zi Qinan, *hao* Baishiweng, Shitian, native of Changzhou (present-day Suzhou, Jiangsu province). Shen came from a prominent literati family and received a classical literary education. He never entered government service but devoted himself to the arts of poetry, calligraphy and painting. Considered to be the leader of the "Four Masters of the Wu School", he was an accomplished painter of landscapes, figures, birds and flowers. His personal style evolved from masterly skill in his middle period to vigourous simplicity in his later years.

1. Twelve Views of Wumen (Suzhou)

Album of twelve leaves, ink on paper
each leaf 25.6×22.5 cm

(1) Huqiu Mountain
With inscription, signature, 1 seal of the artist and 1 collector's seal on facing page.

(2) Xuanmu Mountain
With inscription, signature and 1 seal of the artist on facing page.

(3) Hushan Bridge
With 1 collector's seal on painted page; with inscription, signature and 1 seal of the artist on facing page.

(4) Nanfeng
Same as leaf (2).

(5) Hengtang
Same as leaf (2).

(6) Guangfu Mountain
Same as leaf (2).

(7) Tianchi Mountain
Same as leaf (2).

(8) Hejiu Ridge
Same as leaf (2).

(9) Shangfang Mountain
Same as leaf (2).

(10) Juehai Temple
Same as leaf (2).

(11) Gusu Terrace
Same as leaf (1).

(12) Lianhua Peak
Same as leaf (1).

2 additional leaves with 3 colophons by Zhang Huan, Zhu Longxi and Wu Ziyu.

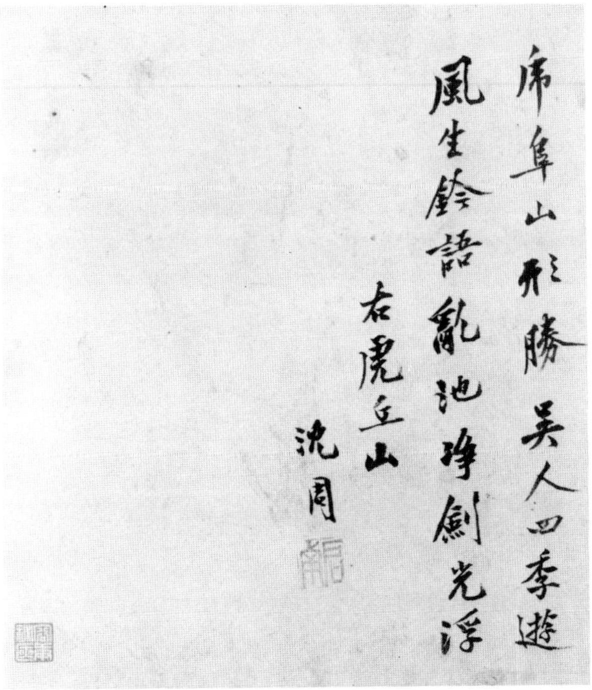

1.1a

1.1

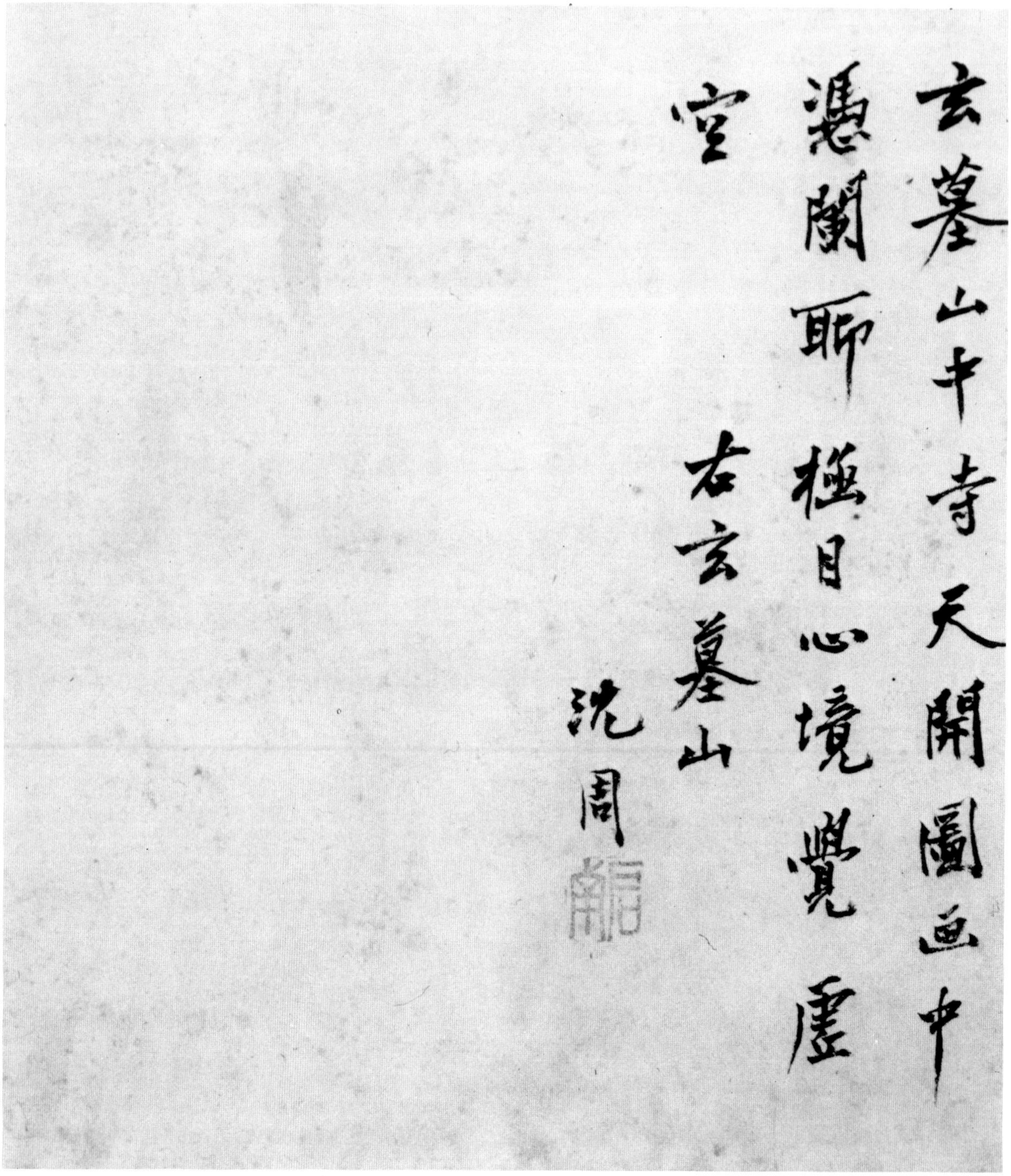

1.2a

1.2

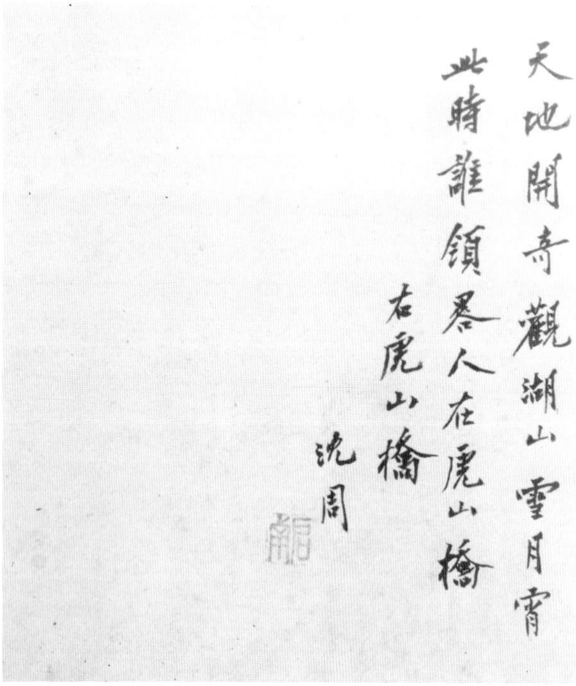
天地開奇觀湖山雪月霄
此時誰領畧人在虎山橋
右虎山橋
沈周

1.3a

1.3

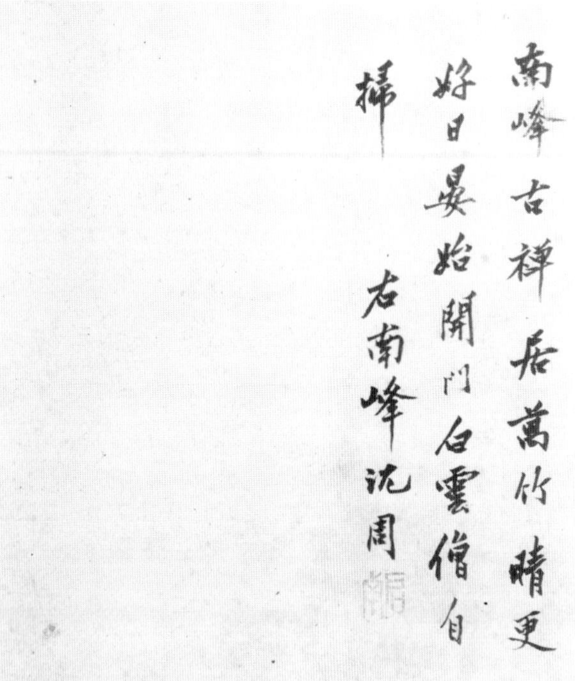
南峰古禅居萬竹晴更
好日晏始開門白雲僧自
掃
右南峰沈周

1.4a

1.4

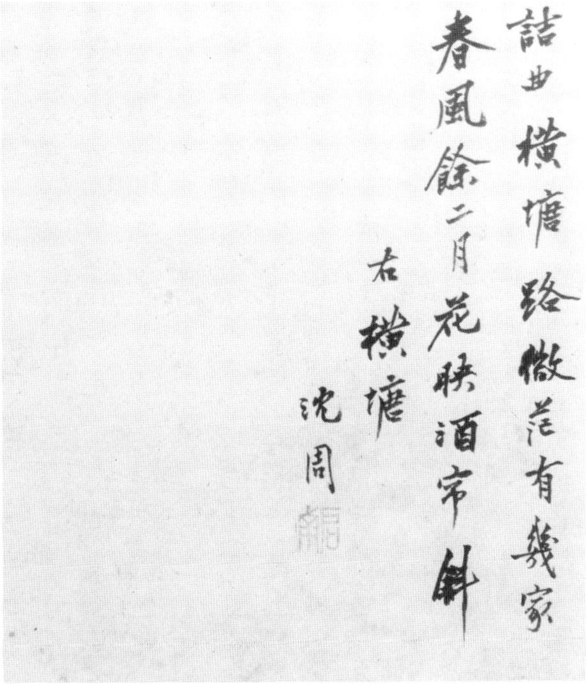
詰曲橫塘路微茫有幾家
春風餘二月花映酒帘斜
右橫塘
沈周

1.5a

1.5

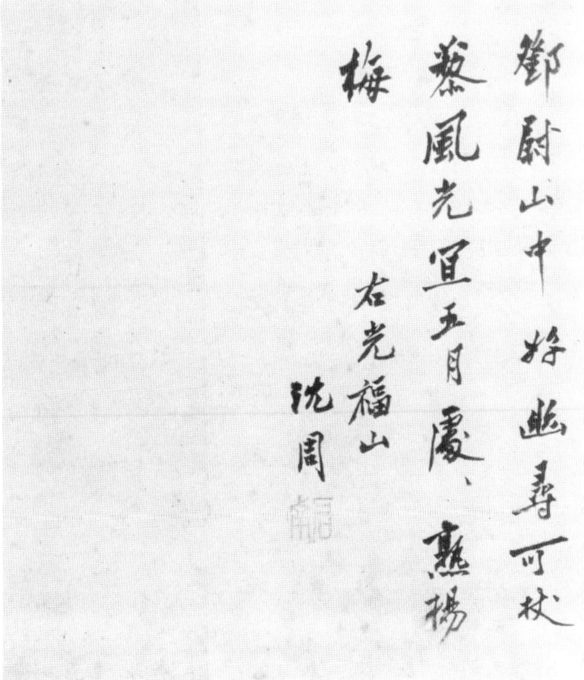
鄧尉山中好幽尋可杖
藜風光宜五月處處熏楊
梅
右光福山
沈周

1.6a

1.6

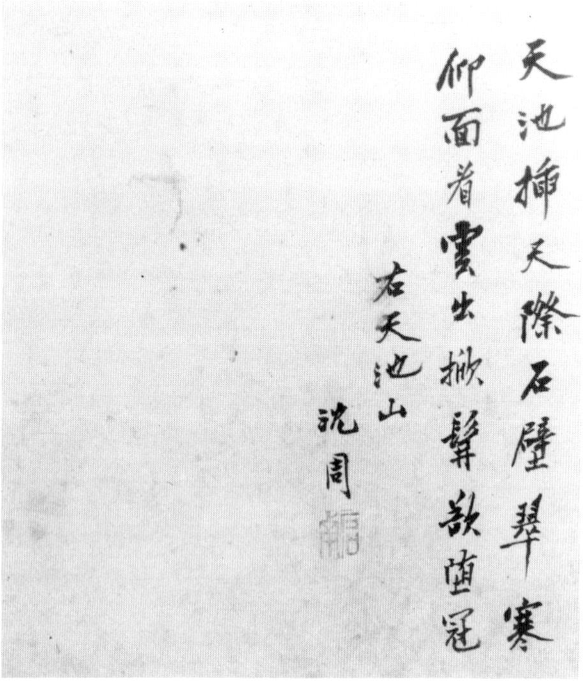
天池插天際石壁翠寒
仰面看雲出掀髯欲墮冠
右天池山
沈周

1.7a

1.7

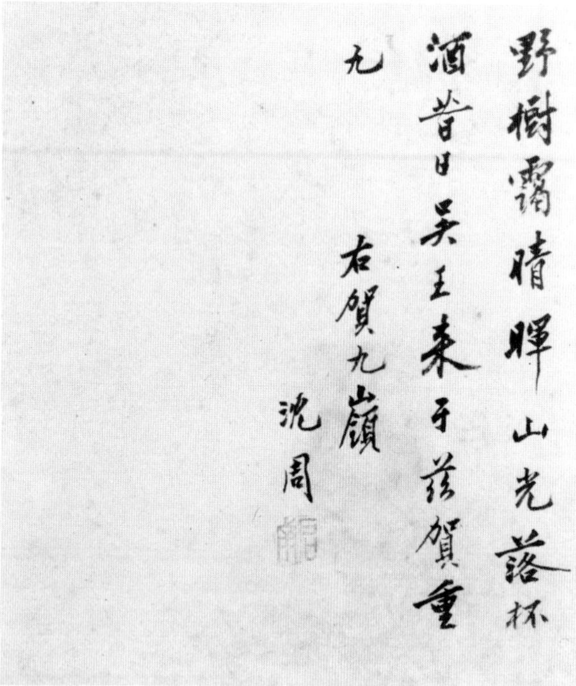
野樹露晴暉山光落杯
酒昔日吳王來于茲賀重
九
右賀九嶺
沈周

1.8a

1.8

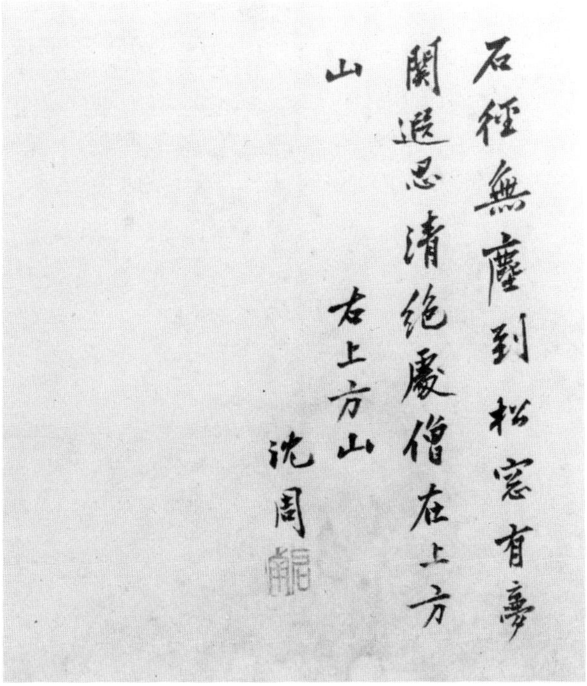

1.9a

1.9

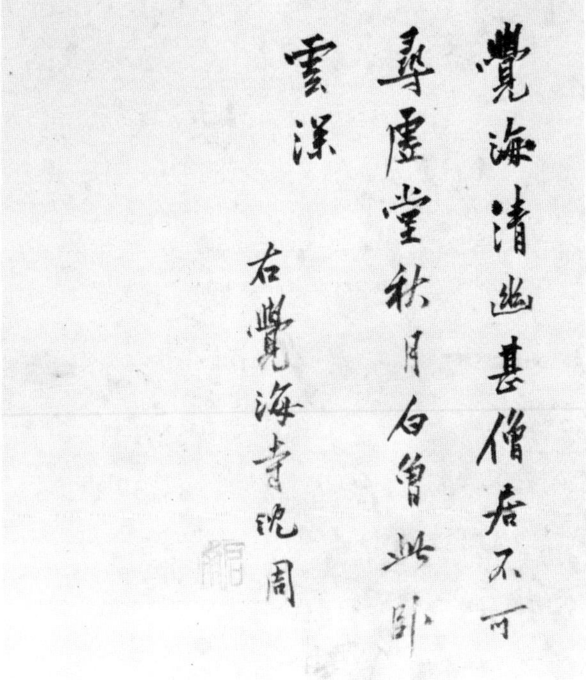

1.10a

1.10

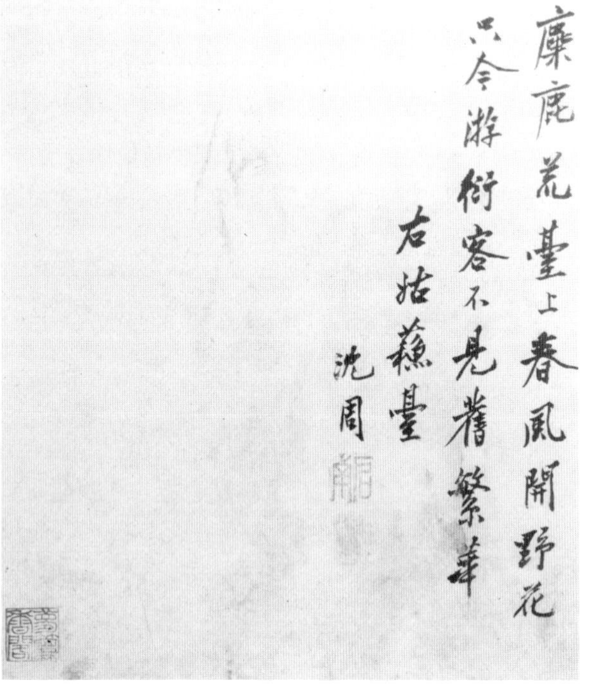

1.11a

1.11

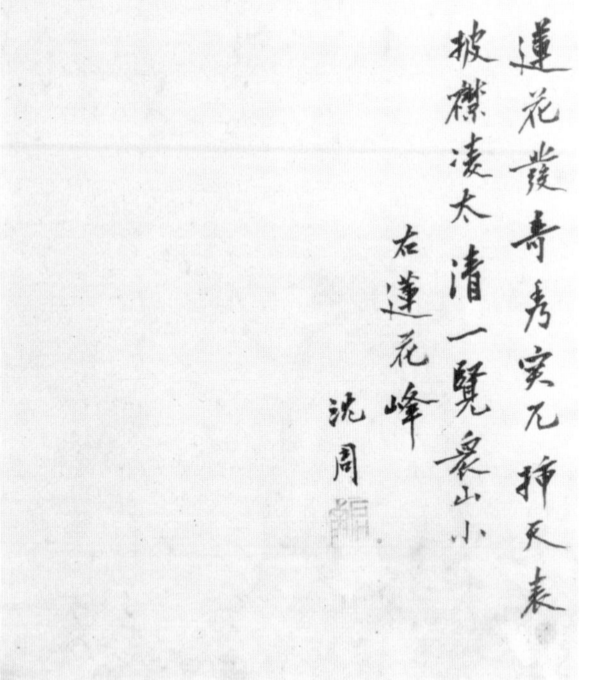

1.12a

1.12

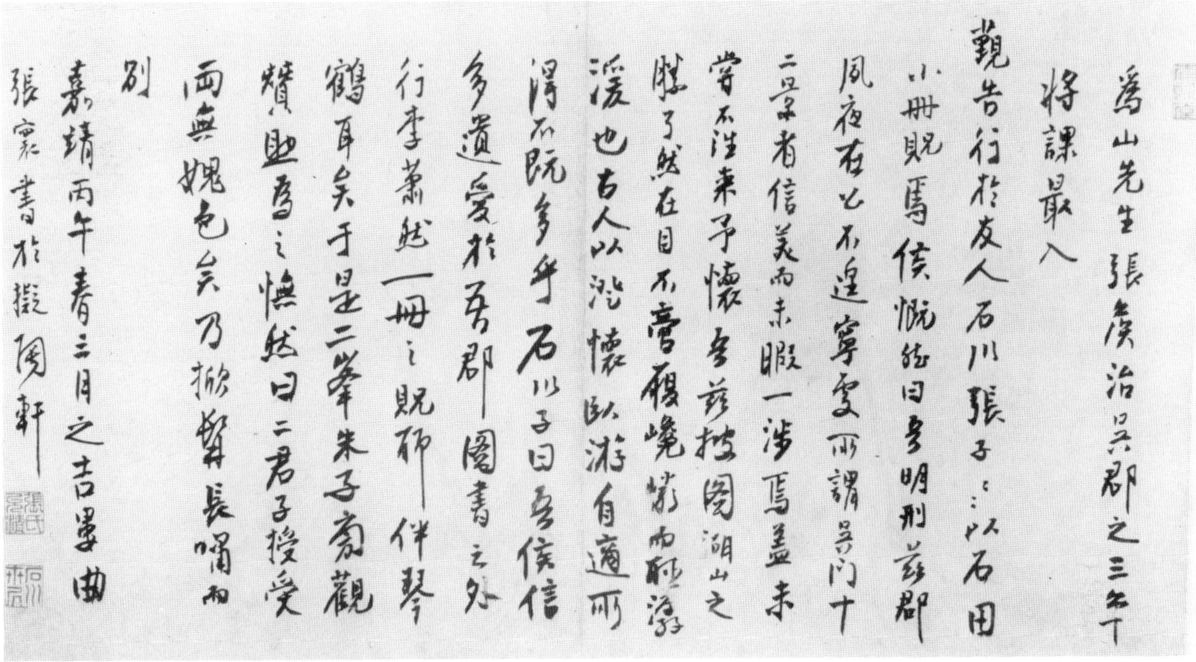

1.13

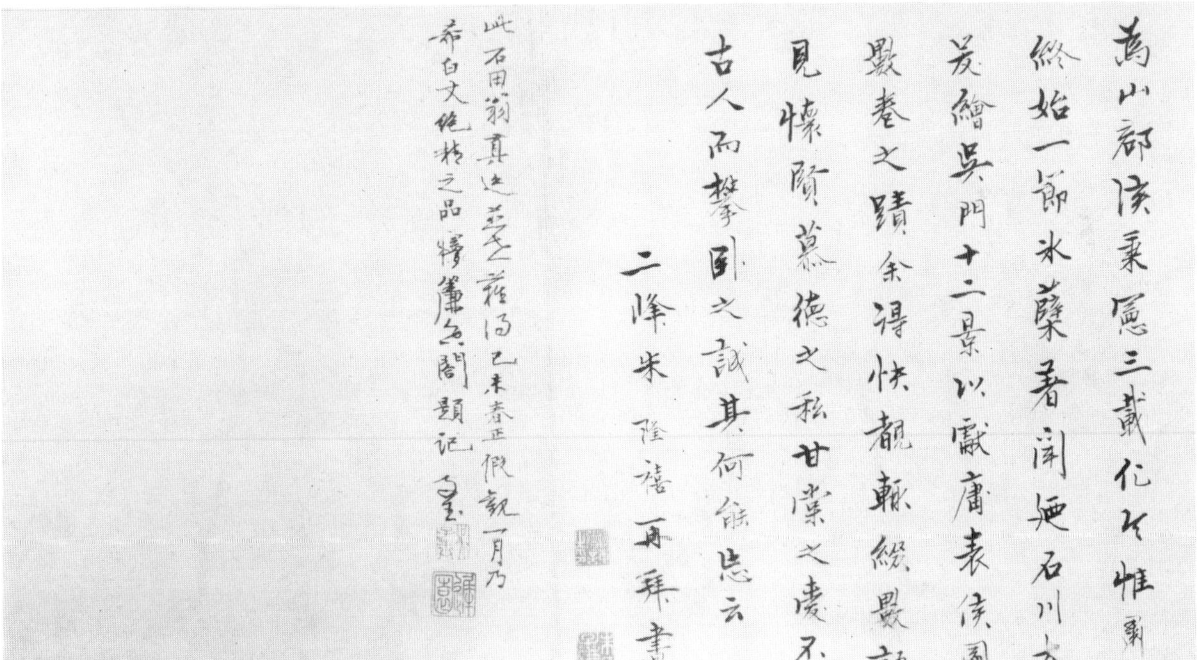

1.14

明　人

2. 山水長卷

紙本設色手卷　50×2073厘米

此畫開卷近處山石攢聚，遠山煙霧迷茫，奇石嶙峋。繼而叢樹竹林，出見溪流，人物騎馬，兩僕前後相隨，正欲過橋，橋邊客舍兩間，漁舟泊岸。小溪出口處，可見開闊大江，煙波浩渺，數小艇來往江中。而近景又出現松林，中有路有橋可通，過橋便入嶺路險峻，大江遠岫均爲所遮，山泉流瀉。稍過又見遠峯浮靄，小溪環繞灣轉，平坡一片。接着又巉巖峻嶺，古木參天，山色迷濛，若隱若顯，江山無盡，意境深遠。此山水卷，從筆法及景緻構思顯然受南宋夏珪（十三世紀前期）《溪山清遠圖卷》影響，有些段落有仿傚跡象。如帶橋亭的長橋一段，幾乎一模一樣。款識原署："錢塘戴進"。按戴進（1388－1462），字文進，號靜庵，錢塘（浙江杭州）人。善畫山水、人物。山水受李唐、夏珪、馬遠影響，喜用斧劈皴，挺勁雄拔，開創了明代浙派畫風。此卷鑑定爲明人作品，風貌和戴進相近，年份也不差太長，是明代浙派山水畫少見長卷。

款識：
錢塘戴進。

印章：
文進（朱文方印）

鑑藏印章：
益夫（朱文方印）
晉陵王氏東齊畫記（朱文方印）
容庚秘匧（白文方印）
李恩慶（朱白文方印）
愛吾廬珍藏印（白文方印）
佟氏珍藏（朱文方印）
王慊（朱文方印）
晉陵王氏東齊畫印（朱文方印）
翰林編收太常少卿（朱文方印）
曾爲北平李季雲收藏（白文方印）

Artist Unknown

Ming dynasty

2. Landscape

Handscroll, ink and colour on paper
50 × 2073 cm

With apocryphal signature and 1 seal of Dai Jin (1388-1462), and 10 collectors' seals.

2

文徵明

明代　1470－1559

初名壁，字徵明，後以字行，改字徵仲，號衡山居士。長洲（江蘇蘇州）人。官翰林待詔。工詩文、書畫，山水法趙孟頫（1254－1322）、吳鎮（1280－1354）、王蒙（1308－1385）。亦善人物花卉，爲"吳門四大家"之一，畫派影響至爲廣遠。

3. 扇面册

金箋紙本設色、水墨扇面六開　各闊29.5厘米

此册山水花鳥共十二開。筆法有工有意，有水墨有設色。具年款及上款各一，諒爲後人集裱成册，其中部份作品尚待確鑑。今選刊其六。

(1) **山水**

款識：
徵明。

印章：
徵、明（朱文聯珠印）

(2) **山水**

款識：
落日浮圖昏，遙鐘隔烟嶺。應有未眠人，冷然發深省。徵明。

印章：
徵、明（朱文聯珠印）

(3) **棘枝雙鳥**

款識：
落木蕭蕭苦竹深，茆簷日煖笑雙禽。棘枝豈是棲遲地，三月春風滿上林。徵明。

印章：
徵、明（朱文聯珠印）

(4) **山水人物**
1531年作

款識：
嘉靖辛卯（1531年）秋日，過孔周書齋，聊作扇景贈之。徵明。

印章：
文徵明印（白文方印）

(5) **樹石**

款識：
徵明。

印章：
徵明（白文長方印）

鑑藏印章：
山曾印信（白文方印）

(6) **赤壁圖**

款識：
徵明。

印章：
文徵明印（白文方印）

Wen Zhengming

Ming dynasty　1470-1559

Original name Bi, *zi* Zhengzhong, *hao* Hengshan Jushi, native of Changzhou (present-day Suzhou, Jiangsu province). Born into a family of scholar-officials, Wen was appointed *daizhao* in the Hanlin Academy in Beijing. He excelled in poetry, calligraphy and painting, following in particular the landscape styles of Zhao Mengfu (1254-1322), Wu Zhen (1280-1354) and Wang Meng (1308-1385). He was one of the ''Four Masters of the Wu School'' and exerted great influence on later generations.

3. Album of Fan Paintings

Album of six folding fans,
ink and colour on gold paper
each fan 31 cm in width

(1) Landscape
With signature and 1 seal of the artist.

(2) Landscape
With inscription, signature and 1 seal of the artist.

(3) Thorn bushes with Birds
With inscription, signature and 2 seals of the artist.

(4) Landscape with Figures
Dated 1531
With inscription, signature and 1 seal of the artist.

(5) Trees by the Stream
With signature and 1 seal of the artist.

(6) The Red Cliff
With signature and 1 seal of the artist.

3.1

3.2

3.3

3.4

3.5

3.6

陳　淳

明代　1483－1544

字道復，後以字行，更字复甫，號白陽山人。吳縣（江蘇蘇州）人。文徵明弟子。工畫水墨花卉、山水，筆法灑落，自成一家。此圖畫荔枝連枝帶葉數顆，雖自稱生平未識其面目，然寫來眞實可摘。

4．荔枝賦圖

紙本設色手卷　28.5×309厘米

引首：
荔枝賦。

鑑藏印章：
金協中（白文方印）

款識（一）：
荔枝賦並敍。

南海郡出荔枝焉。每至季夏，其實乃熟。狀甚瓌詭，味特甘滋，百果之中，無一可比。余往在西掖，嘗盛稱之，諸公莫之知，故未之信。惟舍人彭城劉侯，弱年累遷，經於南海，一聞斯談，倍復嘉嘆，以爲甘美之極也。又謂龍眼凡果，而與荔枝齊名。魏文帝方引葡萄及龍眼相比，是時二方不通，傳聞之大謬也。每相顧閑議，欲爲賦述，世務孳孳，此志莫就。及理郡暇日，追敍往心。夫物以不知爲輕，味以無味而疑，遠不可驗，終焉永屈。况士有未效之用，而身在無譽之間，苟無深知，與彼亦何以異也。因道揚其實，遂作此賦云：
果之美者，厥有荔枝，雖受氣於震方，實稟精於火離。乃作酸於此裔，爰負陽以從宜。蒙休和之所播，涉寒暑而匪虧。下合圍以擢秊，傍蔭畝而抱規，紫文紺理，黛葉緗枝，蓊茸霏霺，環合棼菲。如盖之張，如幬之垂。雲烟沃若，孔翠於斯。靈根所盤，不高不卑。陋下澤之沮洳，惡層崖之險巇。彼前志之或妄，何側生之見疵。爾其勾芒在辰，凱風入律，肇氣含滋，芬敷謐溢。綠穗靡靡，青英苾苾。不豐其花，但甘其實。如有意乎端本，故微文而妙質。蔕藥房而捽萃，皮龍鱗以駢比。膚玉英而含澤，色紅荓以吐日。朱苞剖，明璫出，冏然數寸，猶不可匹。未玉齒而殆銷，雖瓊漿而可軼。彼衆味而有五，此甘滋之不一。伊醇淑之無算，非精言之能悉。聞者歡而竦企，見者訝而驚佗。心恚可以蠲忿，口爽可以忘疾。且欲神於醴露，何比數於甘橘。援蒲萄以具擬，亦古人之深失。若乃華軒洞開，嘉賓四會，時當燠煜，客或煩憒，而斯果在筵，莫不心侈而體泰。信瑀盤之仙液，實玳筵之綺績。有終食於累百，愈益氣而理內，故無厭於所甘，雖不貪而必愛。沉美李而莫取，浮甘瓜而自退。豈一坐之所榮，冠四時而爲最。夫其貴可以薦宗廟，珍可以羞王公，亭十里兮莫致，門九重兮曷通。山五嶠兮白雲，江千里兮青楓。何斯美之揚遠，嗟爾命之不逢。每被銷於凡口，罕獲知於貴躬。柿何稱乎梁侯，梨何幸乎張公，亦因地之所遇，孰能辨乎其中哉。道復。

款識（二）：
荔枝賦，余數年前書。偶閱一過，掩卷茫然。案頭適有朱墨，乃戲作數顆。平生未識眞面目，不過捕風捉影耳。觀者當參諸賦，或自得其眞焉。淳。

印章：
古吳陳淳（白文方印）
白陽山居（白文方印）
陳淳之印（白文方印）
陳道復氏（白文方印）
大姚邨（朱文長方印）
大姚（朱文圓印）
淳（朱文方印）

鑑藏印章：
蓉峯劉恕審定（朱文橢圓印）
閱驅堂印（朱文方印）
長山王曆長審定重裝（白文方印）
金協中（白文方印）
張眞人（朱文方印）
靈后何蘭士藏（朱文長方印）

Chen Chun

Ming dynasty 1483-1544

Zi Daofu, later *zi* Fufu, *hao* Baiyang Shanren, native of Wuxian (present-day Suzhou, Jiangsu province). Chen was a student of Wen Zhengming and excelled in painting landscapes and flowers in ink in a free and spontaneous style.

4. Prose Poem on Lychee

Handscroll, ink and colour on paper
28.5 × 309 cm

With frontispiece, long inscription, signature, 7 seals of the artist and 6 collectors' seals.

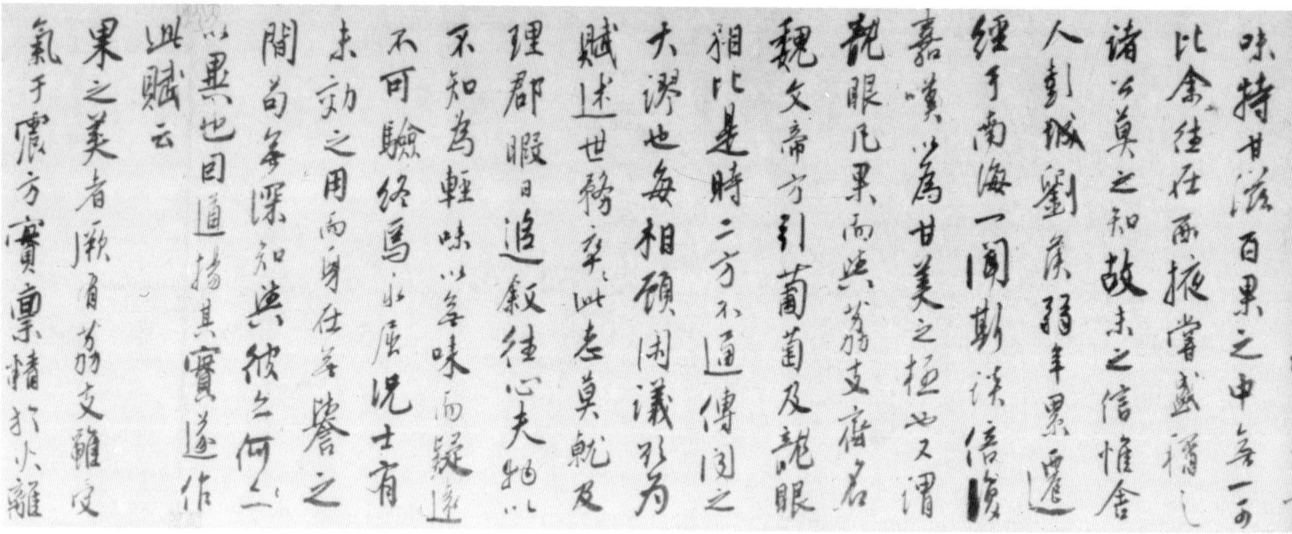
味特甘滋百果之中無一可
比余往在西掖嘗盛稱之
諸公莫之知故未之信惟舍
人彭城劉侯弱年累遷
經于南海一聞斯談倍復
嘉嘆以為甘美之極也又謂
龍眼凡果而與荔支為
魏文帝方引蒲萄及龍眼
相比是時二方不通傳聞之
大謬也每相顧閑議欲為
賦述世務卒卒此志莫就及
理郡暇日追敘往心夫物以
不知為輕味以無味而疑遠
不可驗終焉永屈況士有
未効之用而身在無譽之
間苟無深知與彼亡何以
異也因道揚其實遂作
此賦云
果之美者厥有荔支雖受
氣于震方實稟精於火離

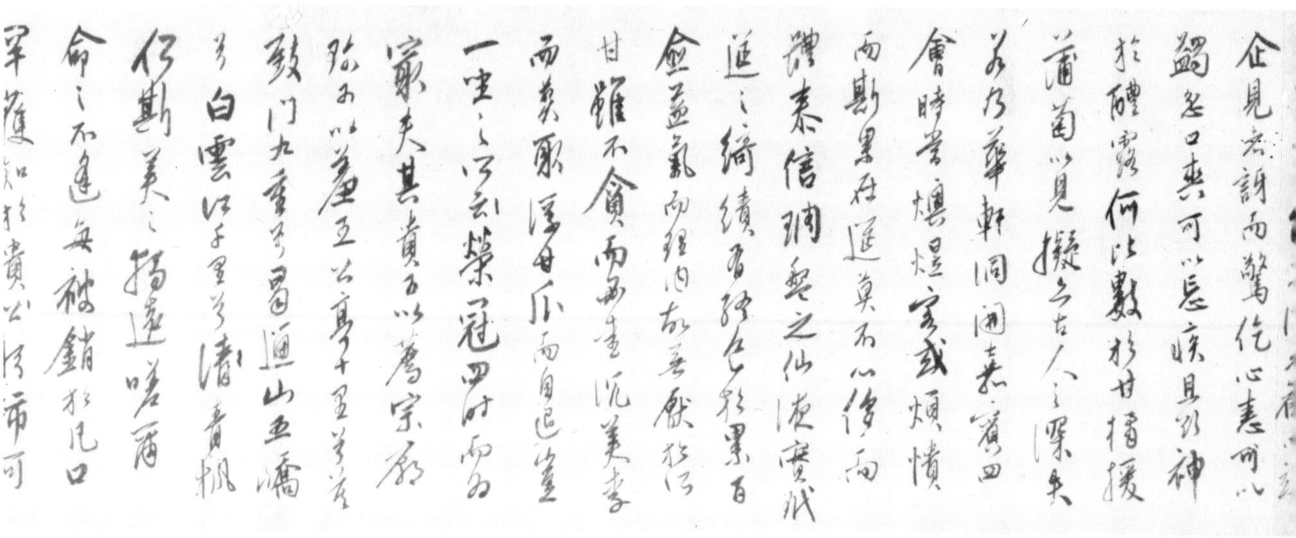

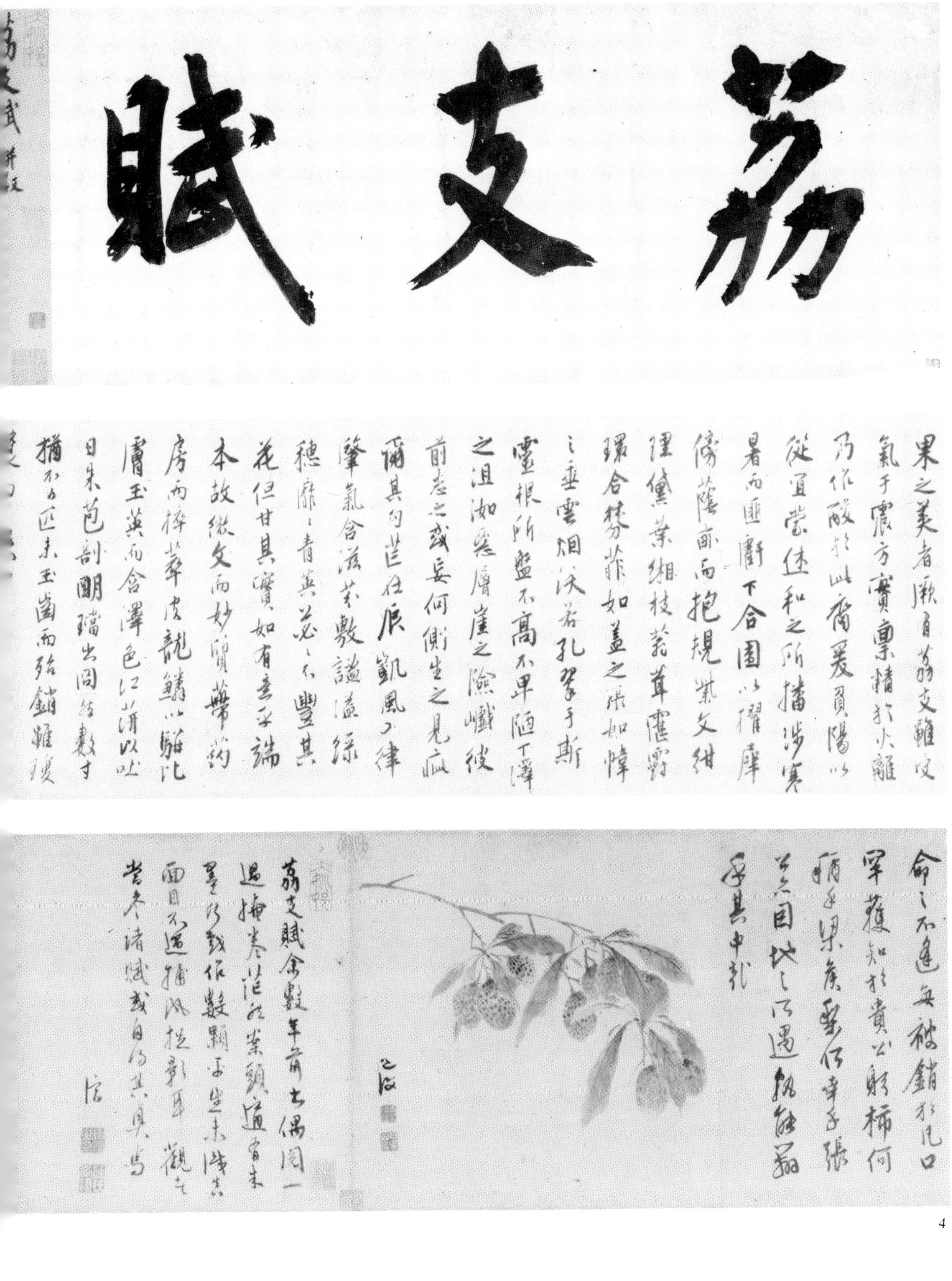

4

謝時臣

明代　1487－1567後

字思忠，號樗仙。吳縣（江蘇蘇州）人。善畫山水，學沈石田而略變更厚重，作巨幛大幅，氣勢雄厚。

5. 匡廬瀑布圖

紙本設色立軸　220×141.4厘米

匡廬在江西星子九江二縣間，相傳時有匡俗兄弟七人結廬於此，故名。

款識：
匡廬瀑布。謝時臣筆。

印章：
謝思忠氏（白文方印）
樗仙（白文長方印）
賜本（朱文長方印）
青宮太保（朱文方印）

鑑藏印章：
海昌錢鏡塘藏（朱文長方印）

Xie Shichen

Ming dynasty　1487-after 1567

Zi Sizhong, *hao* Shuxian, native of Wuxian (present-day Suzhou, Jiangsu province). Xie was best known for his landscape painting, basing his style on that of Shen Zhou but with heavier handling of brush and ink. He painted many monumental paintings which impart a strong and compelling feeling.

5. Waterfall of Mount Lu

Hanging scroll, ink and colour on paper
220×141.4 cm

With inscription, signature, 4 seals of the artist and 1 collector's seal.

匡廬瀑布

仇　英

明代　1494/5－1552

字實父，號十洲。江蘇太倉人，居蘇州。學畫於周臣（約1450－1535後），工人物、山水、花鳥，尤善摹古畫。與沈周、唐寅（1470－1523）、文徵明，並稱爲"吳門四家"。

6. 停琴聽阮圖

紙本設色立軸　112.2×42厘米

此圖寫二人於山坡上停琴聽阮，山石用小斧劈皴，樹葉雙勾。瀑布流泉，氣蒸雲蔚，幽靜清妍。此幀曾爲文徵明家族後人文鼎（1766－1852）收藏，有"後山藏於停雲舊築"題簽。並經鑒藏家李佐賢《書畫鑒影》收錄，後爲廣東鑒藏家何荔甫和黃詠雩收藏。

款識：
仇英實父製。
印章：
十洲（朱文葫蘆印）
仇英之印（白文方印）
鑑藏印章：
李佐賢收藏書畫之印（白文方印）
休易注□□□甫珍藏（朱文長方印）
後山珍藏（長方白文印）
田溪書屋鑑藏（朱文長方印）
麗圃心賞（白文方印）

Qiu Ying

Ming dynasty　1494/5-1552

Zi Shifu, *hao* Shizhou, native of Taicang, Jiangsu province. Qiu lived in Suzhou and studied painting with Zhou Chen (ca. 1450-after 1535). He was an accomplished painter of landscapes, figures, birds and flowers, particularly gifted in copying ancient paintings. Together with Shen Zhou, Tang Yin (1470-1523) and Wen Zhengming, Qiu was regarded as one of the ''Four Masters of the Wu School''.

6. Listening to Music by the Waterfall

Hanging scroll, ink and colour on paper
112.2×42 cm

With signature, 2 seals of the artist and 5 collectors' seals.

仇十洲停琴聽阮圖

文伯仁

明代　1502－1575

字德承，號五峯山人。長洲（江蘇蘇州）人。文徵明姪。工畫山水、人物，以細密見長，是文派筆墨略近王蒙（1308－1385）一路。

7. 谿山仙館圖

1564年作
紙本設色立軸　71×39厘米

此圖寫峯巒鬱茂，谿流清澈，人物橋上停步顧應，山路曲折，濃蔭叢中，館閣隱露。畫筆工細，設色淡雅，是作者晚年佳作。

款識：
谿山仙館。嘉靖甲子（1564年）冬十二月望爲允謙比部寫。五峯文伯仁。

印章：
五峯（朱文方印）
文伯仁（朱文方印）

Wen Boren

Ming dynasty　1502-1575

Zi Decheng, *hao* Wufeng Shanren, native of Changzhou and nephew of Wen Zhengming. Wen painted landscapes and figures and was noted for his detailed and refined manner. He continued the tradition of Wen Zhengming but also showed influence from Wang Meng (1308-1385) of the Yuan dynasty.

7. Pavilion amid Streams and Mountains

Dated 1564
Hanging scroll, ink and colour on paper
71 × 39 cm

With inscription, signature and 2 seals of the artist.

王穀祥

明代　1501－1568

字祿之，號酉室。長洲（江蘇蘇州）人。官至吏部員外郎。文徵明學生。工書畫篆刻，善畫花卉。

8. 花卉卷

1541年作
紙本設色手卷　25.5×496厘米

此卷寫四季折枝花卉十二種，具沈周、文徵明風貌。

引首：
效顰前列。吏部郎王穀祥。

印章：
王祿之印（朱文方印）

款識：
辛丑（1541年）之歲，春多霪雨，寂坐小齋，避濕暄也。漫閱圖籍，頗覺適意。旣而得石田先生所作花卷，自春徂冬，種種不遺。余亦高興，勉寫一過，恐聰明未始能及，見者必笑走也。酉室王穀祥記。

鑑藏印章：
渤海後人（朱文方印），兩方
歐陽竹平（朱文方印），兩方
養齋秘賞（朱文方印），兩方
曾藏喬固庵家（白文方印）
夢香室主秘笈之印（朱文長方印）
皇帝圖書（朱文方印），兩方
寶玩之記（朱白文長方印）
日麗中天之寶（朱文方印）
萬歷之璽（朱文方印）
御府圖書（朱文方印）
正心誠意（朱文方印）
小山書屋（白文方印）
堅白齋（朱文方印）

後幅題跋：
酉室先生人品極高，文章詞翰妙絕一時，而書畫尤爲士夫所重。據《藝苑卮言》謂：先生中年後絕不爲人落筆，而畫傳世尤少。此卷所畫折枝花卉十二種，行筆布墨，秀韻天成；敷色渲染，直窺元人之奥。觀其題識，知其爲平生得意之作。引首四大字，卓健不羣，不媿爲衡翁高足。卷前後均鈐有御璽，是曾經收入內府者，惟所鈐各璽於位置上不大合

，其必出諸寺人之手無疑，殊令覽者不快也。戊辰六月六日晨起閱罷，試洮河石研漫題。養道者頤元。

題跋印章：
養道者（白文長圓印）
寥瑤室主（朱白文長方印）
辛未生（朱文長方印）
長樂（朱文長方印）

Wang Guxiang

Ming dynasty 1501-1568

Zi Luzhi, *hao* Youshi, native of Changzhou (present-day Suzhou, Jiangsu province). Wang was commissioned as Vice-Secretary of the Ministry of Civil Appointments. He studied with Wen Zhengming and was proficient in calligraphy, painting and seal-engraving. His speciality was flower painting.

8. Flowers

Dated 1541
Handscroll, ink and colour on paper
25.5 × 496 cm

With frontispiece, inscription, signature, 1 seal of the artist and 13 collectors' seals, 1 colophon and 4 seals of Yi Yuan on paper separate from painting.

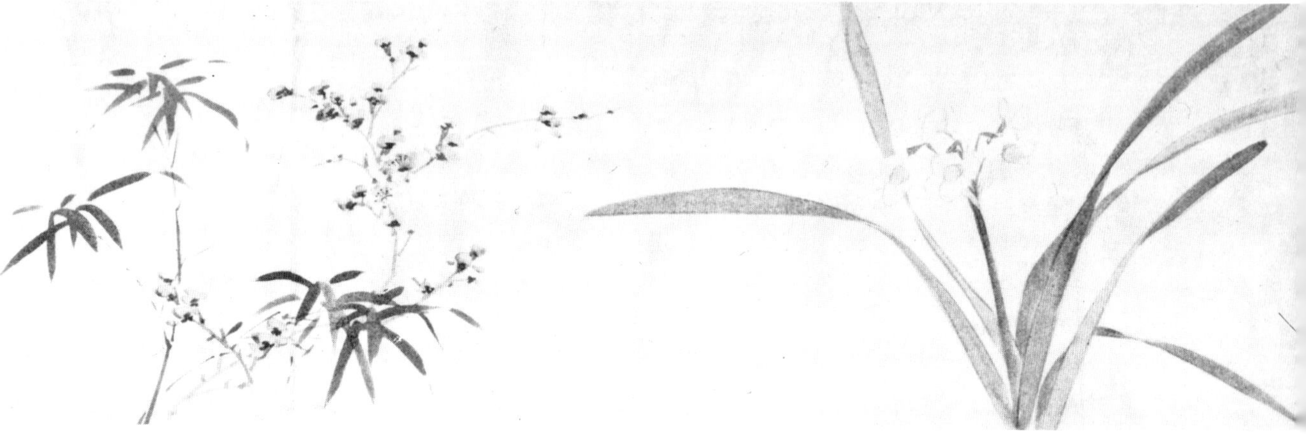

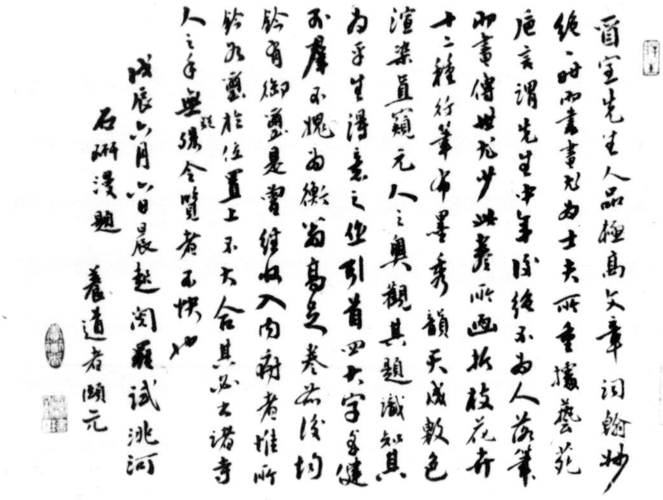
酉室先生人品極高文章詞翰妙
絕一時而書畫尤為士夫所重據藝苑
卮言謂先生中年以後不為人落筆
而書傳世尤少然所畫折枝花卉
十二種行筆布墨秀韻天成數色
渲染直窺元人之奧觀其題識知其
為平生得意之作引首四大字豪健
不群不愧為衡山高足卷後均
鈐有御璽是曾經收入內府者惟所
鈐乃璽於位置上不大合其必出諸寺
人之手無疑損令覽者不快也
戊辰六月六日晨起閱罷試洮河
石研漫題
養遺者頤元

種種不遺余亦高興
勉寫一過以遇聰明來
者能及見者知嘆
走也酉室王穀祥記

8

陳　栝

明代　十六世紀中期

字子正，號沱江。陳淳子。吳縣（江蘇蘇州）人。飲酒放浪，有竹林之習。善畫花卉、山水，能傳家法。

9. 五色蜀葵圖

1550年作
絹本設色立軸　133×66.5厘米

此圖寫五色蜀葵於湖石間。畫右上角有海山錢籍跋，其人待考。

款識：
嘉靖庚戌（1550年）春日，沱江子陳栝寫。

印章：
陳栝之印（白文方印）
子正氏（白文方印）

題跋：
沈約堂前葵似麻，枝枝開出向陽花。根從西蜀移來久，種托東君衍去賒。抱赤不妨同報國，貽謀只許自傳家。願言奕世垂千葉，五色流芳永蔽遮。風詮翁厥子雲文，並舉進士，以忠孝稱，蓋有得於葵者深矣。冢孫復號紹葵，奕葉雲仍，知其未艾，爲賦此。海山錢籍書。

題跋印章：
壬辰進士（朱文方印）

Chen Gua

Ming dynasty　mid-16th century

Zi Zizheng, *hao* Tuojiang, native of Wuxian (present-day Suzhou, Jiangsu province) and son of Chen Chun. Chen was an accomplished painter of flowers and landscapes and successfully perpetuated the family tradition.

9. Hollyhock in Five Colours

Dated 1550
Hanging scroll, ink and colour on silk
133×66.5 cm

With inscription, signature, 2 seals of the artist and 1 colophon with 1 seal of Qian Ji.

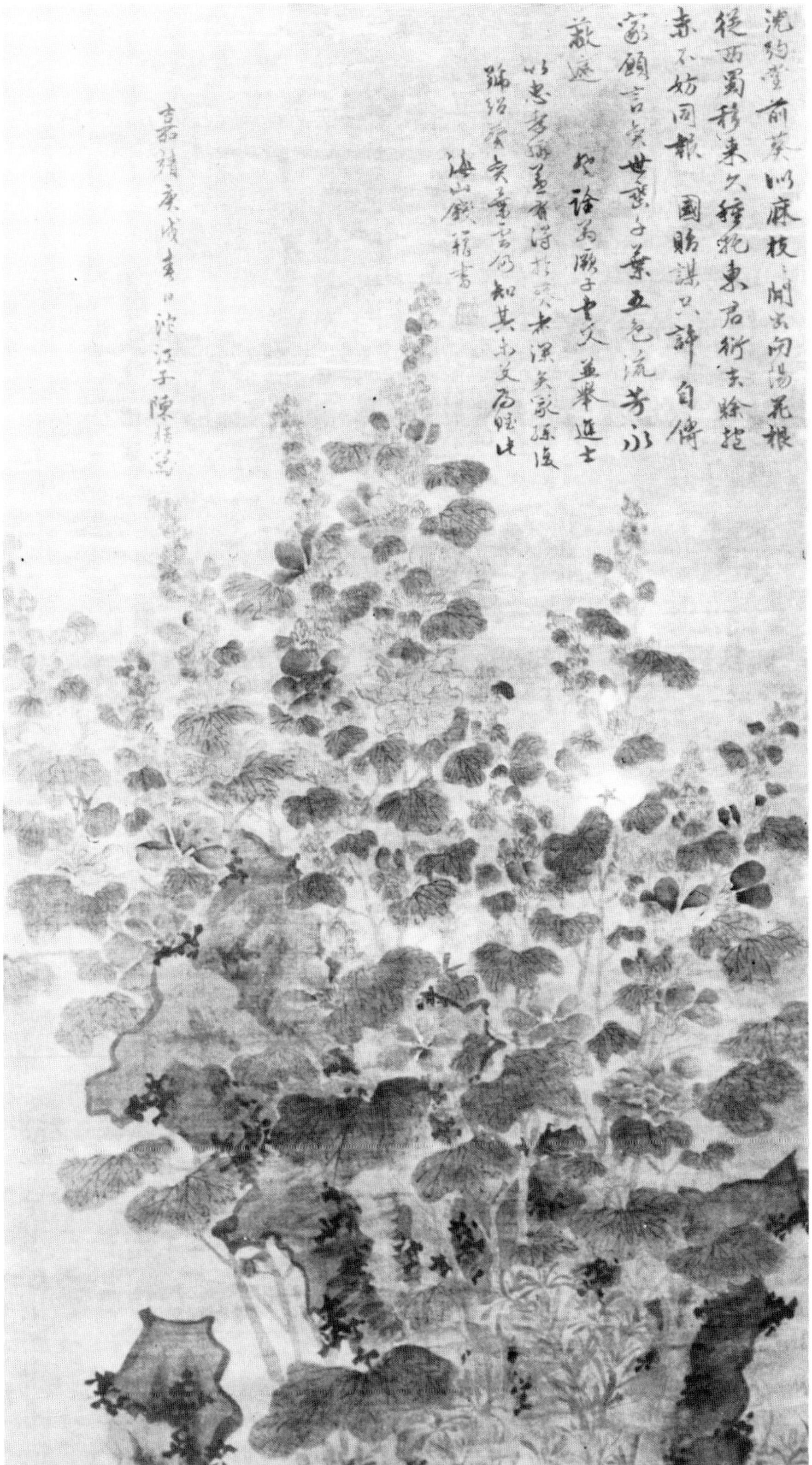

孫克弘

明代　1533－1611

字允執，號雪居，松江（今上海市）人。曾官至漢陽太守。居東郭草堂，列名蹟於秋琳閣。平生善寫山水、花鳥、人物，晚年尤工墨梅，亦有雅尚。

10. 菊竹貓蝶圖

紙本設色立軸　120×31厘米

此圖寫白貓蹲石上，狎蝶爲戲。白貓用筆落粉工緻，與花石寫意手法成對比。

款識：
坐醒羣蝶狎，庭除亦晏如。餘威鈐鼠輩，不患食無魚。雪居。

印章：
雪居（白文方印）
孫允執（白文方印）
漢陽侯印（白文方印）

鑑藏印章：
徵閣鑑藏（朱文長方印）
筱田珍藏（朱文方印）
夫容江館（朱文方印）
甘白張昀鑑定（朱文長方印）
友竹眞賞（朱文長方印）
文桂眞賞（朱文長方印）

Sun Kehong

Ming dynasty　1533-1611

Zi Yunzhi, *hao* Xueju, native of Songjiang (present-day Shanghai). Sun was appointed prefect of Hanyang. He was equally adept in painting landscapes, figures, birds and flowers. In his later years he was noted for his painting of prunus blossoms in ink.

10. Cat and Butterfly with Chrysanthemums and Bamboo

Hanging scroll, ink and colour on paper
120×31 cm

With inscription, signature, 3 seals of the artist and 6 collectors' seals.

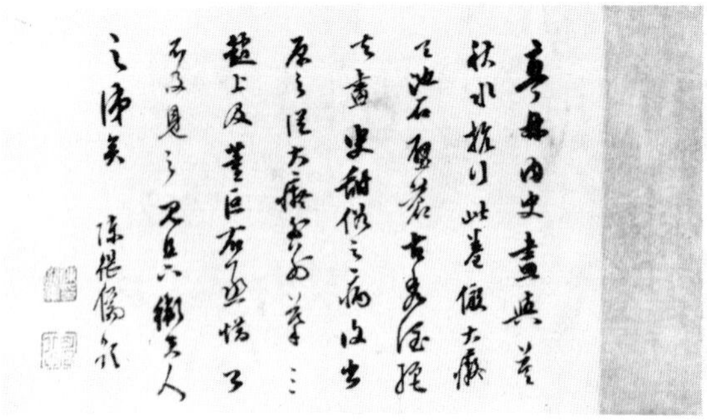

顧正誼

明代　活躍於1573－1620間

字仲方，號亭林，江蘇華亭人。萬曆時仕爲中書舍人，善山水，宗黃公望（1269－1354），家多名蹟，與宋旭（1525－1606尚在）、孫克弘友，窮探旨趣，遂成名家。

11. 仿黃公望天池石壁圖

1596年作
紙本設色手卷　23.2×354.4厘米

此圖作層巒疊嶂，山多作方頂，自有面目。筆法略近董其昌。

款識：
顧正誼寫於寶雲居。丙申（1596年）冬日。

印章：
顧正誼印（白文方印）
仲方子（白文方印）

鑑藏印章：
石渠寶笈（朱文長方印）
小鳳（朱白文方印）
乾隆御覽之寶（朱文圓印）
石渠定鑑（朱文圓印）
寶笈重編（白文方印）
乾淸宮鑑藏寶（朱文長方印）
嘉慶御覽之寶（朱文長圓印）
宣統御覽之寶（朱文長圓印）
乾隆鑑賞（白文圓印）
三希堂精鑑璽（朱文長方印）
宜子孫（白文方印）

後幅題跋：
亭林內史畫與董秋水抗行，此卷倣大痴天池石壁，蒼古秀潤，絕去畫史甜俗之病，復出原之，從大痴外，別摹三趙，上及董巨右丞，惜公不及見之，見且下衞夫人之識矣。陳繼儒題。

題跋印章：
陳繼儒印（白文方印）
眉公（朱文方印）

Gu Zhengyi

Ming dynasty   fl. ca. 1573-1620

Zi Zhongfang, *hao* Tinglin, native of Huating (present-day Suzhou, Jiangsu province). Gu held the position of a drafter in the Central Drafting Office in the Wanli era. He specialized in landscape painting, working in a style reminiscent of Huang Gongwang (1269-1354). He collected old paintings and befriended other literati artists, including Song Xu (1525-after 1606) and Sun Kehong.

11. Stone Cliff at the Pond of Heaven in the Style of Huang Gongwang

Dated 1596
Handscroll, ink and colour on paper
23.2 × 354.4 cm

With inscription, signature, 2 seals of the artist and 11 collectors' seals, 1 colophon with 2 seals of Chen Jiru (1558 1639) on paper separate from painting.

董其昌

明代　1555－1636

字思白，號玄宰。江蘇華亭人。官至南京禮部尚書。精鑑賞，善書，工畫山水，以董源（活躍於937-976間）、巨然（活躍於960－980間）、黃公望（1269－1354）、倪瓚（1301－1374）爲宗。名重一時，後世稱爲"華亭派"。著《畫禪室隨筆》、《畫旨》、《畫眼》、《容臺集》，對中國畫學有深遠影響。

12. 剪江草堂圖

紙本水墨立軸　94.3×25.5厘米

此畫用高麗鏡面箋，化董巨筆法，成平穩秀潤之畫風，爲畫家晚年力作。

款識：
雪浪雲堆勢可呼，移將點綴草堂圖。誰知王宰剪江手，却似初平叱石符。玄宰。

印章：
宗伯學士（白文方印）
董玄宰氏（白文方印）

鑑藏印章：
梅景書屋（朱文方印）
吳湖帆潘靜淑珍藏印（朱文方印）

裱邊題跋：
董思翁晚歲嘗曰："得意時作畫，用高麗鏡面箋，以楷書題字而自存者，每不鈐印章，然對外之作都鈐'董氏玄宰'、'宗伯學士'二玉印。"此圖是也。已脫盡倪黃面目，自有獨特之致。丙子（1936年）之冬吳湖帆識。余生平愛董書畫，所收畫幾十數事，此亦晚年經意作，裝竟鑒題。

題跋印章：
全董室（朱文方印）

裱邊鑑藏印章：
吳氏梅景書屋圖書印（朱文方印）

Dong Qichang

Ming dynasty　1555-1636

Zi Sibai, *hao* Xuanzai, native of Huating, Jiangsu province. Dong served as the high-ranking Minister of the Board of Rites. A connoisseur, theorist, calligrapher and landscape painter, he exerted tremendous influence on his contemporaries as well as succeeding generations. He was considered the patriarch of the Huating school and advocated the study of Song and Yuan Masters, particularly Dong Yuan (fl. ca. 937-976), Juran (fl. ca. 960-980), Huang Gongwang (1269-1354) and Ni Zan (1301-1374).

12. Thatched Cottage of Jianjiang.

Hanging scroll, ink on paper
94.3×25.5 cm

With inscription, signature, 2 seals of the artist, 2 collectors' seals and 1 colophon with 2 seals of Wu Hufan (1894-1968) on mounting silk.

雪浪重堆勢可吁
移將點綴草堂圖
誰知玄宰翻江手
都似初平叱石符
玄宰
董思翁晚歲嘗曰得意詩作畫用高麗鏡面箋以楷書題字而自存者每不鈐印章然對外之作
都鈐董氏玄宰宗伯學士二印此圖是也已晚盡倪黃兩目自有獨特之致 丙子之冬吳湖帆識

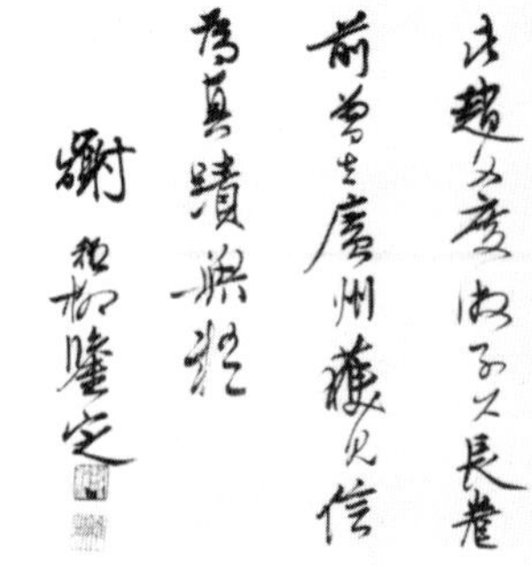

趙　左

明代　1573－1644?

字文度，江蘇華亭人。善畫山水。與宋懋晋（十六世紀晚期至十七世紀早期）俱受業於宋旭（1525－1606尚在）。趙左畫風以惜墨爲特色，其畫宗董源（活躍於937－976間），兼得黃倪兩家之勝，雲山近米氏父子，間亦用焦墨。開蘇松一派。

13. 溪山清遠圖

1619年作
紙本設色手卷　23×530厘米

此卷寫羣山重疊，草木華滋，人物屋舍盎然。溪山清遠，富黃公望筆意，然筆致略爲細碎，具平淡天眞之趣。

款識：
己未（1619年）夏日避暑於婁東僧舍，倣子久筆意作此長卷。趙左。

印章：
趙左（白文方印）
文度（朱文方印）

鑑藏印章：
容庚秘匧（白文方印）
胡晚外鑑定印（朱文長方印）
金陵馬鞠邨鑒賞印（朱文長方印）

後幅題跋：
此趙文度倣子久長卷，前曾在廣州獲見，信爲眞蹟無疑。謝稚柳鑒定。

題跋印章：
謝稚（白文方印）
稚柳（朱文方印）

Zhao Zuo

Ming dynasty 1573-1644?

Zi Wendu, native of Huating, Jiangsu province. A student of Song Xu (1525-after 1606), Zhao specialized in landscape painting. He used ink sparingly, sometimes employing the darkest tone with a dry brush. His personal style was based on that of Dong Yuan (fl. ca. 937-976), incorporating elements from Huang Gongwang, Ni Zan of the Yuan dynasty as well as Mi Fu and Mi Youren of the Song dynasty.

13. Pure and Remote Views of Streams and Mountains

Dated 1619
Handscroll, ink and colour on paper
23 × 530 cm

With inscription, signature, 2 seals of the artist, 3 collectors' seals and 1 colophon with 2 seals of Xie Zhiliu (b. 1909).

李流芳

明代　1575－1629

字長蘅，號檀園。本安徽歙縣人，僑居嘉定（江蘇）。工詩文書畫，善畫山水。風格近黃公望（1269－1354）、吳鎮（1280－1354）等元代畫家，爽朗蒼潤。

14. 山水册

1621年作
紙本水墨册頁十開　各17×26厘米

此册共十開，寫山水小景，枯木寒石，或蕭疏淡遠，或蒼勁潤濕，均爲隨意之作。

⑴、⑶－⑼ 山水

印章：
李流芳印（白文方印）

⑵ 山水

印章：
李流芳印（白文方印）

鑑藏印章：
愼生（白文長方印）
特健藥（朱文長方印）

⑽ 山水

款識：
辛酉（1621年）冬日。李流芳。

印章：
李流芳印（白文方印）

鑑藏印章：
去非審定書畫（朱文長方印）
藥農平生眞賞（朱文長方印）
愼生珍賞（朱文橢圓印）

另附題跋四開：
徐宗浩、啓功、邵章、張伯英及黃賓虹題。

Li Liufang

Ming dynasty　1575-1629

Zi Changheng, *hao* Tanyuan, native of Shexian, Anhui province but lived in Jiading, Jiangsu province. Li was adept in poetry, calligraphy and painting. He painted landscapes in a loose manner, bearing stylistic affinities with Huang Gongwang (1269-1354), Wu Zhen (1280-1354) and other Yuan masters.

14. Landscape Album

Dated 1621
Album of ten leaves, ink on paper
each leaf 17×26 cm

(1), (3)-(9) Landscape
With 1 seal of the artist.

(2) Landscape
With 1 seal of the artist and 2 colectors' seals.

(10) Landscape
With inscription, signature, 1 seal of the artist and 3 collectors' seals.

4 additional leaves with 5 colophons by Xu Zonghao, Qigong, Shao Zhang, Zhang Boying and Wang Binhong.

14.1

14.2

14.3

14.4

14.5

14.6

14.7

14.8

14.9

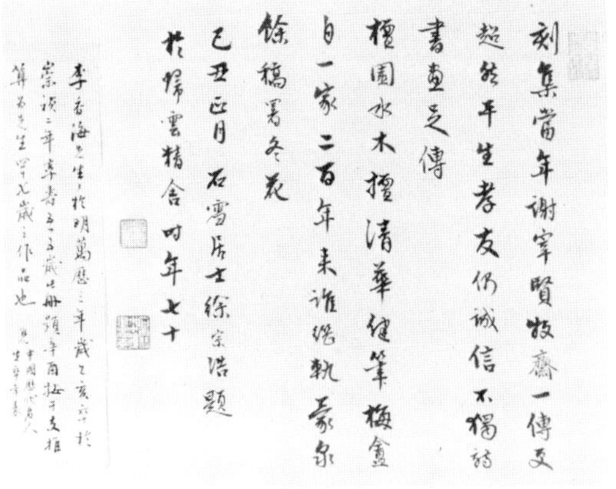

14.11

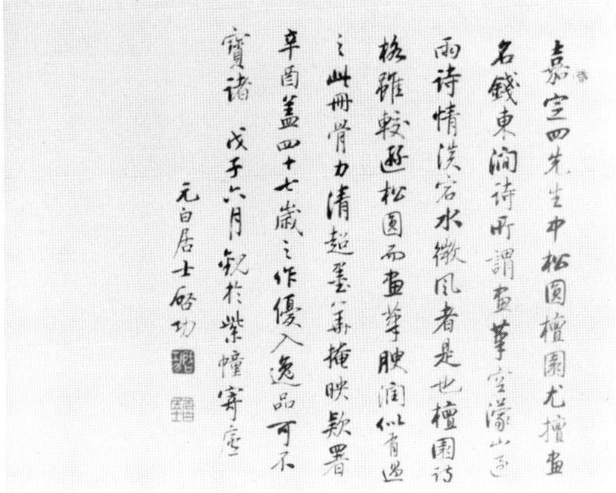

14.12

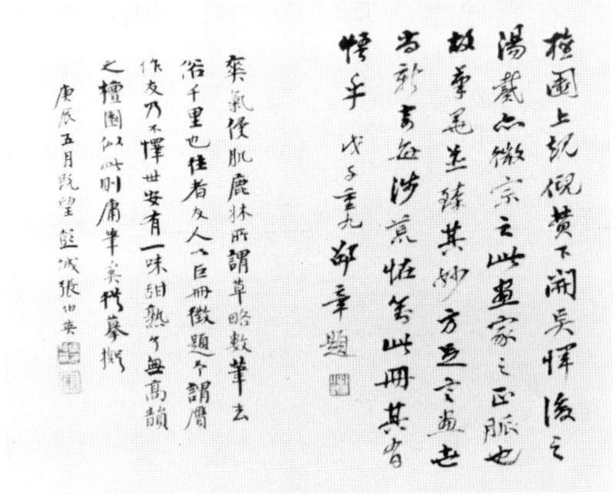

14.13

14.14

14.10

沈士充

明代　活躍於1607－1640後

字子居，江蘇華亭人。善山水，出宋懋晋（十六世紀晚期至十七世紀早期）、趙左門下，屬雲間派。

15 .寒林讀書圖

1632年作
紙本設色立軸　103×30厘米

此圖書寒林屋舍，人物讀書其中，雲氣繞遠峯。用筆疏散。

款識：
壬申（1632年）冬日寫寒林讀書圖。沈士充。

印章：
子居（白文方印）
沈士充印（白文方印）

鑑藏印章：
秋亭汪氏珍藏（白文長方印）

Shen Shichong

Ming dynasty　fl. ca. 1607-after 1640

Zi Ziju, native of Huating (present-day Suzhou, Jiangsu province). As a master of landscape painting Shen was grouped with the Yunjian School and studied with Song Maojin (late 16th to early 17th centuries) and Zhao Zuo.

15. Study in Wintry Forest

Dated 1632
Hanging scroll, ink and colour on paper
103 × 30 cm

With inscription, signature, 2 seals of the artist and 1 collector's seal.

壬申冬日寫寒林讀書圖
沈士充

蔣　靄

明代　十七世紀前期

字志和。江蘇華亭人。善畫山水，學沈士充法。規摹唐宋，皆能神合。嘗言畫家一要人品高，二要師古法，蓋自況云。

16. 峻壁飛泉圖

1622年作
紙本設色立軸　129.5×60厘米

此圖用渴筆畫峻壁高疊，架廊飛泉，人物聽流於中。筆勢多作飛白，墨老多濃，瘦骨堅凝，自成一家。

款識：
峻壁飛泉。壬戌(1622年)小春寫，怡雲野人蔣靄。

印章：
蔣氏志龢（白文方印）
怡雲野人（白文方印）

Jiang Ai

Ming dynasty　first half of 17th century

Zi Zhihe, native of Huating (present-day Suzhou, Jiangsu province). Jiang was a landscape painter who based his style on that of Shen Shichong. He also advocated the study of ancient models, particularly the Tang and Song Masters.

16. Cliffside Spring

Dated 1622
Hanging scroll, ink on paper
129.5 × 60 cm

With inscription, signature and 2 seals of the artist.

峻壁飛泉
壬戌小春寫

劉原起

明代　十七世紀前期

初名祚，後以字行，更字子正，號振之。吳縣（江蘇蘇州）人。工畫山水。師錢穀（1508－約1578），頗肖其神。

17. 城關驟雨圖

1628年作
紙本設色立軸　122×60.5厘米

此圖畫驟雨怒瀉，密樹樓閣中人物相對論書，畫右方有城關一角，牆外江水悠悠。坡石大小攢聚，輪廓皴擦無多，以密苔增點精神，筆法略近文徵明。

款識：
崇禎戊辰（1628年）七夕立秋日寫。劉原起。

印章：
劉氏振之（白文方印）
原起（白文方印）

Liu Yuanqi

Ming dynasty　first half of 17th century

Original name Zuo, *zi* Zizheng, *hao* Zhenzhi, native of Wuxian, Jiangsu province. Liu was noted for his poetry and landscape painting, modelling himself after Qian Gu (1508-ca.1578).

17. Caught in a Shower

Dated 1628
Hanging scroll, ink and colour on paper
122×60.5 cm

With inscription, signature and 2 seals of the artist.

崇禎戊辰七夕立秋日寫

魏　克

明代　十七世紀前期

早年名之克，字和叔。上元（今南京）人。魏之璜弟。善山水、花卉。與兄考叔，賣畫爲生。

18. 松蔭流泉圖

1624年作
金箋紙本設色立軸　142×37.5厘米

此圖畫松林中流泉有聲，雲烟繞繚，一派明靜清幽境界。筆勢流暢滋潤。

款識：
甲子（1624年）冬日魏克寫。

印章：
魏之克印（朱文方印）
𥡴叔（朱文方印）

鑑藏印章：
北平燕雲亭珍藏書畫之印記（朱文方印）

Wei Ke

Ming dynasty　first half of 17th century

Original name Zhike, *zi* Heshu, native of Shangyuan (present-day Nanjing). Wei established his fame as a painter of landscapes and flowers. Together with his brother Zhihuang, he earned his living from painting.

18. Flowing Stream in Pine Forest

Dated 1624
Hanging scroll, ink and colour on gold paper
142×37.5 cm

With inscription, signature, 2 seals of the artist and 1 collector's seal.

甲子冬日魏克寫

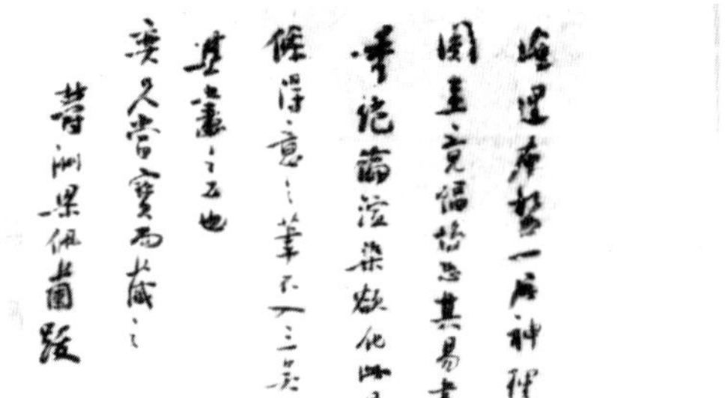

王中立

明代　十七世紀前期

字振之。吳縣（江蘇蘇州）人。善畫花鳥。

19. 花鳥圖

1615年作
紙本設色長卷　28×535厘米

此卷寫桃、梅、菊、芙蓉等十三種花卉及翠鳥等五種小鳥，設色清淡，筆致秀雅，乃王氏少數流傳作品之一。尾紙有梁佩蘭（1629－1705）跋，然未提及王畫，且質地甚殘，而王畫紙質甚完整，是否另有所題仍待攷。

款識：
萬曆乙卯（1615年）十月既望爲秋空禪兄寫。王中立。

印章：
王中立印（白文方印）
玄洲（白文方印）

鑑藏印章：
東老（朱文葫蘆印）
德畬審定（朱文方印）
莨林曾觀（朱文方印）
江左陸郎（朱文方印）
□雨齋圖書記（朱文方印）
□元秘笈（朱文方印）
另一印不可辨。

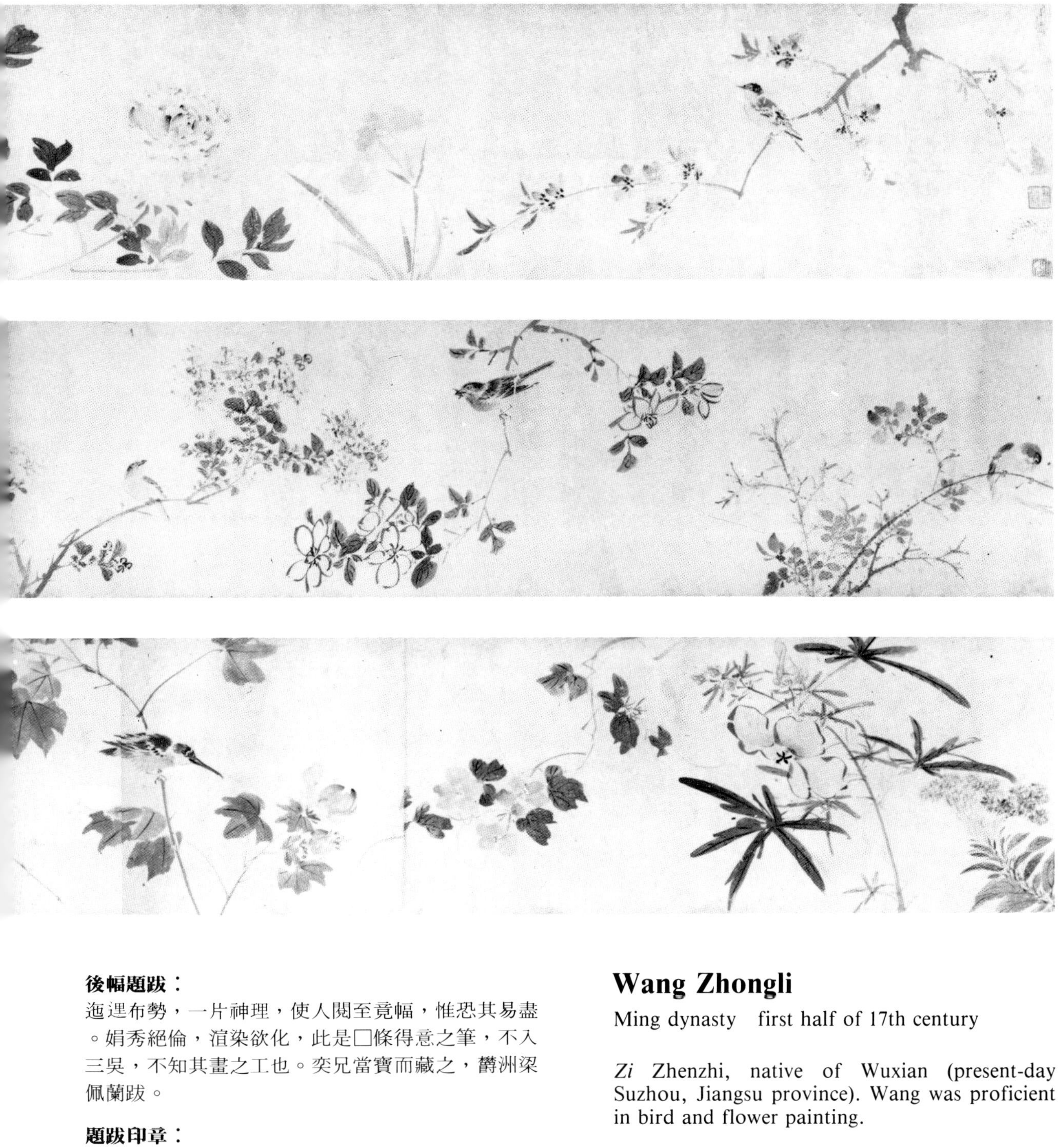

後幅題跋：

迤逦布勢，一片神理，使人閱至竟幅，惟恐其易盡。娟秀絕倫，渲染欲化，此是□條得意之筆，不入三吳，不知其畫之工也。奕兄當寶而藏之，鬱洲梁佩蘭跋。

題跋印章：

梁佩蘭印（白文方印）
藥亭（朱文方印）

Wang Zhongli

Ming dynasty first half of 17th century

Zi Zhenzhi, native of Wuxian (present-day Suzhou, Jiangsu province). Wang was proficient in bird and flower painting.

19. Birds and Flowers

Dated 1615
Handscroll, ink and colour on paper
28 × 535 cm

張　翀

明代　十七世紀前期

字子羽，號圖甬。《明畫錄》作江寧（江蘇南京）人。工畫花卉、人物，筆力疎秀，設色古雅，尤重寫生。

20. 花鳥草蟲册

紙本設色册頁十二開　各29.5×34厘米

此册共十二頁，雀鳥草蟲多用筆工細，草木坡石多下筆豪放。

(1) 毛蟹

款識：
張翀。

印章：
子羽（朱文方印）

(2) 李花

印章：
張翀（白文方印）
子羽（朱文方印）

(3) 紫丁香小鳥

印章：
張翀（白文方印）
子羽（朱文方印）

(4) 芙蓉壽帶：

印章：
張翀（白文方印）
子羽（朱文方印）

(5) 芙蓉

印章：
張翀（白文方印）
子羽（朱文方印）

(6) 秋海棠飛蝶

印章：
張翀（白文方印）
子羽（朱文方印）

(7) 寒樹棲鳥

印章：
子羽（朱文方印）

(8) 春江游鴨

印章：
張翀（白文方印）
子羽（朱文方印）

(9) 蟠桃

印章：
張翀（白文方印）
子羽（朱文方印）

(10) 野菊草蟲

印章：
張翀（白文方印）

(11) 石榴

印章：
張翀（白文方印）
子羽（朱文方印）

(12) 紅蓼草蟲

印章：
張翀（白文方印）
子羽（朱文方印）

Zhang Chong

Ming dynasty　first half of 17th century

Zi Ziyu, *hao* Tuyong, native of Jiangning (present-day Nanjing, Jiangsu province). Zhang excelled in painting flowers and figures, developing a personal style which combines loose brushwork and elegant colouring in the study of nature.

20. Album of Birds, Flowers and Insects

Album of twelve leaves, ink and colour on paper
each leaf 29.5×34 cm

(1) Crab
With signature and 1 seal of the artist.

(2) Plum Blossoms
With 2 seals of the artist.

(3) Bird on Lilac Branch
With 2 seals of the artist.

(4) Bird and Hibiscus
With 2 seals of the artist.

(5) Hibiscus
With 2 seals of the artist.

(6) Butterflies and Begonia
With 2 seals of the artist.

(7) Birds Resting on Wintry Trees
With 1 seal of the artist.

(8) Ducks Swimming in Spring River
With 2 seals of the artist.

(9) Peach
With 2 seals of the artist.

(10) Daisies and Insects
With 1 seal of the artist.

(11) Pomegranates
With 2 seals of the artist.

(12) Insects and Knotgrass
With 2 seals of the artist.

20.1

20.2

20.3

20.4

20.5

20.6

20.8

20.9

20.10

20.7

20.11

20.12

惲　向

明代　1586－1655

原名道生，字本初，以字行，號香山。江蘇武進人。工畫山水，學董源（活躍於937－976間）、巨然（活躍於960－980間、黃公望（1269－1354）。著有《畫旨》。

Yun Xiang

Ming dynasty　1586-1655

Original name Daosheng, *zi* Benchu, *hao* Xiangshan, native of Wujin, Jiangsu province. Yun was renowned for his landscape painting, evolving his personal style from the study of Dong Yuan, Juran and Huang Gongwang.

21. 濯泉自潔圖

紙本水墨立軸　152×53厘米

此圖畫茂樹下人物自濯清泉，頗得雄渾之趣。

款識：

坐茂樹以永日，濯清泉以自潔。摹燕文貴筆。惲向。

印章：

惲本初印（白文方印）
道生（白文方印）

21. Mountain Spring in the Sunlight

Hanging scroll, ink on paper
152×53 cm

With inscription, signature and 2 seals of the artist.

坐茂樹以永日濯清泉以自潔
惲向

沈 顥

明代　1586－1661尚在

字朗倩，號石天。吳縣（江蘇蘇州）人。詩文書畫，無所不能。山水近石田，深於畫理，著有《畫麈》行世。

22．擬南宗各家山水册

絹本水墨册頁十開　各28.3×25.7厘米

此册原爲沈顥集南宗四十家而仿其大概之作，現僅存後十頁，即南宗三十一至四十。各頁題材多爲山林小景，烟霞迷幻，構圖詭奇，題款小字乃自雲林（1301－1374）所來。

⑴ 南宗三十一

款識：
南宗三十一。懷州趙林不識一字，後悟畫理，潛通書籍，其寒林烟岫作淺絳色，有河陽遠神，非庸史也。

印章：
沈、顥（朱白文聯珠印）
（以下各開所鈐印章同）

⑵ 南宗三十二

款識：
南宗三十二。楡次郭鐵子，恕先之後人。呼鐵子者，以剛頑傲物，不近人情，畫亦類之，蕭遠可喜。

⑶ 南宗三十三

款識：
南宗三十三。范寬礬頭不可太作態，以虛靄寒烟吞吐之，便如美人琵琶遮面之意。

⑷ 南宗三十四

款識：
南宗三十四。江參貫道雖得法北苑，其開崖倒瀑，陡木驚松，自出悟道，非倚門旁戶比也。

⑸ 南宗三十五

款識：
南宗三十五。趙山甫飛廊水榭，有偎溪瓌島之致，而筆之淸潤，不落點塵，眞足喜也。

⑹ 南宗三十六

款識：
南宗三十六。霍元鎭初入北苑南宮，後一洗脫，別開活路，此其頂門豁眼處也。

⑺ 南宗三十七

款識：
南宗三十七。龔開淸寒潤邃，胎骨靈異，眞得唐人印綬，謂之北苑兒孫亦屈矣。

⑻ 南宗三十八

款識：
南宗三十八。許龍湫初亦董氏家臣，旣復力袪夙習，別有施設，令煙火兒嚼冰洗眼而近。

⑼ 南宗三十九

款識：
南宗三十九。鄭天民雖爲阿源摩頂，養力日到。亦能謝却筌罤，令觀者神曠。

⑽ 南宗四十

款識：
南宗四十。王詵，字晋卿，雖本摩詰、鵲華秋色皴法，而自有奇妙，入深入細入夷怪，無所不得。此幅予摹想三日夜始落筆，勿謂小技之非大學問也。

另附題跋一開：
方鼎題。

Shen Hao

Ming dynasty　1586-after 1661

Zi Langqian, *hao* Shitian, native of Wuxian (present-day Suzhou, Jiangsu province). Shen was adept in poetry, calligraphy and painting. He was also a theorist, with the treatise entitled *Huazhu* to his credit. His landscape painting showed influence from Shen Zhou.

22. Landscapes after Masters of the Southern School of Painting

Album of ten leaves, ink on silk
each leaf 28.3×25.7 cm

(1)-(10) Southern School Masters (Original numbering 31 to 40)

Each leaf with inscription and 1 seal of the artist.

1 additional leaf with 1 colophon of Fang Ding.

22.1

22.2

22.3

22.4

22.5

22.6

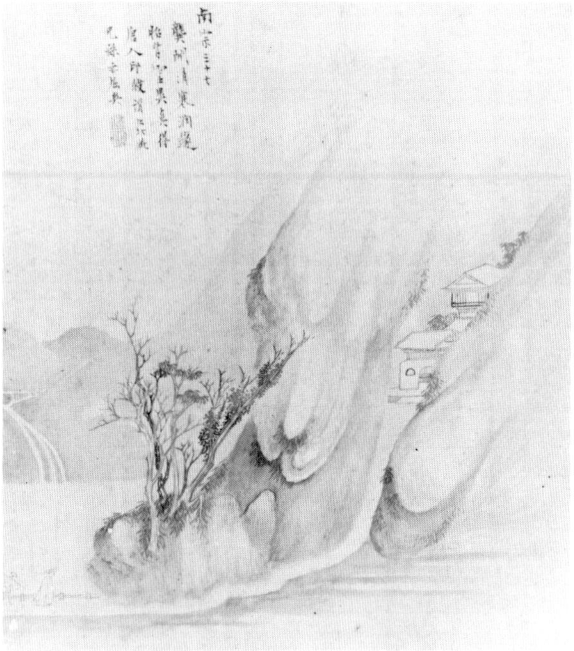

22.7

22.8

22.9

22.10

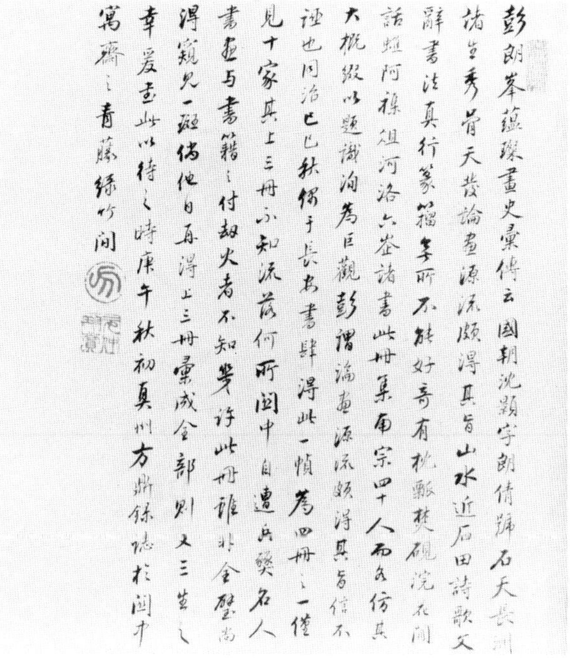
彭朗峯蘊璨畫史彙傳云國朝沈顥字朗倩號石天長洲
諸生秀骨天發論畫源流頗得其旨山水近石田詩歌文
辭書法真行篆籀皆所不能好奇有枕甑焚硯浣衣圊
話蜷阿祿組河洛六荅諸書此冊集南宗四十人而各仿其
大概綴以題識洵為巨觀彭謂論畫源流頗得其旨信不
誣也同治己巳秋得于長安書肆得此一幀為四冊々一僅
見十家其上三冊不知流落何所閩中自遭兵燹名人
書畫与書籍々付劫火者不知幾許此冊雖非全璧尚
得窺見一斑倘他日再得上三冊彙成全部則又三生之
幸爰壹此以待々時庚午秋初真州方鼎錄誌於閩中
寓齋々青藤綠竹間

葛徵奇

明代　？－1645

字無奇，號介龕。浙江海寧人。崇禎元年（1628）進士，善寫山水。

23. 故山尋道圖

1635年作
綾本水墨立軸　188.5×54.5厘米

此圖用筆蒼勁，墨氣清潤，橫筆點苔，筆法略近董其昌。

款識：
空携斗酒與雙□，辜負今年三月三。欲向故山尋道侶，一灣溪水結茅菴。時崇禎乙亥（1635年）春日，寫爲新翁老先生詞宗。赭山葛徵奇。

印章：
葛徵奇印（白文方印）
無奇氏（朱文方印）

Ge Zhengqi

Ming dynasty　?-1645

Zi Wuqi, *hao* Jiekan, native of Haining, Zhejiang province. Ge passed his *jinshi* examination in 1628. He specialized in landscape painting.

23. Mountian Retreat

Dated 1635
Hanging scroll, ink on satin
188.5×54.5 cm

With inscription, signature and 2 seals of the artist.

藍　瑛

明代　1585－1664尚在

字田叔，號蜨叟，晚號石頭陀，又自號東郭老農。錢塘（浙江杭州）人。工畫山水、人物、花鳥。其畫融合宋元人畫法，具有蒼勁、濕潤之致，自成一派。

24. 秋山圖

1644年作
紙本設色立軸　304.7×105.5厘米

此圖畫樹蔭溪流間屋宇，人物對話，近處板橋上一人急行赴會，景緻清新，筆勢蒼勁，設色高雅。爲藍瑛之紙本設色巨幅大作。

款識：
北苑太守畫法於河湄，似士任老社長兄正之。甲申（1644年）冬仲，蜨叟藍瑛。

印章：
田叔（朱文方印）

Lan Ying

Ming dynasty　1585-after 1664

Zi Tianshu, *hao* Dieshou, Shitoutuo, Dongguo Laonong, native of Qiantang (present-day Hangzhou, Zhejiang province). Lan was a versatile artist, equally at ease with landscape, figure, bird and flower painting. He assimilated the brush methods of the Song and Yuan masters evolving a distinctive personal style that is vigourous and expressive.

24. Autumn Mountains

Dated 1644
Hanging scroll, ink and colour on paper
304.7 × 105.5 cm

With inscription, signature and 1 seal of the artist.

陳洪綬

明代　1598－1652

字章侯，號老蓮，後號悔遲。諸暨（浙江紹興）人。善畫花卉、山水，尤工人物，風格雄奇古樸。早年曾學畫於藍瑛，後自成一家。

25. 三松圖

絹本設色立軸　154×49.5厘米

此圖畫三松，雲霧濃厚，後二松中間爲雲氣所遮。枝石略近藍瑛筆勢，爲中年之筆。

款識：
洪綬。

印章：
陳洪綬印（白文方印）

Chen Hongshou

Ming dynasty 1598-1652

Zi Zhanghou, *hao* Laolian, Huichi, native of Zhuji, Zhejiang province. Chen painted landscapes and flowers but he was best known for his figures. His early training in art came from Lan Ying. Subsequently he developed a highly individual style that has an expressive powerful and archaic feeling.

25. Three Pine Trees

Hanging scroll, ink and colour on silk
154×49.5 cm

With signature and 1 seal of the artist.

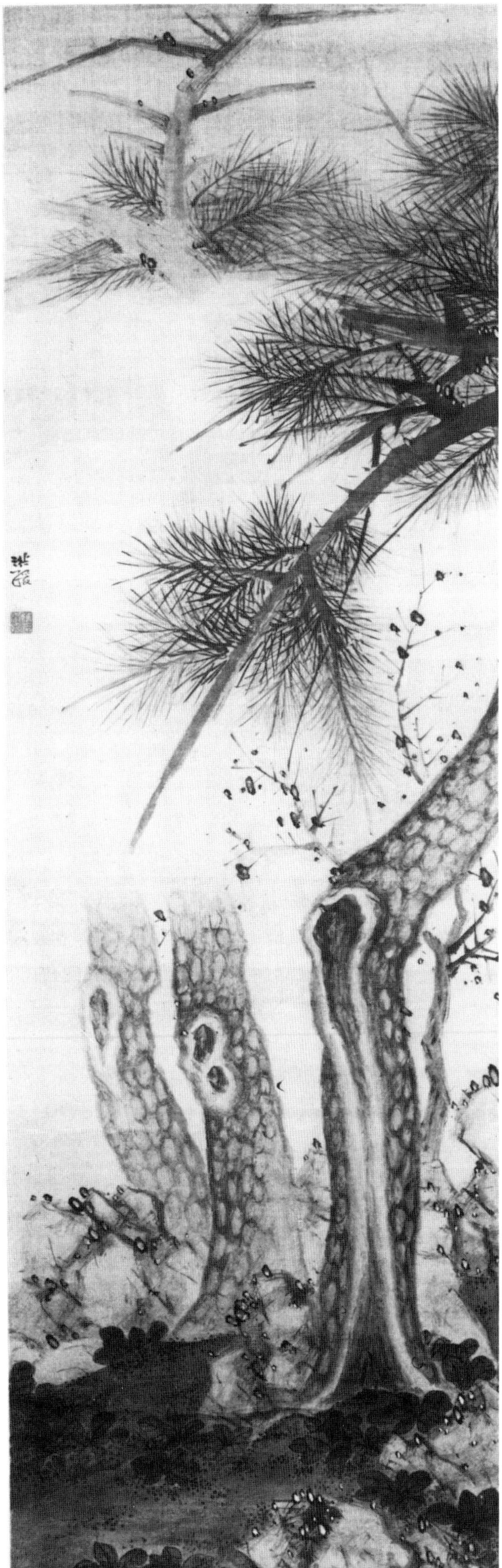

王時敏

清代　1592－1680

字遜之，號烟客，晚號西廬老人。江蘇太倉人。崇禎初，以蔭仕至太常寺少卿，故也稱王奉常。善山水、書法，專師元黃公望（1269－1354）、倪瓚（1301－1374）。明亡後不仕，優游筆墨過日，爲清初“四王”之首。

26. 秋山圖

1674年作
紙本水墨立軸　71×38.3厘米

此畫寫峯巒起伏，林木蔚秀，雲烟飄蕩，用墨乾濕互見，用筆荒率蘊藉，爲王氏晚年隨心適意之作。

款識：
西廬老人時年八十有三。
印章：
王時敏印（白文方印）
鑑藏印章：
願固珍藏（朱文方印）

Wang Shimin

Qing dynasty　1592-1680

Zi Xunzhi, *hao* Yanke, native of Taicang, Jiangsu province. Wang had served at the Ming Court in the position of Sub-director of Rites, but retired shortly before the Ming Government collapsed. Noted for his landscape painting and calligraphy, he was acclaimed as the leader of the "Four Wangs", who were the four most influential figures of the art circules in the early Qing dynasty.

26. Autumn Mountains

Dated 1674
Hanging scroll, ink on paper
71×38.3 cm

With incription, signature, 1 seal of the artist and 1 collector's seal.

西廬老人時年
八十有三

王　鑑

清代　1598－1677

字玄（元或員）照，後改圓照，號湘碧，別署染香庵主。江蘇太倉人。明中葉鴻儒王世貞（1526－1590）曾孫，自幼得觀摩家藏書畫。崇禎年間曾官廉州太守，故人又稱王廉州。畫山水，最擅摹古，筆法圓渾蒼勁。與王時敏齊名，爲清初"四王"之一。

27. 倣各家山水册

1643年作
絹本水墨册頁七開　各25×17.5厘米

此册倣古山水，原八開，其一散失。

(1) 松亭山泉

款識：
倣董北苑筆。王鑑。

印章：
王鑑（朱白文方印）
（以下各開所鈐印章同）

(2) 雲山烟雨

款識：
小米雲山。王鑑。

(3) 春雨山村
倣高房山。王鑑。

(4) 對岸山村

款識：
倣黃子久筆。王鑑。

(5) 山溪板橋

款識：
倣梅華道人。王鑑。

鑑藏印章：
容庚（朱文方印）

(6) 山谿積雪

款識：
山谿積雪。王鑑。

(7) 峯泖烟波

款識：
峯泖烟波。崇禎癸未（1643年）作小景八幅於雲間舟次。王鑑。

另附題跋一開：
謝稚柳（1909－　）題。

Wang Jian

Qing dynasty　1598-1677

Zi Xuanzhao, *hao* Xiangbi, native of Taicang, Jiangsu province. Wang was the great-grandson of Wang Shizheng (1526-1590), a well respected scholar at the Ming Court. He was thus exposed to famous old paintings in the family collection from an early age. He served for a short term in the Ming Government as a Prefect of Lianzhou. He specialized in landscape painting and was often acclaimed for his ability to work in the style of various old masters. He was also one of the "Four Wangs" of the early Qing period, enjoying equal prominence with Wang Shimin.

27. Album of Landscapes

Dated 1643
Album of seven leaves, ink on silk
each leaf 25×17.5 cm

(1) Pavilion by the Stream
With inscription, signature and 1 seal of the artist.

(2) Mountains amid Clouds and Mist
Same as leaf (1).

(3) Mountain Village in Spring Rain
Same as leaf (1).

(4) Mountain Village on the Opposite Bank
Same as leaf (1).

(5) Houses by a Stream
With inscription, signature, 1 seal of the artist and 1 collector's seal.

(6) Streams and Mountains under Snow
Same as leaf (1).

(7) Misty Lake
Same as leaf (1).

1 additional leaf with 1 colophon of Xie Zhiliu (b.1909).

27.1

27.2

27.3

27.4

27.5

山谿積雪
王鑑

27.6

峯泖烟波
崇禎癸未作小景八幅于雲間舟次
王鑑

27.7

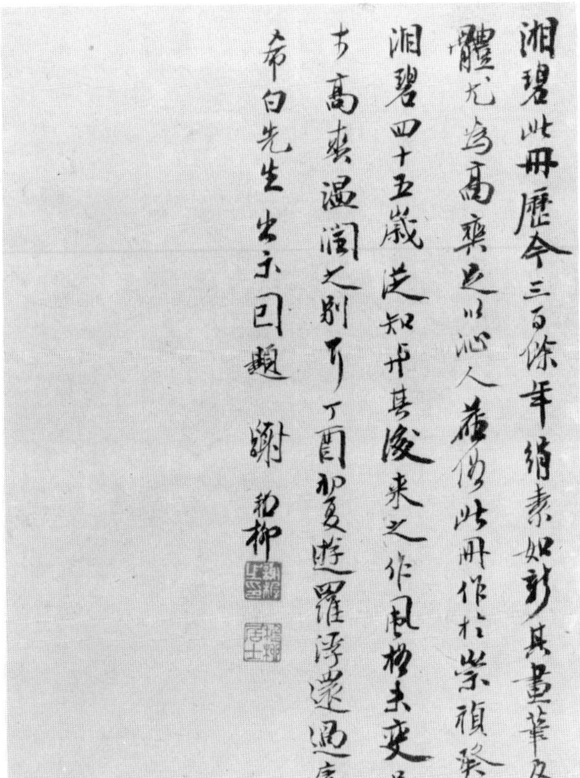
湘碧此冊歷今三百餘年絹素如新其畫筆及書
體尤為高爽足以沁人蓋湘碧此冊作於崇禎癸未為
湘碧四十五歲從知其後來之作風格未變只在
古高爽溫潤之別耳丁酉初夏遊羅浮還過廣州
希白先生出示同觀 謝稚柳

程正揆

清代　1604－1676

初名正葵，字端伯，號鞠陵，又號青溪道人。湖北孝感人。明崇禎四年（1631）進士，官至翰林院編修。入清則官至工部右侍郎，後被革官，遂寄情山水，與石谿（1612－1673）交往最深，人稱"二溪"。工詩書畫，善鑒賞。山水得董其昌指授，後自成一家。喜用禿筆，嘗作《卧遊圖》五百卷，此卷即其第八十卷。

28. 江山卧游圖

1658年作
紙本設色長卷　28.3×242厘米

引首：
青溪道人卧游圖。甲寅夏日。瓢叟。

引首印章：
顏世清印（白文方印）
□□寵（白文方印）

款識：
江山卧游圖，其八十。青溪道人戊戌（1658年）春二。

印章：
程正揆（白文方印）

後幅題跋：
顏世清題。

鑑藏印章：
退耕老人壬戌前藏（朱文長方印）
容庚（朱文方印）
彀齋鑒定（白文方印）
水竹邨藏（朱文方印）

Cheng Zhengkui

Qing dynasty　1604-1676

Zi Duanbo, *hao* Juling and Qingxi Daoren, native of Xiaogan, Hubei province. Cheng passed the civil examination in 1631 and became an official in the Ming government. He also served the Qing Court as Vice President of the Board of Works. After he was removed from office, he devoted himself to travelling and art. Monk Shixi (1612-1673) became his good friend and together they were called the "Two Xis". He was noted for his poetry, calligraphy, painting and connoisseurship. He studied with Dong Qichang but later evolved his own personal style. It has been said that he painted a total of five hundred scrolls of *Dream Journey* and this is the eightieth.

28. Dream Journey among Rivers and Mountains

Dated 1658
Handscroll, ink and colour on paper
28.3 × 242 cm

With inscription, signature and 1 seal of the artist. Frontispiece and 1 colophon of Yan Shiqing and 4 collectors' seals on paper separate from painting.

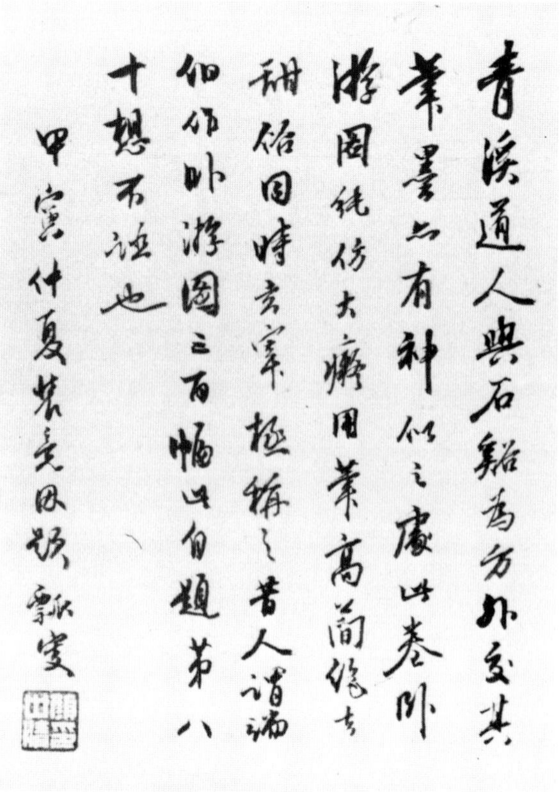

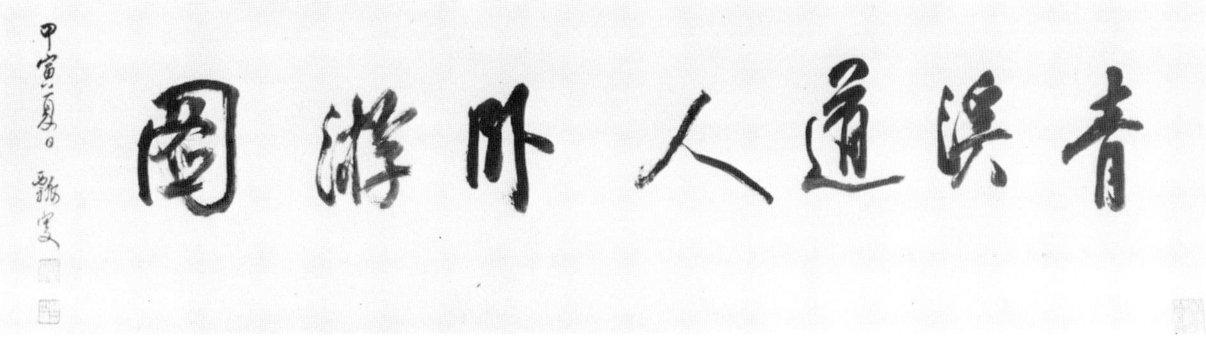
青溪道人卧游圖
甲寅夏日

江山卧游圖 其八十
青溪道人
戊戌春二

江山臥游圖 其八十
青溪道人
戊戌春二

28

弘 仁

清代　1610－1664

號漸江，又號梅花古衲、無智。原姓江，名舫，字鷗盟。一說名韜，字六奇。徽州歙縣（今安徽歙縣）人。明亡後出家爲僧。工詩文，平生愛寫黃山景物，尤喜畫松石。山水學倪瓚（1301－1374），山石輪廓則簡練過之。巨幅作品結構雄奇壯偉，又出倪畫之外。爲新安畫派代表人物，又與朱耷、原濟、髡殘並列爲清初"四畫僧"。

29. 黃山始信峯圖

1663年作
紙本設色立軸　314×84厘米

作者是年本擬與戴本孝等人共遊黃山，因雪阻不克，於呂士鶴之且讀齋度歲，爲呂氏之父應昉作此圖。

款識：
始信峯圖。癸卯（1663年）春弘仁爲旦先居士作於番陽之且讀齋。

印章：
漸江學人（白文方印）

題跋：
紫雲千堵削秋容，不信人間有此峯。記與老人松畔立，至今眉髩帶煙濃。壬癸間，予客芝陽，漸公自黃山來。偕予將往匡廬，留寓且讀齋，爲主人呂君圖此，而予題識之。廣粱樵王艮。

題跋印章：
不菴（白文方印）
王艮第三（白文方印）

鑑藏印章：
錢君匋審定印（朱文長方印）
文農審定（白文方印）
王氏文農收藏金石書畫之印（白文長方印）

Hongren

Qing dynasty　1610-1664

Hao Jianjiang, Meihua Guna, Wuzhi, all Buddhist titles taken as a monk at the fall of the Ming dynasty. The original name of Hongren was said to be Jiang Fang, *zi* Oumeng, or Jiang Tao, *zi* Liuji. He was a native of Shexian, Anhui province. He had made several trips to Mount Huang where the mountains and trees became his favourite themes. His landscape style evolved from Ni Zan (1301-1374), achieving even greater simplicity in the outlines of rocks. The monumental compositions in his large-sized hanging scrolls are also beyond the narrow scope of Ni Zan. He was the leading artist in the Xin'an School and was grouped with Zhu Da, Yuanji and Shixi as the ''Four Monk Painters'' of the early Qing period.

29. The Shixin Peak of Mount Huang

Dated 1663
Hanging scroll, ink and colour on paper
314 × 84 cm

With inscription, signature, 1 seal of the artist, 1 colophon and 2 seals of Wang Gen and 3 collectors' seals.

始信峯圖
癸卯春弘仁為
旦先居士作于番
昜之且讀齋

查士標

清代　1615－1698

字二瞻，號梅壑。安徽休寧人。明亡後棄舉子業，專事書畫。家富珍藏，遂精鑒別。書學董其昌，畫宗元四家，特好倪瓚（1301－1374）筆。畫山水清勁秀逸；後人稱其與弘仁、孫逸（十七世紀中期）、汪之瑞（十七世紀中期）並稱〝新安四大家〞。

30. 寒樹奇峯圖

紙本水墨立軸　134×60.5厘米

此圖寫寒林秋山，行人持杖，一片索寞景色，氣韻荒寒。畫法介乎倪瓚與董其昌間。

款識：
面面奇峯琢削成，瘦添寒樹幾枝横。溪雲晚照橋邊路，盡洗嵐光影水聲。查士標畫並題。

印章：
士標私印（白文方印）
查二瞻（朱文方印）

Zha Shibiao

Qing dynasty　1615-1698

Zi Erzhan, *hao* Meihe, native of Xiuning, Anhui province. Zha gave up any thought of entering an official career after the fall of the Ming dynasty. He devoted his life to painting, calligraphy and connoisseurship, building up an art collection at the same time. He modelled his calligraphy on Dong Qichang's and his painting followed the styles of the four masters of the Yuan dynasty, particularly Ni Zan. He was known as one of the "Four Masters of Xin'an".

30. Wintry Trees and Strange Peaks

Hanging scroll, ink on paper
134×60.5 cm

With inscription, signature and 2 seals of the artist.

面面奇峰琢削成夜添
寒樹幾枝橫淡雲晚照
查士標畫并題

梅　清

清代　1623－1697

字淵公，號瞿山。安徽宣城人。順治十一年（1654）舉人。工畫山水，多畫黃山勝景，尤善松梅，枝幹奇古，自有特色。

31. 山水通景

1693年作
絹本設色十屏　181.5×493.6厘米

此通景十屏，右起山崖崔巍，漸漸舒緩，至左則平山重疊。近溪屋宇，更有人物聚談，另山中小徑與溪上石橋，各有一人携童子，或持酒，或牽琴，赴會於途。

款識：
百歲惟傳黃大癡，雲山亂石供題詩。狂來潑墨同傾酒，誰道遊仙不畫師。癸酉（1693年）九月望前三日寫於茶峽草堂。瞿山梅清並題。

印章：
瞿硎清（白文方印）
淵公（朱文方印）

鑑藏印章：
曾經詠葵珍藏（朱文方印）
養齋珍藏（白文方印）

Mei Qing

Qing dynasty 1623-1697

Zi Yuangong, *hao* Qushan, native of Xuancheng, Anhui province. Mei passed the provincial civil service examination in 1654 but failed in the higher-level examinations. He then returned home and spent his entire life in Anhui province. He was a landscapist, noted for his depictions of Mount Huang. He was also skilled in painting prunus and pines.

31. Landscape Panorama

Set of ten hanging scrolls, ink and colour on silk
181.5 × 493.6 cm

With inscription, signature, 2 seals of the artist on the last two scrolls and 2 collectors' seals.

朱 耷

清代　1626－1705

明寧王朱權後裔，别號很多，明亡後出家爲僧，號傳綮、個山、雪個、個山驢等，又號八大山人。工詩文，書法魏晋，喜用禿筆。畫山水學董其昌。花鳥則放縱雄奇，别樹一幟，影響清代花鳥畫極大。

32. 花鳥雜畫册

紙本水墨册頁十二開　各25×20.9厘米

此水墨雜册十二開，筆墨精簡，神氣完足。所畫禽鳥游魚，生動有致；花卉怪石，筆法老健。款署〝八〞字作二點寫法，當爲朱氏晚年作品。

⑴ 水仙

印章：
八大山人（朱文花押）

鑑藏印章：
子韶審定（朱文方印）
藏張長史節官記之室（朱文長方印）
香源珍賞（朱文方印）

⑵ 鷓鴣

款識：
涉事。

印章：
可得神仙（白文方印）

鑑藏印章：
香源珍賞（朱文方印）
另一印不可辨。

⑶ 游魚

印章：
八大山人（朱文花押）

鑑藏印章：
香源珍賞（朱文方印）
另一印不可辨。

⑷ 蘭

印章：
八大山人（朱文花押）

鑑藏印章：
香源珍賞（朱文方印）
子韶審定（朱文方印）
另一印不可辨。

⑸ 奇石

款識：
八大山人寫。

印章：
可得神仙（白文方印）

鑑藏印章：
香源珍賞（朱文方印）
另一印不可辨

⑹ 雄鷄

印章：
八大山人（朱文花押）

鑑藏印章：
藏張長史節官記之室（朱文長方印）
香源珍賞（朱文方印）
子韶審定（朱文方印）

⑺ 黄頭雀

印章：
八大山人（白文方印）

鑑藏印章：
香源珍賞（朱文方印）

⑻ 墨荷

印章：
八大山人（朱文花押）

鑑藏印章：
香源珍賞（朱文方印）

⑼ 萱花

款識：
八大山人寫。

印章：
可得神仙（白文方印）

鑑藏印章：
子韶審定（朱文方印）
香源珍賞（朱文方印）

⑽ 鸜鵒

款識：
八大山人寫。

印章：
可得神仙（白文方印）

鑑藏印章：
香源珍賞（朱文方印）

另一印不可辨。

⑾ **茶花**

款識：
八大山人寫。

印章：
可得神仙（白文方印）

鑑藏印章：
子韶審定（朱文方印）
香源珍藏（朱文方印）
另一印不可辨。

⑿ **白鴒鳥**

款識：
八大山人寫。

印章：
可得神仙（白文方印）

鑑藏印章：
江左□氏（朱文方印）
貽泉所藏（朱文方印）
藏張長史節官記之室（朱文長方印）
子韶審定（朱文方印）
香源珍賞（朱文方印）
另一印不可辨。

另附題跋一開：
李天馬、黃金海題。

Zhu Da

Qing dynasty 1626-1705

Zhu Da was a descendent of a branch of the royal family of the Ming dynasty. At the fall of the Ming dynasty, he entered the Buddhist monastic order and adopted many other names, such as Chuanqi, Geshan, Xuege, Geshanlu, etc. In his late years, he used Bada Shanren by which he was best known. He studied calligraphy from the masterpieces of the Wei and Jin periods (AD 220-420) and studied landscape from the works of Dong Qichang. His energetic and expressive style, as seen in his paintings of birds and flowers, exerted a great influence throughout the Qing dynasty.

32. Album of Birds, Flowers and Miscellaneous Subjects

Album of twelve leaves, ink on paper
each leaf 25 × 20.9 cm

(1) Narcissus
With 1 seal of the artist and 3 collectors' seals.

(2) Francolin
With inscription, 1 seal of the artist and 1 collector's seal. 1 additional seal unidentified.

(3) Fish Swimming
With 1 seal of the artist and 1 collector's seal. 1 additional seal unidentified.

(4) Orchid
With 1 seal of the artist and 2 collectors' seals. 1 additional seal unidentified.

(5) Strange Rock
With signature, 1 seal of the artist and 1 collector's seal. 1 additional seal unidentified.

(6) Cock
With 1 seal of the artist and 3 collectors' seals.

(7) Birds
With 1 seal of the artist and 1 collector's seal.

(8) Lotus
With 1 seal of the artist and 1 collector's seal.

(9) Tawny Daylilies
With signature, 1 seal of the artist and 2 collectors' seals.

(10) Myna Bird
With signatre, 1 seal of the artist and 1 collector's seal. 1 additional seal unidentified.

(11) Camellia
With signature, 1 seal of the artist and 2 collectors' seals. 1 additional seal unidentified.

(12) Bird on Branch
With signature, 1 seal of the artist and 5 collectors' seals. 1 additional seal unidentified.

1 additional leaf with 2 colophons of Li Tianma and Huang Jinhai.

32.1

32.2

32.3

32.4

32.6

32.5

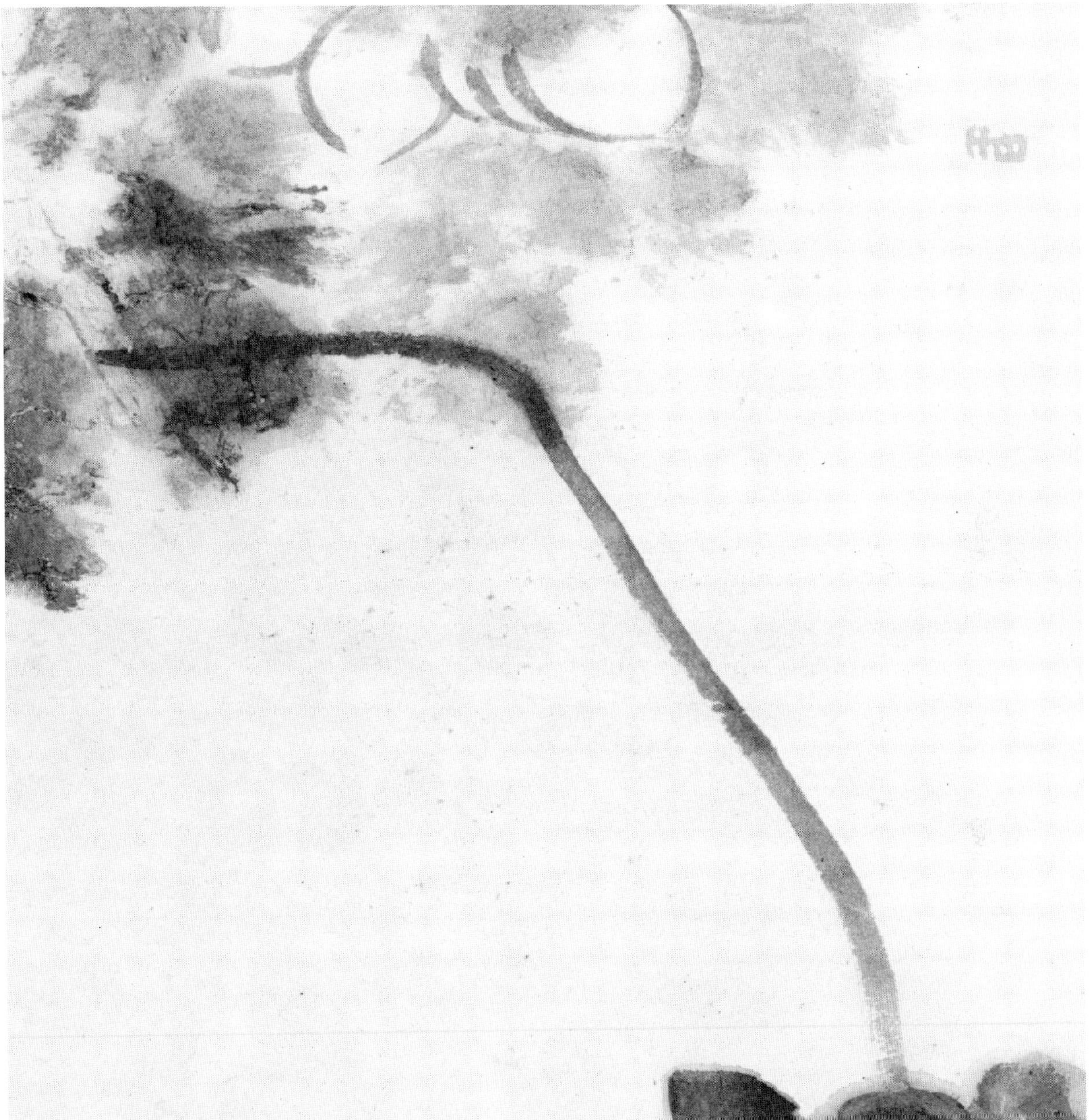

32.8

32.7

32.9

32.10

32.11

32.12

原　濟

清代　1642－1707

字石濤，號清湘老人、大滌子、苦瓜和尚等。原姓朱，名若極，小字阿長，明靖江王朱贊儀十世孫，籍廣西全州，明亡出家，先後流寓江西、浙江、安徽、江蘇等地，卒於揚州。工詩文書畫，天才橫溢，倡"我自有我在"，自成一家。精畫理，著《畫語錄》。

33. 愛蓮圖

紙本設色橫披　46×77.8厘米

此圖雙勾畫蓮塘荷花盛開，隸書自錄周敦頤《愛蓮說》文（不錄）。

款識：
秋日並書爲聖老年道長兄先生博教。清湘遺人大滌子極。

印章：
清湘老人（朱文圓印）
贊之十世孫阿長（朱文長方印）
頭白依然不識字（白文長方印）
藏之名山（白文方印）
齊莊中正（朱文方印）

鑑藏印章：
景祺堂（朱文方印）
瑞亭氏珍藏（朱文方印）
海昌錢鏡塘藏（朱文長方印）
裕齋（白朱文小聯珠印）

Yuanji

Qing dynasty　1642-1707

Zi Shitao, *hao* Qingxiang Laoren, Dadizi, Kugua Heshang, native of Quanzhou (present-day Guilin, Guangxi province). A twelfth-generation descendant of one of the princes of the first Ming emperor, his original name was Zhu Ruoji. After the fall of the Ming empire, he became a Buddhist monk and devoted himself to the arts. Subsequently he led a wandering life, travelling in the provinces of Jiangxi, Anhui, Zhejiang and Jiangsu and painting at many mountain sites. However, in his old age he retired to Yangzhou, where he died. He was acclaimed the most original and prolific artist of the Qing dynasty. His theories in art were recorded in a book entitled *Huayulu*.

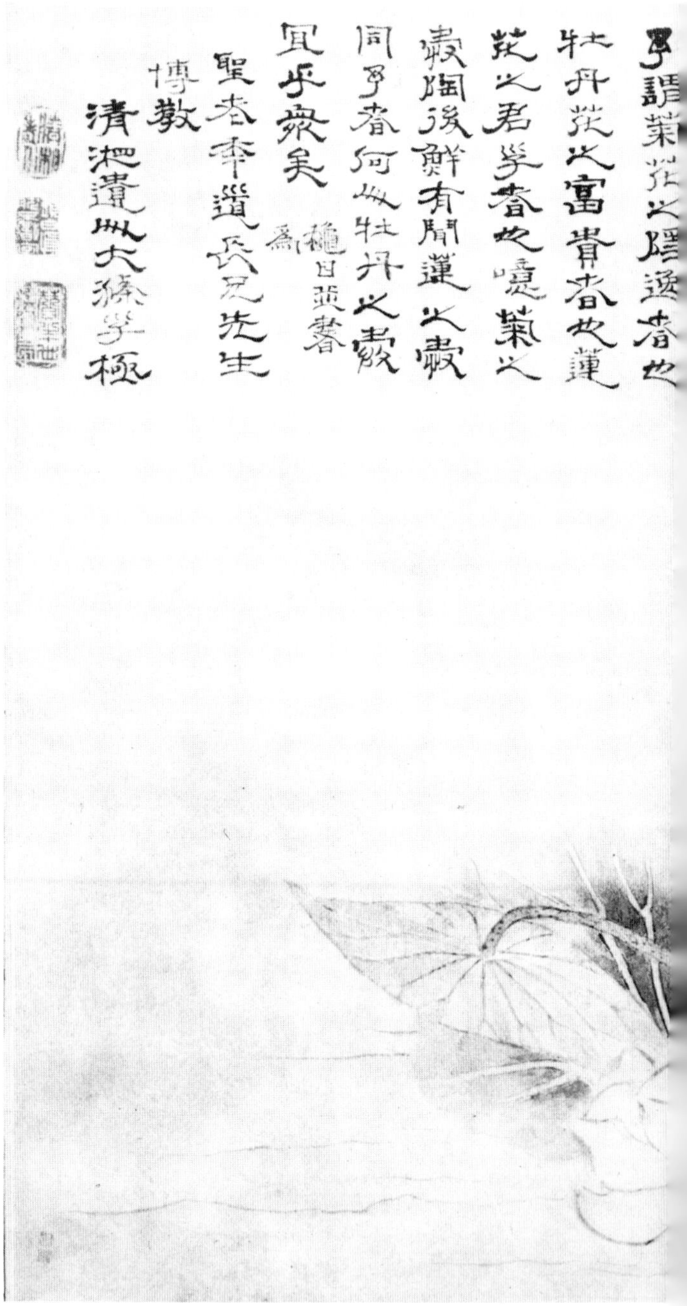

33. Lotuses

Horizontal scroll, ink and colour on paper
46×77.8 cm

With inscription, signature, 5 seals of the artist and 4 collectors' seals.

水陸艸木之花可愛者
甚蕃晉陶淵明獨愛菊
自李唐來世人甚愛牡
丹予獨愛蓮之出淤
泥而不染濯清漣而
不妖中通外直不蔓不

原　濟

小傳見前。

34. 詩畫册

紙本設色册頁（畫八開、書六開）各38×24.5厘米

此册有山水八頁、書蹟六頁。其中三頁有年款，分別爲庚午（1690年）癸酉（1693年）及丁丑（1697年）。文字款識，皆情思充沛，畫則極變化生動之致。此册曾經廣東嶽雪樓孔廣陶珍藏，並具廣東書畫家張維屏（1780－1859）、熊景星（1791－1856）、陳其錕書題，張大千（1899－1983）跋。

扉頁：
清湘墨妙。伯晴。

印章：
笛江（朱文方印）

⑴ 風雨山樓

款識：
感時催朽木，疎雨浸邗溝。意與誰同識，畫來破我愁。春生茶鼎沸，花落酒杯浮。遙憶隔谿水，歸雲殿閣收。依東只來韻復圖此。苦瓜老人濟。

印章：
瞎尊者（朱文長方印）

鑑藏印章：
孔氏鑑定（朱文長方印）

對題：
張維屛題。

⑵ 行人持杖

款識：
諸方乞食苦瓜僧，戒行全無趨小乘。五十孤行成獨往，一身禪病冷如冰。庚午（1690年）長安寫此。

印章：
瞎尊者（朱文方印）

鑑藏印章：
少唐審定（朱文方印）

⑶ 獨立蒼茫

印章：
原濟（白文方印）
石濤（朱文方印）

鑑藏印章：
少唐審定（朱文方印）

對題：
孔廣陶題。

⑷ 草舍流泉

款識：
畫到無聲，何敢題句。清湘苦瓜老人濟。

印章：
瞎尊者（朱文方印）

鑑藏印章：
嶽雪樓鑒藏金石書畫圖籍之章（朱文方印）

對題：
張維屛題。

⑸ 秋雨淋漓

款識：
雨也淋漓風也癡，風風雨雨到秋時。閑向松窗取雨意，一天風雨繪秋詩。苦瓜老人濟。

印章：
瞎尊者（朱文方印）

鑑藏印章：
嶽雪樓印（朱文長方印）

對題：
熊景星題。

⑹ 清流覓句

款識：
秋空山霽寒，清流滙谿碧。輸與簪冠人，吟詩坐苔石。小乘客苦瓜濟。

印章：
釋元濟印（白文方印）

鑑藏印章：
少唐審定（朱文方印）

對題：
熊景星題。

⑺ 荒煙秋城

款識：
離離禾黍動愁深，無語憑欄淚不禁。老去悲秋懷宋玉，行來覓句効依林（唐休公高弟）。三千客路水雲夢，九月窮途感慨心。賴有文場諸長者，潛陰詩賦大家音。杜集西園送秋分得十二侵。苦瓜和尚濟。

印章：
釋元濟（白文方印）

鑑藏印章：
少唐心賞（白文方印）

對題：
孔廣陶題。

⑻ 山亭喜雨

款識：
五月六月六十日，□□南風抱雙膝。但聞霹靂火雲堆，枕簟如焚望山鷸。城中豪富十萬家，米貴金多何用嗟。農子吞聲互相泣，相逢道看秋胡麻。五日禁屠三日開，歡聲飽肉轟如雷。立壇禱雨雨不至，壇收雨下天河催。天有至道非人力，安坐但聽空中極。空中極極不極，大罈小甕飽我休，世外何勞空太息。時癸酉（1693年）夏日客吳山亭，喜雨，戲作此紙。湘源老人苦瓜濟。

印章：
釋元濟印（白文方印）

鑑藏印章：
少唐心賞（白文方印）

對題：
陳其錕題。

⑼ 七言律詩

釋文：
黎明努力趣輕舟，休待東昇暑氣投。文筆一峯天使駐，廣陵渡口客星留。吟詩調古驚林壑，談笑風生動九洲。憶得坡公與顛癖，倒翻墨海研田遊。訪狄向濤於文星閣。

印章：
瞎尊者（朱文方印）

⑽ 古詩：

釋文：
揚子橋邊江水泛，柳絲弄色不管人白頭。一春雨雪阻遊屐，梅花尚可清明留。老去無聊藉朋輩，年來星散逐波鷗。汪子無端向我發長嘯，吾將縱覽閩海之奧妙。請君置我先向畫圖看，眼前立壑都一掃。千里萬里毫端見，非墨非烟聊寄傲。君家嚴親百代才，一言奏對驚風雷。天子非常賜顏色，瀛臺稱旨今南來。多少寒灰待君活，看君作意爲龍媒。題畫贈汪牧庭之閩海，兼呈思白學使者。

印章：
原濟（白文方印）
半個漢（朱文方印）
頭白依然不識字（白文長方印）

⑾ 七言古詩

釋文：
丁丑（1697年）三月上巳晴，清湘野老眼方明。手拖籐杖出門去，興教寺前訪舊盟。登堂拜揖驚大笑，密移一步快生平。十年淚盡故交散，此地逢君不易評。客裏吟成才八斗，夢中頭白酒千傾。人生適意解眞樂，世事輸贏朝暮情。有詩盡付枝人讀，西去長安紙價爭。上巳日過興教寺訪陳定九。瞎尊者原濟。

印章：
老濤（朱文長方印）

⑿ 七言古詩：

釋文：
二月已過三月中，梅花不放抱犢翁。翁喜梅花有奇骨，梅亦對翁多古風。廣陵思煞好朋輩，恨不見翁猶我同。高談雄辯耳邊近，身未渡江神已功（原註功字錯）。鐵畫草能開百代，玉鉤新月掛高空。好將一幅摩天紙，試展翁畫始盡雄。懷韋華江寧不至。大滌山人濟。

印章：
老濤（朱文長方印）

⒀ 七言古詩：

釋文：
一春雨雪二月杪，病夫小閣巢如鳥。擁被高眠懶下床，齒長疎痛食漸少。念子將歸還不歸，夜來夢入

神漂渺。知己無多遠間隔，筆墨雖快成寮倒。請君一笑解相思，揚帆來者清湘老。寄懷石友兄之龍沙。

印章：
半個漢（朱文方印）
贊之十世孫阿長（朱文長方印）

⒁ 七言律詩：

釋文：
醒癡香罷澆愁茗，助我幽懷二千頃。招手啣杯風雪來，仰天大笑摩冰冷。此時對雪呼高人，吾欲隨之飄有神。閣小風高恐吞去，濃香苦茗心無塵。項子贈我名香佳茗，春雪忽狂，呼筆索笑。清湘老人濟草青蓮小閣。

印章：
贊之十世孫阿長（朱文長方印）

另附題跋一開：
張大千題。

Yuanji

For biography see cat. no. 33.

34. Album of Paintings and Poems

3 leaves dated 1690, 1693 and 1697, respectively
Album of eight leaves of painting, six leaves of calligraphy, ink and colour on paper
each leaf 38×24.5 cm

(1) Mountain Cottages in the Rain
With inscription, signature and 1 seal of the artist.
1 colophon of Zhang Weiping (1780-1859) on facing page.

(2) Solitary Traveller
Dated 1690
With inscription, 1 seal of the artist and 1 collector's seal.

(3) Mountain Retreat
With 2 seals of the artist and 1 collector's seal.
1 colophon of Kong Guangtao (1832-?) on facing page.

(4) Thatched Cottage by the Stream
With inscription, signature, 1 seal of the artist and 1 collector's seal.
1 colophon and 1 seal of Zhang Weiping on facing page.

(5) Autumn Rain
With inscription, signature, 1 seal of the artist and 1 collector's seal.
1 colophon and 1 seal of Xiong Jingxing (1791-1856) on facing page.

(6) Seeking Poetry by the Stream
With inscription, signature, 1 seal of the artist and 1 collector's seal.
1 colophon and 1 seal of Xiong Jingxing on facing page.

(7) City Dwellings in Autumn
With inscription, signature, 1 seal of the artist and 1 collector's seal.
1 colophon and 1 seal of Kong Guangtao on facing page.

(8) Mountain Rain
Dated 1693
With inscription, signature, 1 seal of the artist and 1 collector's seal.
1 colophon and 1 seal of Chen Qikun on facing page.

(9) Poem
With 1 seal of the artist.

(10) Poem
With 3 seals of the artist.

(11) Poem
Dated 1697
With 1 seal of the artist.

(12) Poem
With 1 seal of the artist.

(13) Poem
With 2 seals of the artist.

(14) Poem
With 1 seal of the artist.

2 additional leaves of frontispiece by Xiong Jingxing, 1 additional leaf of colophon by Zhang Daqian (1899-1983).

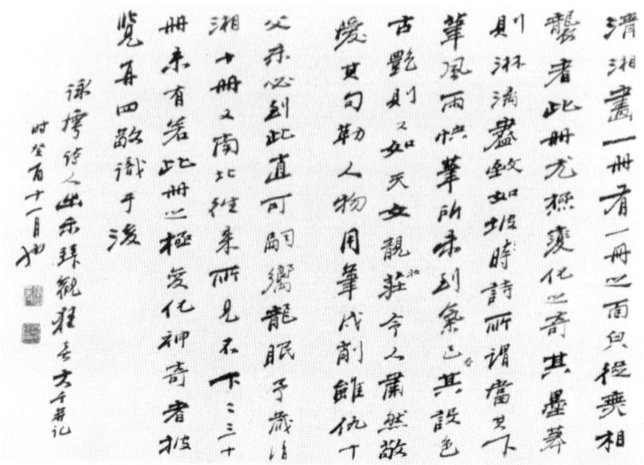

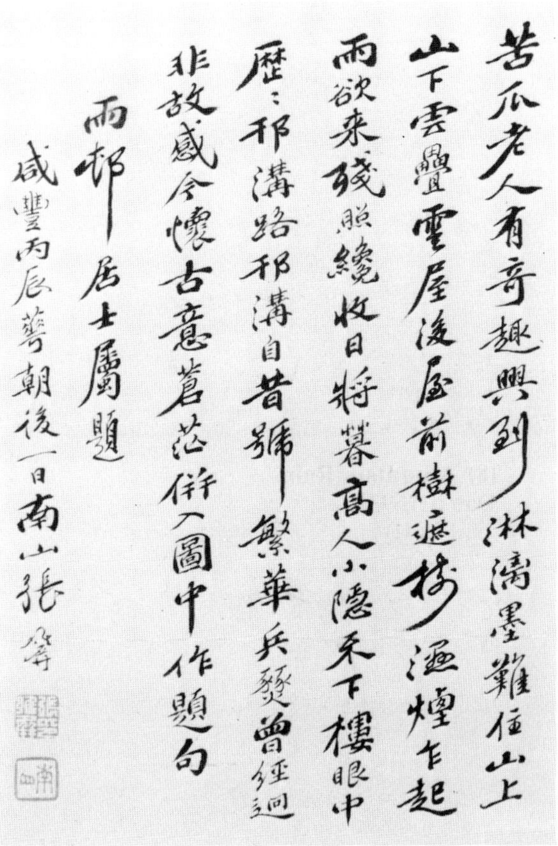
苦瓜老人有奇趣興到淋漓墨難住山上
山下雲疊疊屋後屋前樹遮樓涵煙乍起
雨欲來殘照繞收日將暮高人小隱不下樓眼中
歷歷邗溝路邗溝自昔稱繁華兵發曾經迴
非故感今懷古意蒼茫併入圖中作題句
雨邨居士屬題
咸豐丙辰華朝後一日南山張崟

34.1a

34.1

34.2

34.3a

34.3

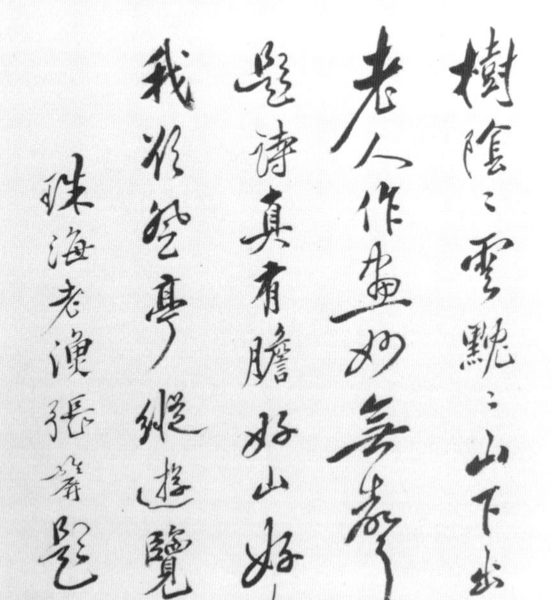

34.4a

34.4

34.5

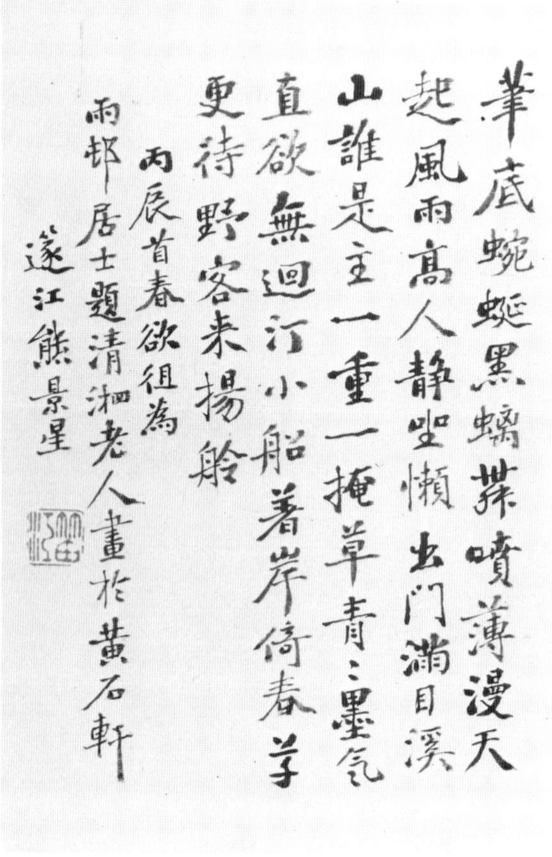

34.5a

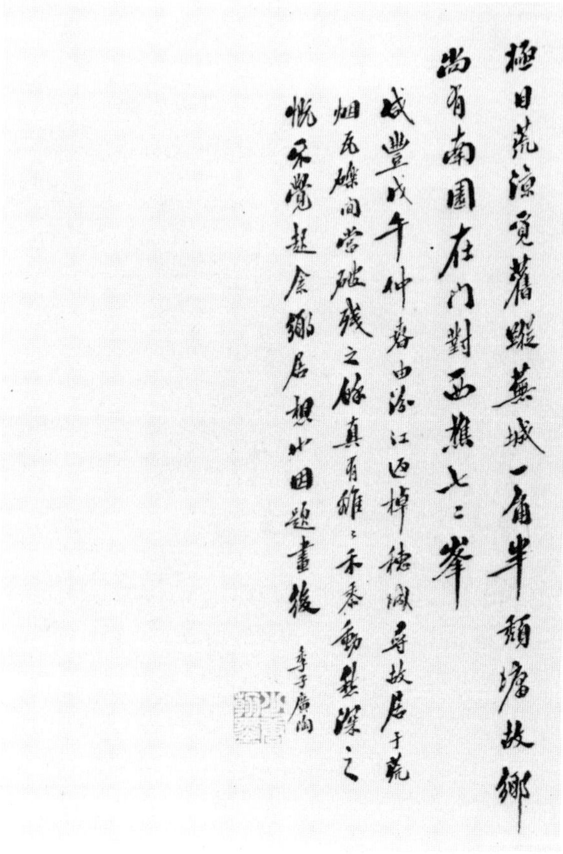

34.7a

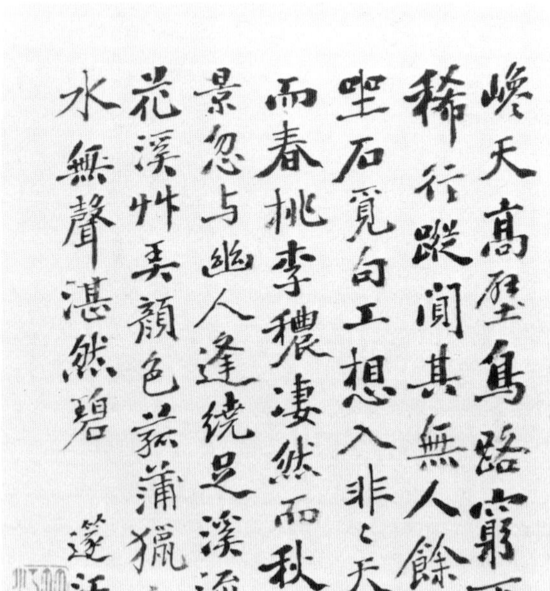

34.6a

34.6

34.7

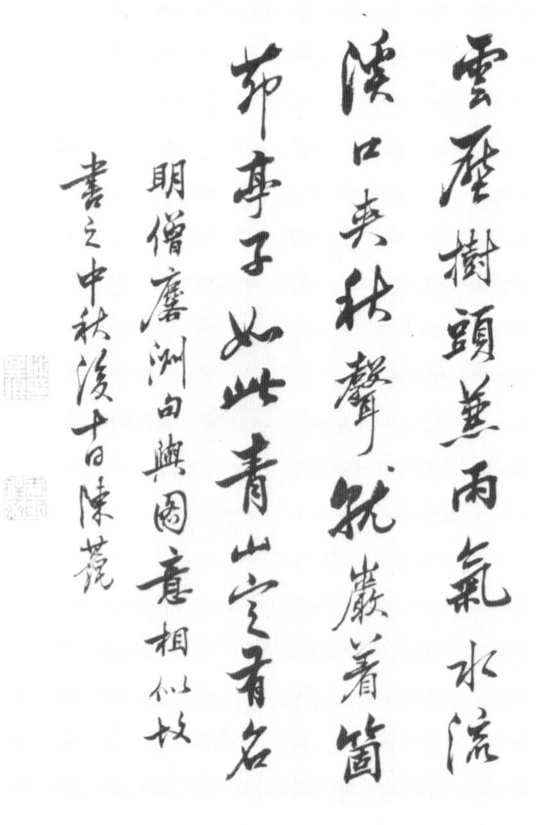

34.8a

34.8

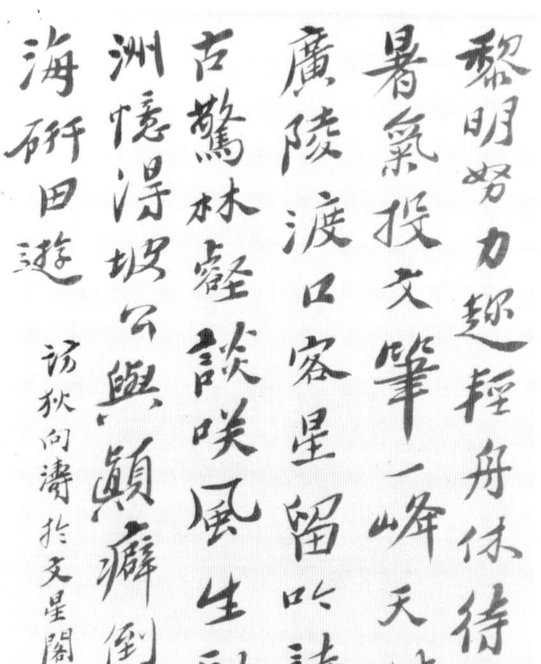

34.9

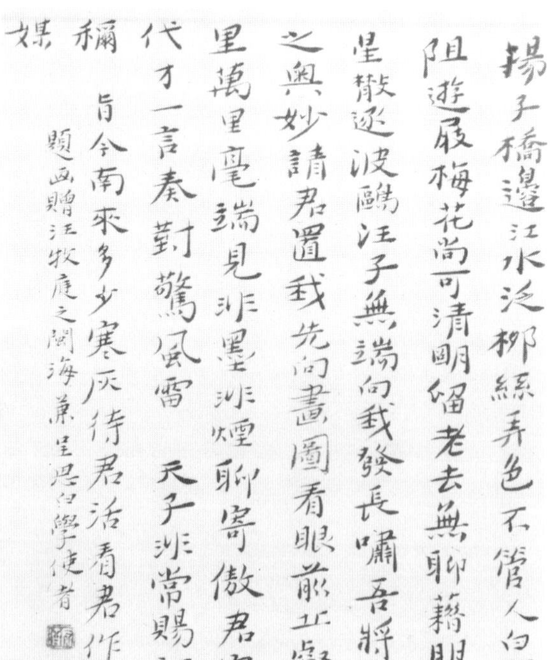

34.10

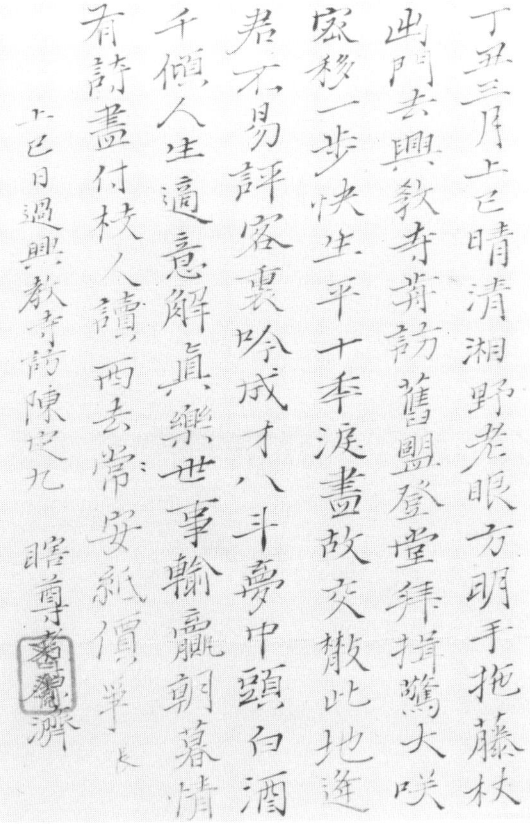

34.11

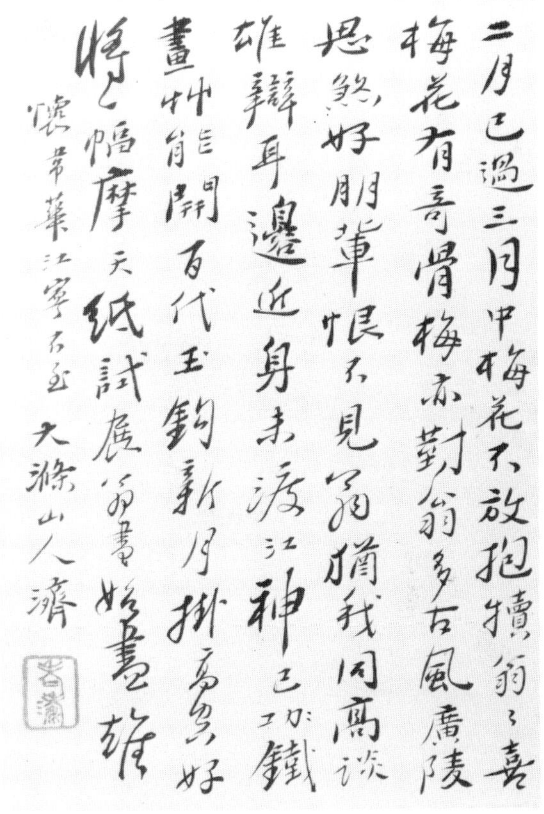

34.12

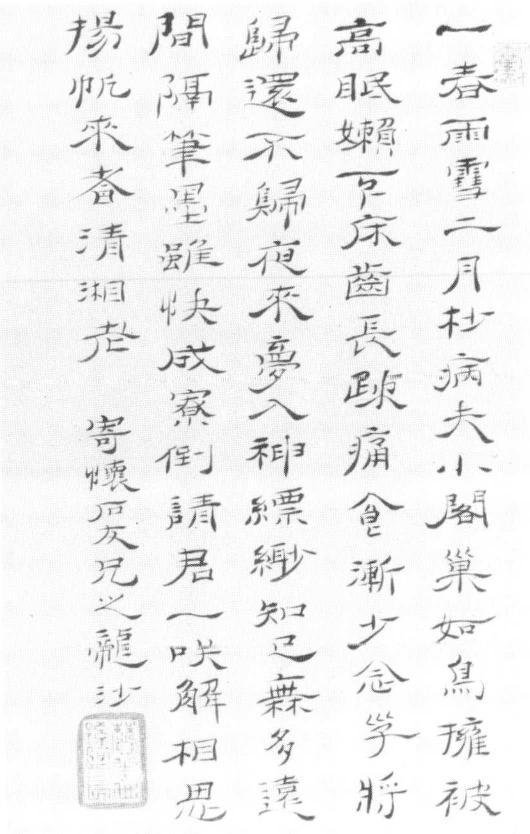

34.13

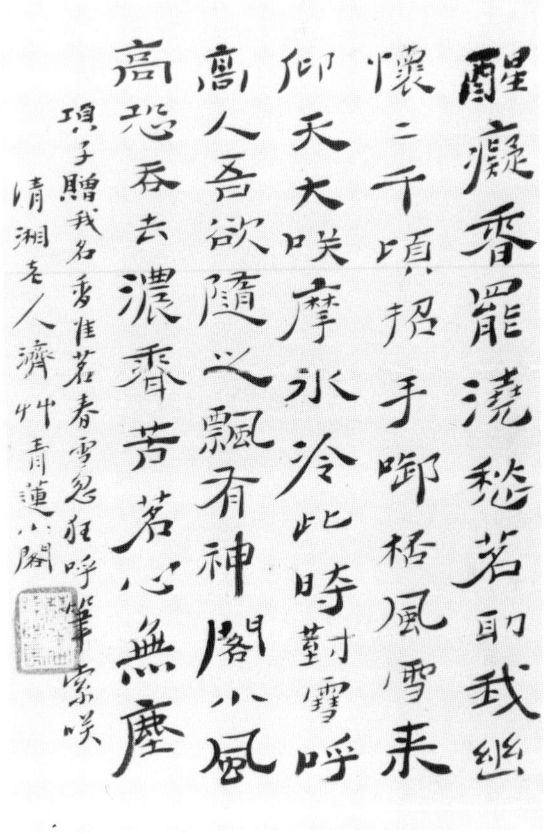

34.14

龔　賢

清代　1619－1689

又名豈賢，字半千，又字野遺（或作野逸），號半畝，柴丈人。江蘇崑山人，寓居南京。工詩文書法，善畫山水，畫法自董源巨然出，墨色渾厚，筆勢雄奇，自成一家。後世推爲"金陵八家"之一。

35. 秋山飛瀑圖

1676年作
綾本設色立軸　177×71厘米

此圖畫青山疊翠，流瀑下叢林屋舍，筆墨厚重，設色工整，爲龔賢傳世僅見綾本青綠設色畫。

款識：
半畝居人年近六十，未嘗一爲設色畫，蓋非素習也。而酷好余畫者，數以青綠見索，遂有糟粕可厭如斯。雖亦遠慕古人，實則不如用墨之盡善，因誌數言，就大方指正。龔賢。丙辰（1676年）四月。

印章：
龔賢（朱文方印）

Gong Xian

Qing dynasty　1619-1689

Alias Qixian, *zi* Banqian, Yeyi, *hao* Banmu, Chaizhangren. Though a native of Kunshan, Jiangsu province, Gong spent most of his life in Nanjing. Deriving from the style of the old masters, Dong Yuan and Juran, he created a highly personal landscape which was achieved by repeated brush strokes and layers of wash in a very strong and solid manner. He was acclaimed as one of the "Eight Masters of Nanjing".

35. Cascade in the Autumn Mountains

Dated 1676
Hanging scroll, ink and colour on satin
177 × 71 cm

With inscription, signature and 1 seal of the artist.

龔　賢

小傳見前。

36. 雲山結樓圖

紙本水墨立軸　251×99.5厘米

此畫寫結樓山居，用墨深厚，層次分明，意境眞切。淡墨遠山，見墨見筆，尤具新意，可稱龔賢傑作。

款識：
不必三山住，寧從五嶽遊。儘多哨水石，別有大春秋。度險頻修棧，淸空更結樓。自憐飛湯盞，一嘯碧天頭。龔賢畫並題。

印章：
龔賢（朱文方印）
鍾山野老（白文方印）

Gong Xian

For biography see cat. no. 35.

36. Dwelling among Clouds and Mountains

Hanging scroll, ink on paper
251×99.5 cm

With inscription, signature and 2 seals of the artist.

葉　欣

清代　十七世紀中期

字榮木，華亭人。流寓金陵（南京），工畫山水，“金陵八家”之一。

37. 山水册

1663年作
紙本設色册頁八開　各20×27.5厘米

此册用筆極精細，設色淡雅，各具意趣。

扉頁：
葉榮木山水册精品。荆林居士屬題。芝僊。

印章：
常芝僊（朱文方印）

⑴ **棧廊繞山**

印章：
欣（朱文方印）

鑑藏印章：
秋枚寶愛（朱文方印）

⑵ **垂柳御溝**

款識：
垂柳御溝新。欣。

印章：
葉、欣（朱文聯珠印）

⑶ **荻叢送別**

印章：
欣（朱文方印）

⑷ **出獵覓虎**

款識：
虎嘯深谷底。

印章：
欣（朱文方印）

⑸ **浪湧舟隨**

印章：
榮木（白文長方印）

⑹ **石橋轎過**

印章：
榮木（白文長方印）

⑺ **亭臺遊春**

款識：
春曉。葉欣。

印章：
欣（朱文方印）

鑑藏印章：
蕭壽民印（朱文方印）

⑻ **叢林石寺**

款識：
癸卯（1663年）清和月寫爲松士盟長正。葉欣。

印章：
榮木（白文長方印）

裱邊鑑藏印章：
延齡心賞（朱文方印）
癖於斯（朱文方印）

另附題跋一開：
芝軒題。

鑑藏印章：
古滇蕭壽民藏（朱文方印）

Ye Xin

Qing dynasty mid-17th century

Zi Rongmu, native of Huating, Jiangsu province. A landscapist living in Nanjing, Ye was acclaimed as one of the "Eight Masters" of this city.

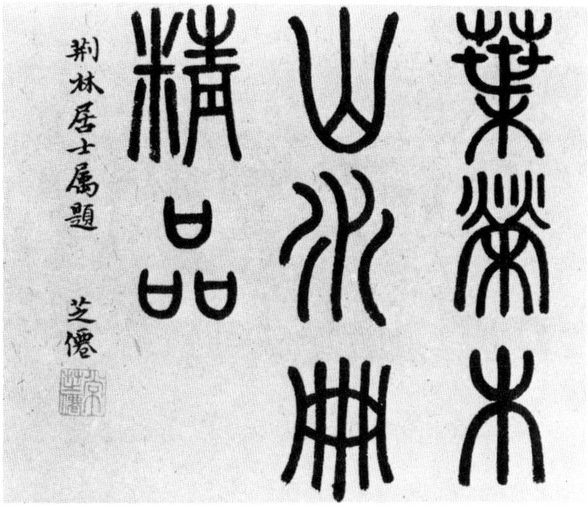

37. Album of Landscapes

Dated 1663
Album of eight leaves, ink and colour on paper
each leaf 20 × 27.5 cm

(1) Covered Walkway Encircling the Mountains
With 1 seal of the artist and 1 collector's seal.

(2) Willows by the Royal Water-course
With inscriptions, signature, and 2 seals of the artist.

(3) Farewell by the Shore
With 1 seal of the artist.

(4) Tiger Hunting
With inscription and 1 seal of the artist.

(5) Boat in Storm at Sea
Same as leaf (3).

(6) Crossing the Stone Bridge
Same as leaf (3).

(7) Spring Morning
With inscription, signature, 1 seal of the artist and 1 collector's seal.

(8) Temple in the Forest
With inscription, signature and 1 seal of the artist.

2 additional leaves with frontispiece and 1 colophon of Chang Zhixuan and 1 collector's seal.

37.1

37.2

37.3

37.4

37.5

37.6

37.7

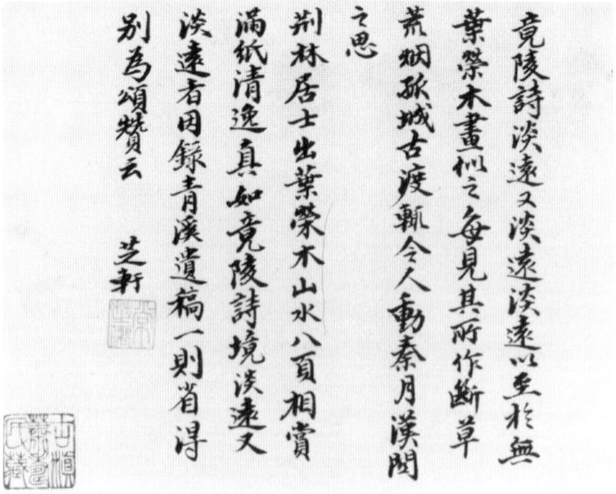

37.8

金陵畫家

清代　十七世紀後期

龔　賢

小傳見　35。

吳　宏

？ －1668

一作弘，字遠度。原籍江西，僑寓江寧（今南京），後爲金陵人。

文　濶

生平不詳。

高　遇

十七世紀中後期

即高適，字雨吉。浙江杭州人，寓金陵（今南京）。高阜子。山水師其叔高岑。

王　槩

活躍於1677－1705間

字安節。原秀水（浙江嘉興）人，僑居南京。善畫山水，龔賢弟子，手摹《芥子園畫譜》山水部份。

高　岑

十七世紀中後期

字蔚生。浙江杭州人，客寓金陵。工詩，善畫山水。

樊　圻

1616－約1695

字會公。江寧(今南京)人。工畫山水、花卉人物。

38. 山水册

紙本水墨設色册頁(畫八開、書一開)
各15.7×19.2厘米

此册書畫共九頁，"金陵八家"之龔賢、樊圻、高岑、吳宏俱在其中。一頁無款無印，未明誰作；從畫風看來，爲金陵派畫家作品無疑。另龔賢書題一頁有年款，乃壬子（1672年）所書。

⑴ 龔賢：叢林重山

印章：
柴丈（朱文長方印）

裱邊鑑藏印章：
山陰任氏所藏（朱文長方印）

⑵ 吳宏：秋林策杖

印章：
吳、宏（朱文聯珠印）

⑶ 文濶：江岸舟船

印章：
文、濶（朱文聯珠印）

⑷ 高遇：山間觀雲

款識：
鍾山高遇

印章：
遇（白文方印）

⑸ 王槩：山崖飛瀑

款識：
自一榕廟上釣嶺登門寺，沿石關轉白龍潭，幽折如此。繡水王槩。

印章：
朱文方印一，未可辨。

⑹ 高岑：竹蔭暢話

印章：
高、岑（白文聯珠印）

⑺ 佚名：溪橋人家

⑻ 樊圻：舟中眺雁

印章：
樊圻之印（白文方印）
字曰會公（朱文方印）

⑼ 龔賢：五言詩

1672年作

釋文：
歲歉多聞見，山中倍寂然。可堪春又雪，莫禁夜憂天。到戶客無跡，經時爨少烟。只愁梅蕊盡，飢鳥尙翩翩。壬子（1672年）春早起摹僧巨然畫，因憶夜來所得五言近體一首，並書之於此。

印章：
龔賢印（白文方印）

另附題跋一開：
此予友樊君會公筆，會公名圻，予携其畫入都，孟津王公笑渼，以爲無一筆不合古人，無一筆不引人勝地。但誤書其字曰洽公，君遂以洽公行，人之重知己之感如是哉。周亮識。

印章：
櫟下周亮（白文方印）
減齋（朱文方印）
壬□（朱文長方印）

裱邊鑑藏印章：
常淸靜室（白文方印）
九籐仙館書畫（白文方印）

Nanjing Masters

Qing dynasty second half of 17th century

Gong Xian (cf. cat. no. 35)

Wu Hong

(?-1668)

Zi Yuandu, native of Jiangxi province but moved to settle in Nanjing. Wu was one of the "Eight Masters of Nanjing".

Wen Yuan (Biography unknown).

Gao Yu

Second half of 17th century

Also known as Gao Shi, *zi* Yuji, native of Hangzhou but lived in Nanjing. Gao was the son of Gao Fu, who was also an artist, and studied landscape painting with his uncle, Gao Cen.

Wang Gai

fl. 1677-1705

Zi Anjie, native of Jiaxing, Zhejiang province but lived in Nanjing. As a student of Gong Xian, Wang was noted for his landscape painting. He was the chief editor of *The Mustard Seed Garden Painting Manual* and he painted all the landscape illustrations in the book.

Gao Cen

Second half of 17th century

Zi Weishang, native of Hangzhou, Zhejiang province but settled in Nanjing where he made his name as one of the "Eight Masters of Nanjing". Gao was well versed in poetry and landscape painting.

Fan Qi

1616-ca. 1695

Zi Huigong, native of Jiangning (present-day Nanjing). Fan was skilled in painting landscape, flower and figure. He was also grouped with the "Eight Masters of Nanjing".

38. Album of Landscapes

Album of eight leaves of painting, one leaf of calligraphy, ink and colour on paper

each leaf 15.7 × 19.2 cm

(1) Gong Xian: Forest and Hills
With 1 seal of the artist and 1 collector's seal.

(2) Wu Hong: Wandering in the Autumn Forest
With 2 seals of the artist.

(3) Wen Yuan: Boats on the River
With 2 seals of the artist.

(4) Gao Yu; Watching Clouds in the Mountains
With signature and 1 seal of the artist.

(5) Wang Gai: Cliffside Waterfall
With inscription and signature of the artist. 1 seal unidentified.

(6) Gao Cen: Conversation under the Shade of Bamboo
With 2 seals of the artist.

(7) Anonymous: Houses by the Stream
Unsigned and with no seals.

(8) Fan Qi: Watching Wild Geese in Flight
With 2 seals of the artist.

(9) Gong Xian: Calligraphy
Dated 1672
With 1 seal of the artist.

1 additional leaf with 1 colophon by Zhou Lianggong (1612-1677) and 2 collectors' seals.

38.6

38.8

38.1

38.2

38.3

38.4

38.5

38.7

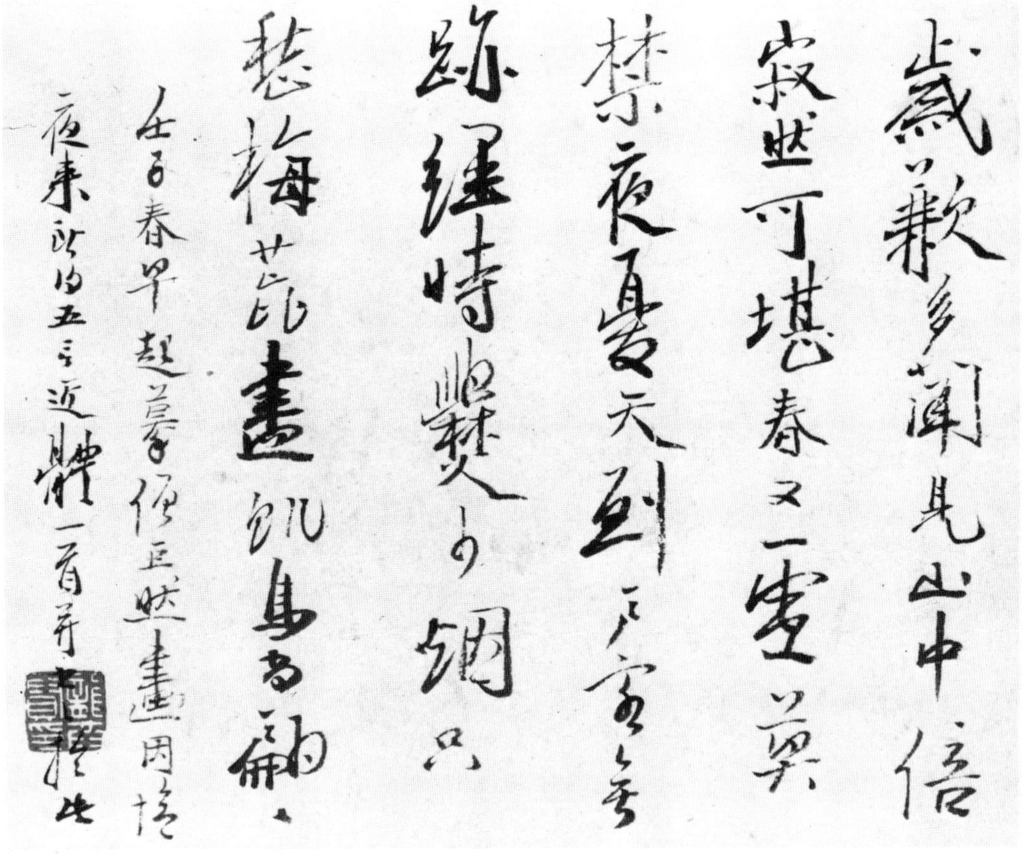

38.9

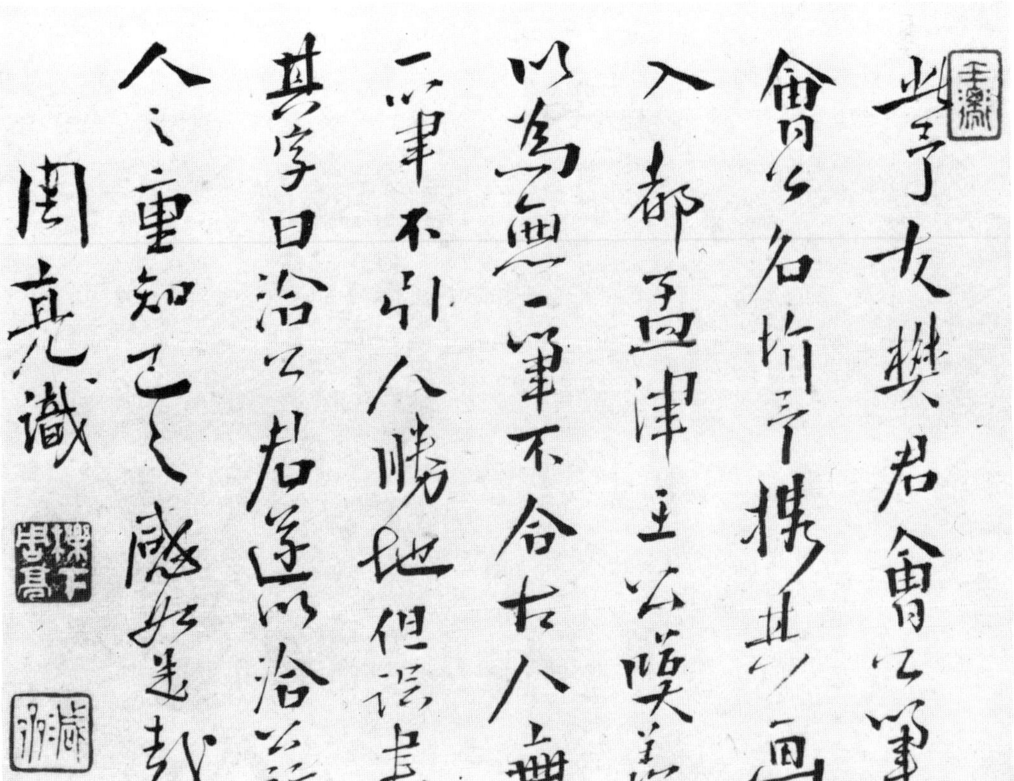

38.10

陳　舒

清代　1612－1682

字原舒，號道山。浙江嘉善人，移居江寧（南京）。順治六年（1649）進士，官至布政使參議。工畫花鳥草蟲，間亦作山水。

39. 芙蓉一甲圖

絹本設色立軸　137.5×46厘米

此畫描寫塘邊一景，芙蓉蘆草雜生，一鴨踟躕欲下。設色淡雅，別有恣趣。

款識：
清江多逸徑，斜炤淡芙蓉。此外漁樵興，高流靜自逢。原野。

印章：
道山（朱文方印）

Chen Shu

Qing dynasty　1612-1682

Zi Yuanshu, *hao* Daoshan, native of Jiashan, Zhejiang province but moved to live in Jiangning (Nanjing). Chen passed the *jinshi* examination in 1649, followed by various official posts in the Qing government. He specialized in bird and flower painting.

39. Duck and Hibiscus

Hanging scroll, ink and colour on silk
137.5×46 cm

With inscription, signature and 1 seal of the artist.

張　穆

清代　1607－1686後

字爾敂，號穆之，又號鐵橋。廣東東莞人。少好騎射，善擊劍；曾參加張家玉軍抗清失敗，明亡；遂隱居東安縣（今雲浮縣），建東溪草堂。擅畫馬，家養名駒以供寫生，所畫馬匹，肌肉結實，骨格剛硬。年八十餘，仍步履如飛，一日無病卒。

40. 春柳三馬圖

1663年作
紙本水墨立軸　139.5×50厘米

此圖畫黑、白、灰三馬，立於柳下；體態準確，筆致清勁。

款識：
癸卯（1663年）花朝寫似冲翁老先生。羅浮張穆。

印章：
張穆私印（白文方印）
鐵橋道人（白文方印）

Zhang Mu

Qing dynasty　1607-after 1686

Zi Erqi, *hao* Muzhi, Tieqiao, native of Dongguan, Guangdong province. As a youth, Zhang was skilled in swordsmanship and riding. When the Ming rule ended, he joined with Zhang Jiayu to recruit soldiers to fight against the Qing army. This failed and he retired to his home village. A poet in his own right, he was also noted for his painting. Hie speciality was horses which were kept in a stable for him to sketch from life.

40. Horses by the Willow Trees

Dated 1663
Handscroll, ink on paper
139.5 × 50 cm

With inscription, signature and 2 seals of the artist.

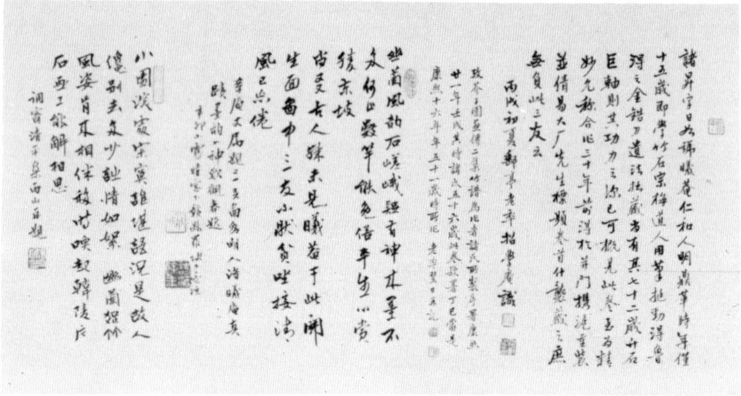

諸　昇

清代　1618－1689後

字日如，號曦庵。浙江仁和（今杭州）人。善畫蘭竹石，師魯得之，筆勁利。

41．三友圖

1677年作

紙本水墨手卷　31×265厘米

此圖水墨畫蘭竹石，用筆勁挺。

引首：
三友圖。學庵藏家屬。丙寅八月朔，大厂居士題。

引首印章：
大厂居士（白文方印）

款識：
丁巳（1677年）花朝寫爲樸老道兄指正。諸昇。

印章：
諸昇之印（白文方印）
日如（朱文方印）

後幅題跋：
招學庵、羅球、張盤及梁山舟題。

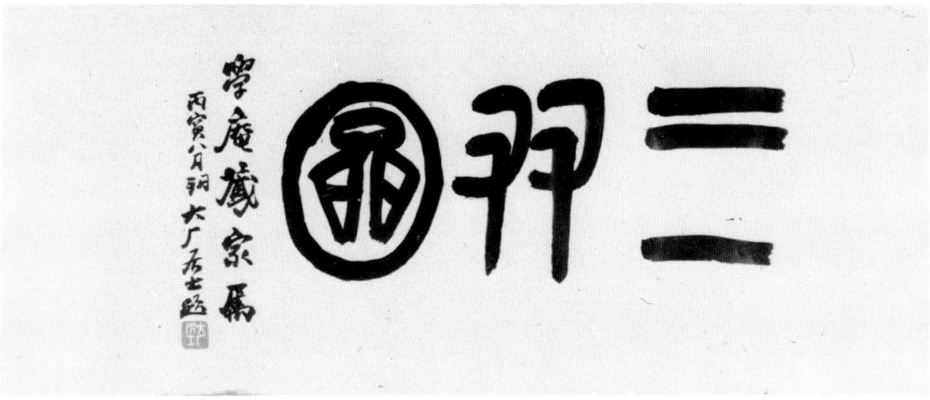

Zhu Sheng

Qing dynasty 1618-after 1689

Zi Riru, *hao* Xi'an, native of Renhe (present-day Hangzhou, Zhejiang province). Zhu was noted for his vigorous manner in painting orchids, bamboo and rocks. He studied with Lu Dezhi, a specialist in these subjets.

41. Three Friends

Dated 1677
Handscroll, ink on paper
31 × 265 cm

With inscription, signature and 2 seals of the artist. Frontispiece by I Da'an, 4 colophons by Zhao Xue'an, Luo Qiu, Zhang Pan and Liang Shanzhou on paper separate from painting.

戴明說

清代　十七世紀中期

字道默，號嚴犖，晚號定圃。滄州（今河北滄縣）人。崇禎七年（1634）進士。入清官戶部尚書，順治十七年（1660）去官。工詩文，善畫墨竹，學吳鎮法，意態生動。亦善山水。

42. 墨竹圖

1675年作
綾本水墨立軸　179×30厘米

此畫寫水邊墨竹一梢，搖舞飄風，簡潔清勁。

款識：
乙卯（1675年）戴明說畫。

印章：
鐵帚老翁（白文方印）
另一印不可辨。

鑑藏印章：
容庚（朱文方印）
另一印不可辨。

Dai Mingshuo

Qing dynasty　mid-17th century

Zi Daomo, *hao* Yanluo, Dingpu in his late years, native of Cangzhou (present-day Cangxian, Hebei province). Having passed the *jinshi* examination in 1634, Dai entered government service. His official career continued until 1660 in spite of the dynastic change. He was accomplished in poetry, essay writing and painting of landscape and bamboo. He took Wu Zhen of the Yuan dynasty as his model for his bamboo painting.

42. Bamboo

Dated 1675
Hanging scroll, ink and colour on satin
179 × 30 cm

With signature, 1 seal of the artist and 1 collector's seal. 2 seals unidentified.

章　谷

清代　十七世紀中期

字言在，號古愚。浙江仁和（今杭州）人。善篆、隸，工畫山水及人物肖像。筆致清勁，烘染尤妙。

43. 八景册

1659年作
絹本設色册頁八開　各28.5×22.3厘米

此册八景均由作者自書畫題，並鈐"章谷"印。

(1)

款識：
赤壁夜遊。

印章：
章谷（朱文長圓印）
（以下各開所鈐印章同）

(2)

款識：
桃源避世。

鑑藏印章：
容庚（朱文方印）

(3)

款識：
帝城春雨。

(4)

款識：
天目雲海。

(5)

款識：
澗道寒泉。

(6)

款識：
麯院荷香。

(7)

款識：
竹林高士。

(8)

款識：
峨嵋積雪。己亥（1659年）秋九月古愚章谷寫。

Zhang Gu

Qing dynasty　mid-17th century

Zi Yanzai, *hao* Guyu, native of Renhe (present-day Hangzhou, Zhejiang province). Zhang was skilled in calligraphy, landscape and figure painting. His painting is always executed with fine lines and delicated gradations of tone values.

43. Album of Eight Views

Dated 1659
Album of eight leaves, ink and colour on silk
each leaf 28.5×22.3 cm

Each leaf with inscription and 1 seal of the artist.

(1) A Night Visit to the Red Cliff

(2) Peach Blossom Spring

(3) Spring Rain in Baidicheng

(4) Sea of Clouds at the Mount Tianmu

(5) Crossing the Stream

(6) Lotus Pond at Quyuan

(7) Sages of the Bamboo Grove

(8) Snow on Mount Emei
With inscription, signature and 1 seal of the artist.

43.1

43.2

43.3

43.4

43.5

43.6

43.7

43.8

王　翬

清代　1632－1717

字石谷，號耕煙散人、清暉主人等，江蘇常熟人。初爲王鑑賞識，收爲弟子，後又從學王時敏。善山水，工力精深，筆氣清秀，世稱虞山派。

44. 竹窩圖

1698年作
紙本設色立軸　94×40厘米

此軸畫叢竹繞山而長，一人獨坐亭中靜憩，入口處有桂花一樹，泉流有聲，境界清幽雅逸。

款識：
歲次戊寅（1698年）六月廿又八日，客窗坐雨，觀王舍人竹窩小卷，髣髴寫此，似莊溪同學先生清玩。耕煙散人王翬。

印章：
王翬之印（朱白文方印）
石谷子（朱文方印）
清暉（朱文方印）
富春高寄（白文方印）
耕煙散人（朱文方印）

鑑藏印章：
醇士鑑藏（朱文長方印）
芸葉庵（朱文方印）

Wang Hui

Qing dynasty　1632-1717

Zi Shigu, *hao* Gengyan Sanren, Qinghui Zhuren, native of Changshu, Jiangsu province. Wang's talent in painting was first recognized by Wang Jian who accepted him as his student and introduced him to Wang Shimin. Wang led a successful professional life in painting and later became the founder of the Yushan school. He specialized in landscape and enjoyed fame as a superb draughtsman with a refreshing and elegant style.

44. Bamboo Grove

Dated 1698
Hanging scroll, ink and colour on paper
94×40 cm

With inscription, signature, 5 seals of the artist and 2 collectors' seals.

惲壽平

清代　1633－1690

初名格，字壽平，後以字行，改字正叔，號南田，又號雲溪外史，東園草衣，白雲外史等。毗陵（江蘇常州）人。工詩書畫，詩格超脫，書法俊秀，畫筆清雅。尤於花卉，精研秀潔，別開生面，人稱常州派。

唐宇昭

清代　1602－1672

字孔明，雲客，號半園，武進（江蘇常州）人，崇禎九年（1636）舉人。明亡遂隱，工詩善畫，所畫淡逸飄擧，與惲壽平爲金石交。

45．蘭蓀柏子圖

1669年作
紙本設色立軸　96×42.5厘米

此圖意態飄灑秀拔，筆致清發。

款識：
蘭蓀柏子圖。己酉（1669年）十月半園先生、南田草衣合作，與上子存鑒。

印章：
壽平（朱文方印）
惲正叔（白文方印）

鑑藏印章：
煦齋藏擧（朱文方印）
介文珍藏（朱文方印）
甘潭朱氏（白文長方印）
爲弼（朱文長方印）
經齋注經（白文方印）

Yun Shouping

Qing dynasty　1633-1690

Original name Ge, *zi* Shouping, Zhengshu, *hao* Nantian, Yunxi Waishi, Dongyuan Caoyi, Baiyun Waishi. Yun, a native of Biling (present-day Changzhou, Jiangsu province), was a poet, calligrapher and painter. He was best known for painting flowers in colour in the "boneless manner". Widely followed by contemporary artists and subsequent generations, his style came to be known as the Changzhou school.

Tang Yuzhao

Qing dynasty　1602-1672

Zi Kongming, Yunke, *hao* Banyuan, native of Wujin (present-day Changzhou, Jiangsu province). Tang passed the *juren* examination in 1636 but lived a life of seclusion after the collapse of the Ming empire. A poet and a painter, he was a good friend of Yun Shouping. His painting displays a feeling of lightness and elegance.

45. Orchids and Cypress

Dated 1669
Hanging scroll, ink and colour on paper
96×42.5 cm

With inscription, 2 seals of Yun Shouping and 5 collectors' seals.

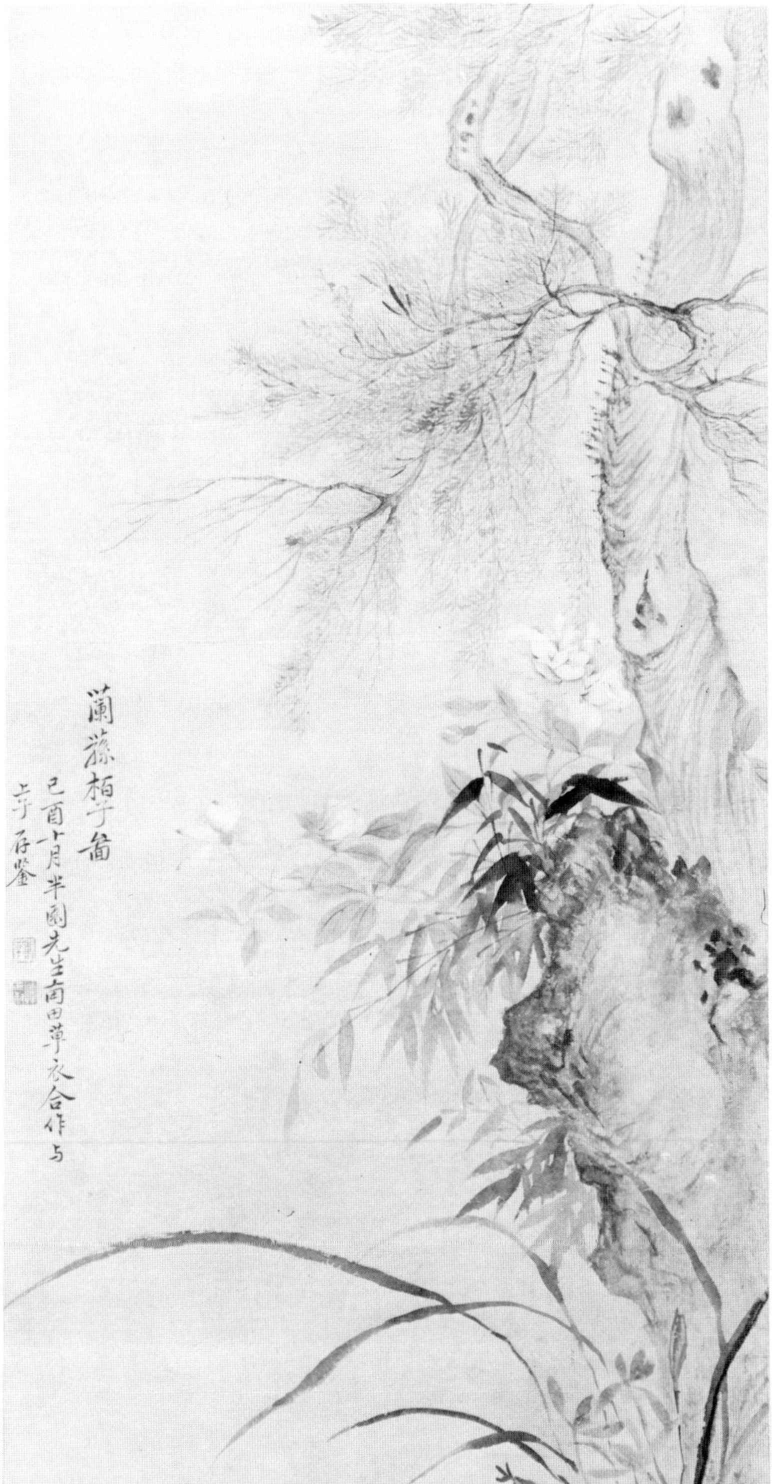

惲南田唐半園合作蘭蓀栢子圖

上　睿

清代　1634－1724後

僧，字尋濬，號目存，又號蒲室子、童心道人。吳縣（江蘇蘇州）人。王翬弟子，工畫山水、人物，近唐寅（1470－1523）筆意。

46．採芝圖

1660年作
紙本水墨設色立軸　187.5×49厘米

款識：
松竹蒼蒼石徑斜，飛泉界嶺鎖雲霞。閒尋芝朮歸來晚，露濕一株仙桂花。庚子（1660）仲秋畫並題，奉祝子文道翁先生八十大壽，並祈教正。童心道人蒲室叡。

印章：
目存睿（白文方印）
童心和尚（朱文方印）
卧雲人（朱文圓印）

鑑藏印章：
海昌錢鏡塘藏（朱文方印）

Shangrui

Qing dynasty　1634-after 1724

Zi Xunrui, *hao* Mucun, Pushizi, Tongxin Daoren, native of Wuxian (present-day Suzhou, Jiangsu province) and a monk. Shangrui was a student of Wang Hui. He painted mainly landscapes, but when he turned to figures, his style was reminiscent of Tang Yin (1470-1523).

46. Picking Fungus

Dated 1660
Hanging scroll, ink and colour on paper
187.5×49 cm

With inscription, signature, 3 seals of the artist and 1 collector's seal.

王原祁

清代　1642－1715

字茂京，號麓臺。江蘇太倉人。王時敏孫，揆（時敏次子）子，秉承家學。康熙九年（1670）進士，政績卓著，累獲升遷，官至戶部左侍郎。精鑑別，曾供奉內廷，爲聖祖寫畫並鑑別古畫。康熙四十四年（1705）《佩文齋書畫譜》纂輯，又奉旨任總裁職。善山水，宗法黃公望，厚重高曠，別具氣格，從學者多，人稱婁東派。

47．倣大癡山水

1713年作
紙本水墨立軸　52×38厘米

此圖爲王氏晚年七十二歲之作，李世倬於詩堂題跋中稱賞〝是幅筆力千鈞，又爲公之最佳者。”

款識：
癸巳（1713年）夏日倣大癡筆。麓臺祁。

印章：
蒼潤（白文長方印）
王原祁印（白文方印）
麓臺（朱文方印）
西廬後人（白文方印）

詩堂題跋：
李世倬題。

鑑藏印章：
世卓（朱文方印）
敬原長（白文方印）
安儀周家珍藏（朱文長方印）
王永譽字孝□圖書印（朱文方印）

Wang Yuanqi

Qing dynasty　1642-1715

Zi Maojing, *hao* Lutai, native of Taicang, Jiangsu province. Wang was the grandson of Wang Shimin. Having passed the *jinshi* examination in 1670, he achieved an illustrous career in the civil service, ultimately becoming the Vice-chancellor of the Census Department. He was also a connoisseur of painting and served as an advisor of the imperial art collection. In 1705, he was appointed the chief compiler of the *Peiwen zhai shuhua pu*. He was an expert in landscape painting and as the founder of ''Loudong School'' commanded a large following. His landscape style can be credited to that of Huang Gongwang, the Yuan master.

47. Landscape after Huang Gongwang

Dated 1713
Hanging scroll, ink on paper
52×38 cm

With inscription, signature, 4 seals of the artist and 4 collectors' seals.
2 colophons by Li Shizhuo on separate sheet of paper above painting (*shitang*).

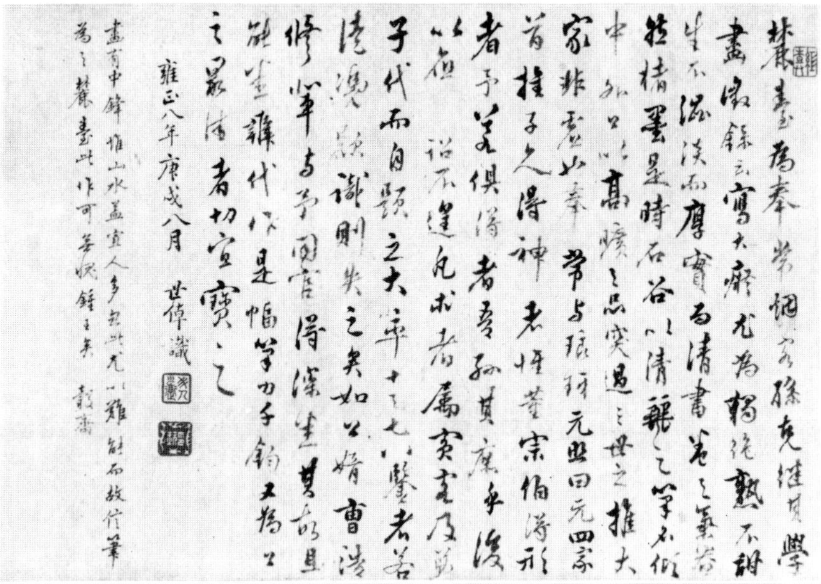
雍正八年庚戌八月 世倬識

癸巳夏日倣
大癡筆
麓臺祁

文　點

清代　1633－1704

字與也，號南雲山樵。長洲（江蘇蘇州）人，文徵明後人。畫山水傳家法，用筆細秀，點染暈潤。兼工人物及松竹小品。

48. 山水册

紙本水墨册頁六開　各23.4×31.2厘米

(1) **山徑通幽**

款識：
仿梅花菴主。

印章：
點（朱文方印）

(2) **停琴共話**

款識：
高山流水，舉世無知。

印章：
香心禪性（朱文方印）
南雲菴（朱文長方印）

(3) **松蔭山亭**

款識：
無數松陰匝地鋪，山深泉閙草亭孤。高人穩卧清溪曲，指點谿山似畫圖。

印章：
點（朱文方印）

(4) **桐陰軒齋**

款識：
梧桐栽向小軒齋，萬斛秋聲伴醉眠。落葉點階憑拾取，剪珪封作散神仙。

印章：
竹塢草廬（朱文方印）

(5) **蘆荻放舟**

款識：

蘆荻蒼茫水漫流，淺深隨處下魚鈎。問他何地風波穩，日暖溪澄好放舟。

印章：
點（朱文方印）

鑑藏印章：
容庚秘匧（白文方印）
㮮潛（白文方印）

(6) **石城積雪**

款識：
石城積雪。仿先太史。

印章：
文點（白文方印）

Wen Dian

Qing dynasty　1633-1704

Zi Yuye, *hao* Nanyun Shanqiao, native of Changzhou (present-day Suzhou, Jiangsu province). Wen was a descendant of Wen Zhengming whose family had exerted great influence on the Suzhou art scene in the Ming dynasty. In continuing the family tradition, Wen also employed elegant brush strokes with delicate ink washes in his landscape painting. His painting of figures, pines and bambooes are also highly regarded.

48. Landscape Album

Album of six leaves, ink on paper
each leaf 23.4×31.2 cm

(1) Secluded Mountain Path
With inscription and 1 seal of the artist.

(2) Conversation after Music Playing
With inscription and 2 seals of the artist.

(3) Pavilion by the Pine Trees
Same as leaf (1).

(4) Studio in the Shade of Paulownia Trees
Same as leaf (1).

(5) Boating among the Reeds
With inscription, 1 seal of the artist and 2 collectors' seals.

(6) Snow Landscape
With inscription and 1 seal of the artist.

48.1

48.2

48.3

48.4

48.5

48.6

顧符稹

清代　1634－1716後

（一作禎），字瑟如，號小癡。江蘇興化人。工書，畫山水、人物，工緻精細。

49. 漢中勝覽圖

絹本設色手卷　36.3×602厘米

此卷循游覽路線畫三國時蜀漢漢中郡地理勝景。每一名蹟勝景，有文字記明。全卷自二里關起，至褒城縣止。

款識：

松巢老人顧符稹畫。

印章：

符、稹（白文聯珠印）

題簽：

顧小癡漢中勝覽圖卷。書博老弟所藏，己丑夏吳湖帆題。

鑑藏印章：

松竹草堂（朱文橢圓印）
任世樸字書博珍藏印（白文長方印）
任書博（朱白文方印）
任世樸珍藏印（朱文長方印）

Gu Fuzhen

Qing dynasty　1634-after 1716

Zi Seru, *hao* Xiaochi, native of Xinghua, Jiangsu province. Gu excelled in calligraphy, landscape and figure painting. He worked in a detailed and complex manner.

49. Famous Views of Hanzhong

Handscroll, ink and colour on silk
36.3×602 cm

With signature, 2 seals of the artist and 4 collectors' seals.

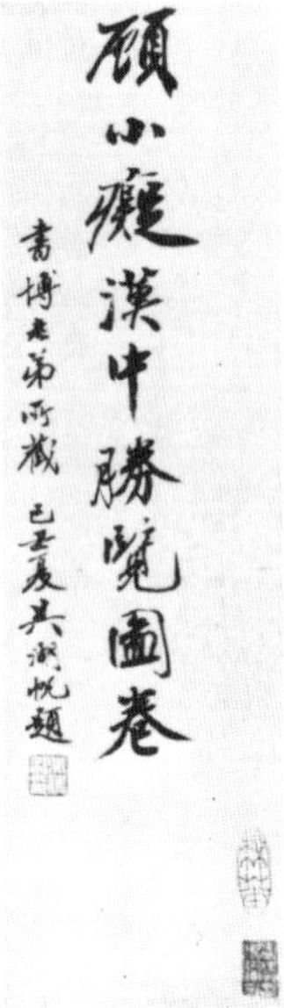

梅翀

清代　十七世紀晚期

字培翼，號文脊山人，安徽宣城人。梅清從孫，畫松石有奇趣。

50. 文殊院觀海圖

紙本設色立軸　218×49厘米

此圖寫黃山文殊院（又稱玉屏峯）觀雲海景象，全幅用流動蜷曲之細線描畫，以筆勢疏密及墨色濃淡，誇張山形之上重下輕，又配以空濛雲濤，顯示虛幻仙境。

款識：
夢想蓬瀛境是仙，仙槎何日泛天邊。今朝黃嶽峯頭坐，滃蕩雲濤思惘然。文殊院觀海，仿黃鶴山樵筆意。鹿墅梅翀。

印章：
梅翀（朱文橢圓印）
培翼（白文長方印）
文脊山人（白文方印）
清玩草堂（朱文長方印）

鑑藏印章：
崔穀忱收藏書畫章（白文方印）
穀忱心賞（白文方印）
穀忱鑑藏（朱文方印）
瑞[作]鑑賞書畫之印（朱文方印）

Mei Chong

Qing dyansty　late 17th century

Zi Peiyi, *hao* Wenji Shanren, native of Xuancheng, Anhui province. Mei was the great-grandson of Mei Qing and was noted for his individualistic style in depicting pine and rock.

50. Sea of Clouds at Wenshuyuan of Mount Huang

Hanging scroll, ink and colour on paper
218×49 cm

With inscription, signature, 4 seals of the artist and 4 collectors' seals.

王　晋

清代

字玉峯，江蘇崑山人。工畫山水、人物。

51. 松濤携琴圖

紙本設色立軸　199×104.5厘米

此圖畫松蔭小路，人物携琴訪友，用筆精細。若大畫寫景一角，極具眞實感。

款識：
玉峯王晋寫。

印章：
王晋之印（白文方印）
日接（朱文方印）

Wang Jin

Qing dynasty

Zi Yufeng, native of Kunshan, Jiangsu province. Wang was a landscape and figure painter.

51. Carrying *Qin* in a Pine Forest

Hanging scroll, ink and colour on paper
199×104.5 cm

With signature and 2 seals of the artist.

陳　書

清代　1660－1736

號上元弟子，晚號南樓老人。上元（江蘇南京）人。善畫花卉、草蟲。設色清姸明麗，秀雅挺拔。

52. 花卉册

1729年作
紙本設色册頁十二開　各25×33.9厘米

此册畫桃、梨、芍藥、紫丁香、罌粟、蜀葵、薔薇、桂、菊、秋海棠、雁來紅及梅等十二種花卉，乃陳書七十歲時作。每頁均有胡九思題詩，時維道光壬午（1822年）。其後復另紙書跋（題詩及跋不錄），識其流傳經過。

(1) **桃花**

印章：
上元弟子（朱文方印）
衞管夫人皆我師（白文方印）

鑑藏印章：
英惠之印（白文方印）
桂慶印（白文方印）
寶奎（白文方印）
五峯（朱文方印）

(2) **梨花**

印章：
南樓老人（白文方印）
陳書之印（白文方印）

鑑藏印章：
英惠之印（白文方印）
桂慶印（白文方印）
福壽之印（白文方印）

(3) **芍藥**

印章：
南樓老人（朱文方印）

鑑藏印章：
英惠之印（白文方印）
桂慶印（白文方印）

(4) **紫丁香**

印章：
南樓老人（白文方印）

鑑藏印章：
英惠之印（白文方印）
桂慶印（白文方印）
雙竹研齋（朱文方印）

(5) **罌粟**

印章：
上元弟子（朱文方印）

鑑藏印章：
尋鄉室（朱文橢圓形印）
英惠之印（白文方印）
桂慶印（白文方印）
福壽之印（白文方印）
澍樵（朱文方印）

(6) **蜀葵**

印章：
衞管夫人皆我師（白文方印）

鑑藏印章：
尋鄉室（朱文橢圓形印）
英惠之印（白文方印）
桂慶印（白文方印）
福壽之印（白文方印）

(7) **薔薇**

印章：
上元弟子（朱文方印）

鑑藏印章：
澍樵（朱文方印）
英惠之印（白文方印）
桂慶印（白文方印）
秋月（白文方印）

(8) **桂花**

印章：
女史、陳書（朱白文聯珠印）

鑑藏印章：
英惠之印（白文方印）
桂慶印（白文方印）
尋鄉室（朱文橢圓印）
福壽之印（白文方印）

(9) **菊**

印章：
上元弟子（朱文方印）
陳書之印（白文方印）

鑑藏印章：
澍樵（朱文方印）
英惠之印（白文方印）
桂慶印（白文方印）

福壽之印（白文方印）

⑽秋海棠

印章：
南樓老人（朱文長方印）

鑑藏印章：
尋鄉室（朱文橢圓形印）
桂慶印（白文方印）
福壽之印（白文方印）

⑾ 雁來紅

印章：
陳書之印（白文方印）
上元弟子（朱文方印）

鑑藏印章：
英惠之印（白文方印）
桂慶印（白文方印）

⑿ 梅花

款識：
雍正己酉（1729年）秋九月聽松閣摹古。
南樓老人陳書。

印章：
女史、陳書（朱白文聯珠印）
上元弟子（朱文方印）
衞管夫人皆我師（白文方印）

鑑藏印章：
尋鄉室（朱文橢圓形印）
英惠之印（白文方印）
桂慶印（白文方印）
福壽之印（白文方印）
五峯珍藏（白文方印）
秋月（白文方印）
容庚（朱文方印）

另附題跋一開：
胡九思題。

Chen Shu

Qing dynasty 1660-1736

Hao Shangyuan Dizi, Nanlou Laoren, native of Shangyuan, Jiangsu province. A specialist in painting flowers and insects, Chen was noted for the delicacy and elegance in her art.

52. Album of Flowers

Dated 1729
Album of twelve leaves, ink and colour on paper
each leaf 25 × 33.9 cm

(1) Peach Blossoms
With 2 seals of the artist, 1 colophon by Hu Jiusi and 4 collectors' seals.

(2) Pear Blossoms
With 2 seals of the artist, 2 colophons by Hu Jiusi and 3 collectors' seals.

(3) Peonies
With 1 seal of the artist, 2 colophons dy Hu Jiusi and 2 collectors' seals.

(4) Lilac
With 1 seal of the artist, 1 colophon by Hu Jiusi and 3 collectors' seals.

(5) Poppies
With 1 seal of the artist, 2 colophons by Hu Jiusi and 5 collectors' seals.

(6) Hollyhocks
With 1 seal of the artist, 1 colophon by Hu Jiusi and 4 collectors' seals.

(7) Roses
With 1 seal of the artist, 2 colophons by Hu Jiusi and 4 collectors' seals.

(8) Osmanthus
With 1 seal of the artist, 1 colophon by Hu Jiusi and 4 collectors' seals.

(9) Chrysanthemum
With 2 seals of the artist, 1 colophon by Hu Jiusi and 4 collectors' seals.

(10) Begonia
With 1 seal of the artist, 2 colophons by Hu Jiusi and 3 collectors' seals.

(11) Tricolour Amaranth
With 2 seals of the artist, 1 colophon by Hu Jiusi and 2 collectors' seals.

(12) Prunus Blossoms
With inscription, signature, 3 seals of the artist, 2 colophons by Hu Jiushi and 7 collectors' seals.

1 additional leaf with 1 colophon of Hu Jiusi.

52.1

52.2

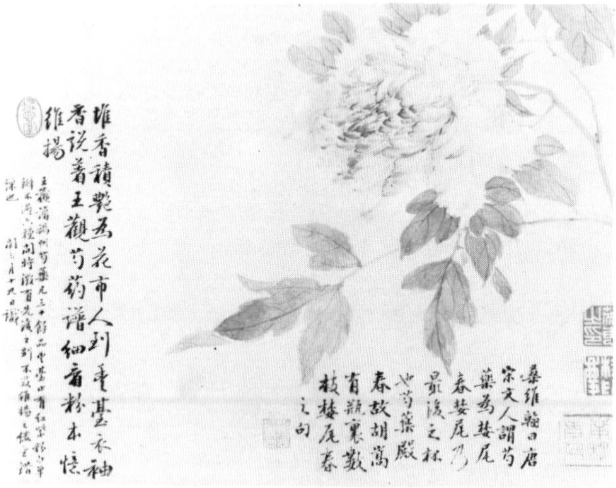

52.3

52.4

52.5

52.6

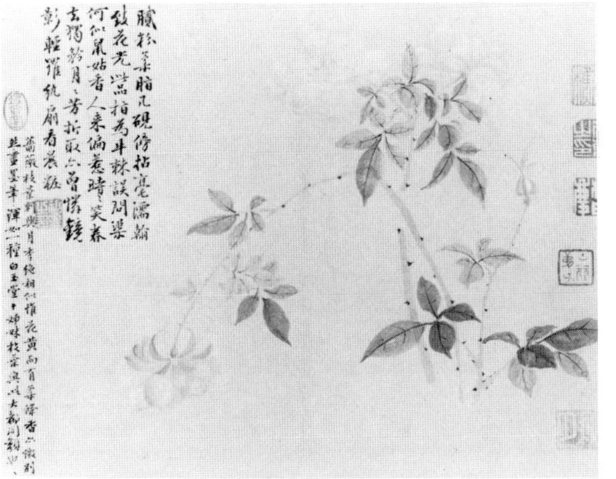

52.7

52.8

52.9

52.10

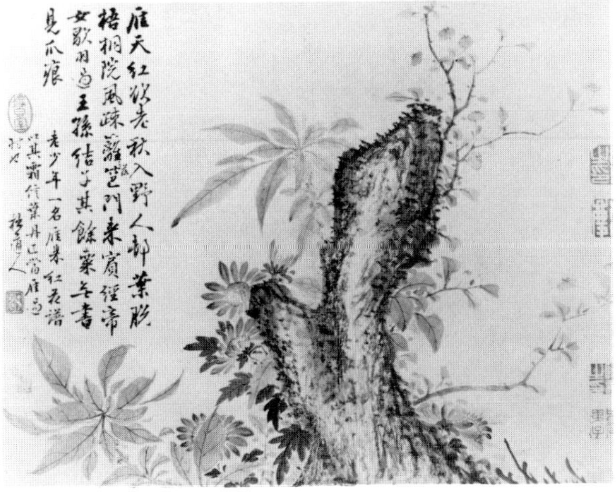

52.11

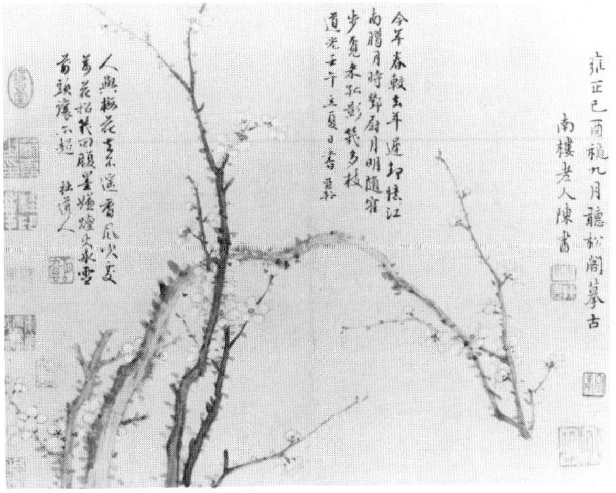

52.12

楊　晉

清代　1644－1728

字子和，一字子鶴，號西亭，自號谷林樵客、鶴道人，又署野鶴。江蘇常熟人。王翬學生。善山水、花鳥，尤工點景人物。傳石谷作畫點景人物、輿轎、牛馬，多出其手筆。

53. 仿李營丘溪山雪霽圖

1708年作
絹本設色立軸　199×50.5厘米

此畫寫溪山雪止時，山村人物四出活動景象。樹石盡得石谷筆法，乃楊氏六十五歲之作。

款識：
溪山雪霽，仿李營丘筆。戊子（1708年）中秋，虞山楊晉。

印章：
楊晉私印（白文方印）
子鶴（朱文方印）

鑑藏印章：
海昌錢鏡塘藏（朱文長方印）
吳下王大炘方芬夫婦同欣賞（白文方印）
冰鉄戡西美学記（朱文方印）

Yang Jin

Qing dynasty　1644-1728

Zi Zihe, *hao* Xiting, Gulin Qiaoke, Hedaoren, Yehe, native of Changshu, Jiangsu province. Yang was skilled in painting landscape, flower and bird, especially figures set in landscape. A student of Wang Hui, Yang was generally believed to have painted the figures, animals and vehicles that appeared in Wang's landscape paintings.

53. Streams and Mountains after Snow after Li Cheng

Dated 1708
Hanging scroll, ink and colour on silk
199×50.5 cm

With inscription, signature, 2 seals of the artist and 3 collectors' seals.

黃　鼎

清代　1650/60－1730

字尊古，號曠亭，又號閑甫，別號獨往客，晚號淨垢老人。江蘇虞山人。王原祁弟子。

54. 山水

1717年作
紙本水墨手卷　24.5×145厘米

此畫寫溪山清秀，筆意蒼潤，咫尺之間，有萬里之勢。

款識：
丁酉（1717年）春二月倣一峯老人筆法，爲希老道先生清鑒。獨往客鼎。

印章：
黃鼎（白文方印）
尊古（朱文方印）
山水中人（朱文方印）
獨往客（朱文方印）
自怡（朱文橢圓印）

Huang Ding

Qing dynasty　1650/60-1730

Zi Zungu, *hao* Kuangting, Xianfu, Duwanke, Jinggou Laoren in his later years, native of Yushan, Jiangsu province. Huang was a student of Wang Yuanqi.

54. Landscape

Dated 1717
Handscroll, ink on paper
24.5×145 cm

With inscription, signature and 5 seals of the artist.

丁酉春二月
倣一峯老人
筆法為
希老道先生
清鑒
獨往客鼎

沈宗敬

清代　1669－1735

字恪庭，又字南季，號獅峯。華亭人。精音律，善畫山水，風格淸淡，在倪瓚和沈周間。

55. 濃蔭山莊圖

綾本水墨立軸　165×46.5厘米

此畫寫山坡小亭，石山崒屼，以欹斜取勢，遠藏樓閣，屋頂僅見。

款識：
濃蔭山莊一徑通，隔溪亭子受淸風。乾坤浩蕩元無外，紫翠光分泉石中。御頒畫扇，恭題應制之一，寫其意爲燕老年翁正之。華亭沈宗敬。

印章：
沈宗敬（白文方印）
客庭（朱文方印）
秋來亭（白長文方印）

鑑藏印章：
御賜煙嵐高曠（朱文圓印）

Shen Zongjing

Qing dynasty　1669-1735

Zi Keting, Nanji, *hao* Shifeng, native of Huating, Jiangsu province. Shen was an expert in music as well as in painting. He developed his landscape style from assimilating the characteristics of Ni Zan and Shen Zhou.

55. Mountain Retreat amid Trees

Hanging scroll, ink on satin
165×46.5 cm

With inscription, signature, 3 seals of the artist and 1 collector's seal.

高其佩

清代　1672－1734

字韋之，號且園。鐵嶺（遼寧）人。隸漢軍鑲黃旗。以蔭官至刑部侍郎。善指畫，凡花木、鳥獸、人物、山水無不工。畫後渲染，或復用筆，意態生動。

56. 指畫雜册

1710年作
紙本水墨册頁十二開　各23.5×37.2厘米

此册指畫山水、人物、花鳥，各具意趣。

⑴ **茶花**

款識：
庚寅（1710年）二月自武林返甌署，見一種花，恍若對西子之面，殆不知洋茶中復有此種。其佩。

印章：
手即是筆（朱文方印）

鑑藏印章：
陳公穆父珍藏（朱文長方印）

⑵ **寒江小屋**

印章：
指頭蘸墨爲之（白文方印）

⑶ **竹**

印章：
鐵嶺高其佩指頭畫（白文方印）

⑷ **携琴圖**

印章：
指頭寫意（朱文方印）

⑸ **懸崖飛鳥**

印章：
指頭生活（朱文方印）

⑹ **山外飛蓬**

款識：
歲內滯蘭江，幾日往坐橫山之半，却望見山外飛蓬。至今乃圖其意，其佩。

印章：
以手爲[此]（朱文方印）

⑺ **蘭**

印章：
手筆（白文方印）

⑻ **啼鳥**

印章：
鐵嶺高其佩指頭畫（白文方印）

⑼ **獨石**

款識：
梅椿開過臏叉丫，一石橫斜致可誇。爲此梅椿不入畫，待生春草又開花。其佩。

印章：
佩（白文方印）
閒爲詩以紀之（白文長方印）
古怪（朱文橢圓印）

⑽ **牆頭花貓**

印章：
指頭畫（朱文長方印）

⑾ **孤帆**

款識：
武林三日達金華，最快意，料他人看布帆迅數(速)，當別是一種心眼。我當之，復圖之，又復忘之。其佩。

印章：
其佩（白文方印）
且園（朱文方印）
指頭畫（白文方印）

⑿ **梅、竹、蕉**

款識：
禿蕉茁茁吐新胎，殘竹蕭條憶早梅。不道紙窗高處破，春風送入杏紅來。庚寅（1710年）二月寫養恬精舍之好趣，致大免却尋物事供畫手也。其佩。

印章：
其佩（白文方印）
且園（朱文方印）
原非有意斯人（白文扁方印）
閒爲詩以紀之（白文長方印）

Gao Qipei

Qing dynasty 1672-1734

Zi Weizhi, *hao* Qieyuan, native of Tieling, Liaoning province. Gao was a high government official as well as a painter. He was noted for his finger painting, and he was able to paint any subject, achieving original and extraordinary effects.

56. Album of Finger Painting

Dated 1710
Album of twelve leaves, ink on paper
each leaf 23.5 × 37.2 cm

(1) Camellia
With inscription, signature, 1 seal of the artist and 1 collector's seal.

(2) Cottage by the River
With 1 seal of the artist.

(3) Bamboo
Same as leaf (2).

(4) Figure Carrying *Qin*
Same as leaf (2).

(5) Bird in Flight
Same as leaf (2).

(6) Sailing Boat beyond the Mountain
With inscription, signature and 1 seal of the artist.

(7) Orchids
Same as leaf (2).

(8) Bird on Branch
Same as leaf (2).

(9) Rock
With inscription, signature and 3 seals of the artist.

(10) Cat
Same as leaf (2).

(11) Boat Sailing
Same as leaf (9).

(12) Prunus Blossoms, Banana and Bamboo
With inscription, signature and 4 seals of the artist.

56.1

56.2

56.3

56.4

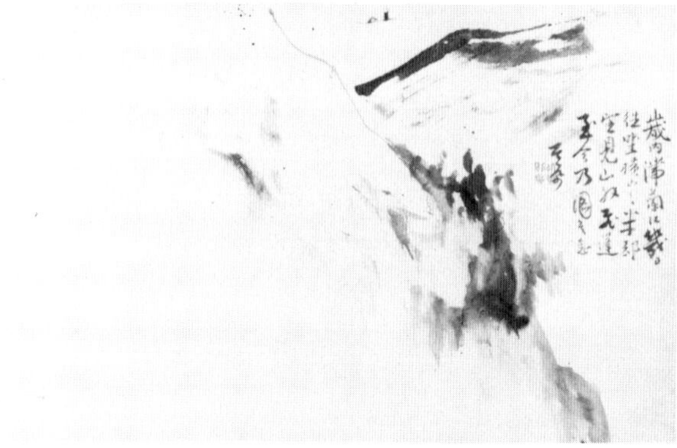

56.6

56.7

56.5

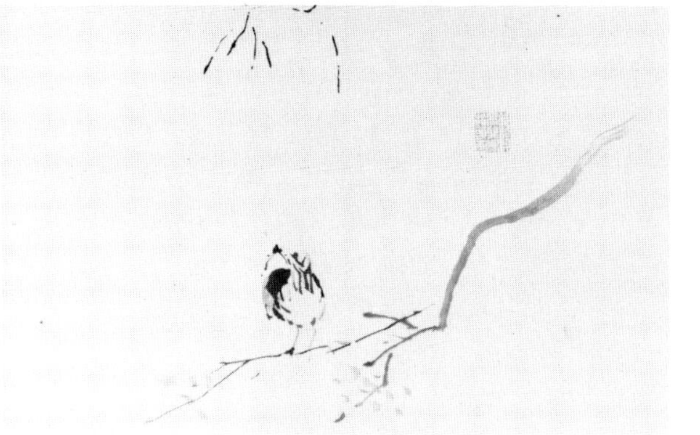
56.8

56.9

56.10

56.11

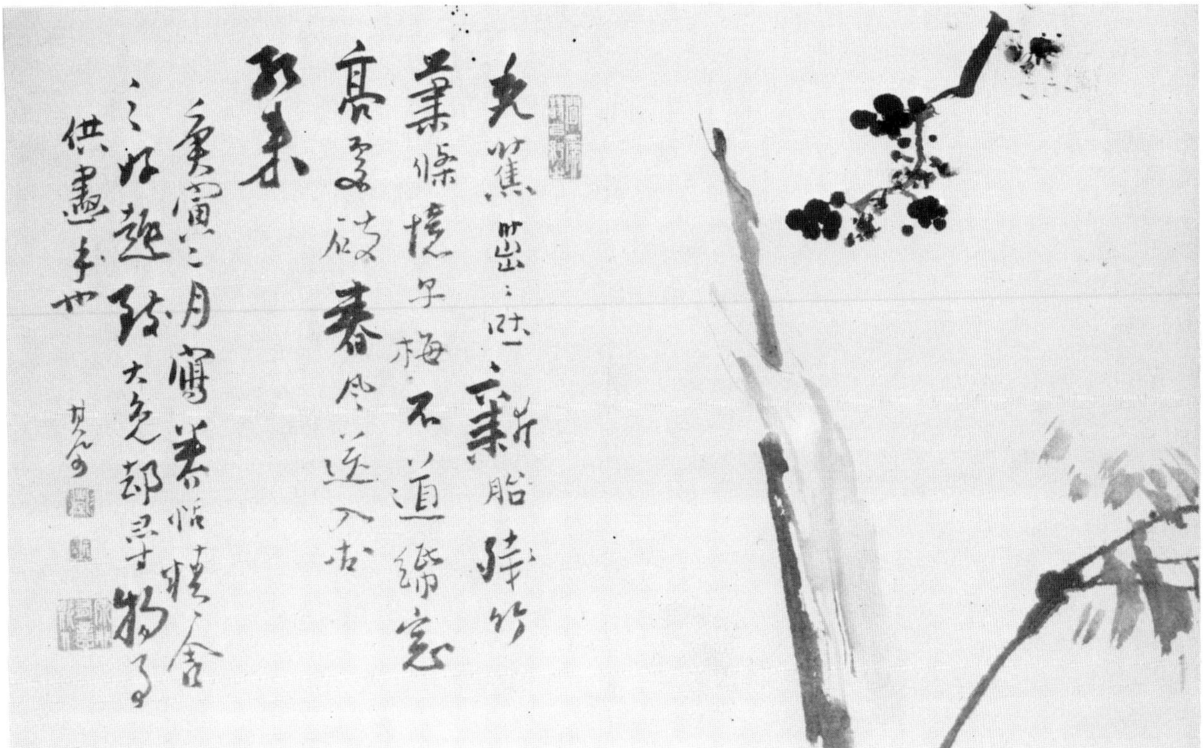
56.12

唐　岱

清代　1673－1751尚在

字毓東，號靜巖，又號默莊。滿州人。善畫山水，出王原祁門。康熙御賜畫狀元。乾隆時祇候內廷，爲弘歷所重。

57. 仿大癡山水圖

1730年作
絹本設色立軸　89.3×46厘米

款識：
大癡畫平淡天眞，不求筆工而意趣橫生，學者從此參之，可入大癡之門矣。庚戌（1730年）冬日，靜巖唐岱並識。

印章：
古唐捪氏（白文方印）
岱字毓東（白文方印）
北窗（朱文橢圓印）

Tang Dai

Qing dynasty　1673-after 1751

Zi Yudong, *hao* Jingyan, Mozhuang, Manchu in origin. Tang was a pupil of Wang Yuanqi and was noted for his landscape painting. He was honoured by Emperor Kangxi with the title *huazhuangyuan* (''first in painting''). He was also held in high regard by Emperor Qianlong who entrusted him with major projects of the painting academy at court.

57. Landscape after Huang Gongwang

Dated 1730
Hanging scroll, ink and colour on silk
89.3×46 cm

With inscription, signature and 3 seals of the artist.

大癡畫平淡天真不求筆工而
意趣横生學者從此參之可入
大癡之門矣
庚戌冬日
靜巖唐岱書

張宗蒼

清代　1686－1756

字默存，一字墨岑，號篁村。吳縣（江蘇蘇州）人。乾隆間入內廷祇候，授戶部主事。工畫山水，學師於黃鼎，喜用乾筆皴擦。

Zhang Zongcang

Qing dynasty　1686-1756

Zi Mocun, Mocen, *hao* Huangcun, native of Wuxian (present-day Suzhou, Jiangsu province). Zhang served as a court painter in the Qianlong era. He was a pupil of Huang Ding and was fond of using dry brushwork in his landscape painting.

58. 雪景山水圖

紙本設色立軸　88×111.5厘米

此圖畫寒林雪景。筆致工整，景象深邃。

款識：
臣張宗蒼恭繪。

印章：
張、宗蒼（朱文聯珠印）

題跋（乾隆御題）：
珠貝林柯薝葡園，琉璃殿閣玉爲垣。飛流不共寒江凍，爲識雲中別有源。御題。

題跋印章（御璽）：
得象外意（朱文方印）
乾隆宸翰（白文方印）

58. Snowy Landscape

Hanging scroll, ink and colour on paper
88×111.5 cm

With signature, 2 seals of the artist and 1 colophon by Emperor Qianlong with two imperial seals.

珠貝林柯薝
蔔園琉璃殿
閣玉爲垣苑
添不與寒江
凍爲淺雲中
別有源
御題

董邦達

清代　1699－1769尚在

字孚存，號東山。富陽（浙江）人。工畫山水。官至禮部尚書。乾隆年間任修編《石渠寶笈》、《秘殿珠林》、《西淸古鑑》等書襄事。

59. 仿王紱溪山深秀卷

紙本水墨手卷　23.5×232厘米

款識：
谿山深秀。臣董邦達恭仿王紱筆意。

印章：
臣、達（朱白文聯珠印）

鑑藏印章：
乾隆御覽之寶（朱文橢圓印）
石渠寶笈（朱文長方印）
石渠定鑑（朱文圓印）
寶笈重編（白文方印）
御書房鑑藏寶（朱文橢圓印）
嘉慶御覽之寶（朱文橢圓印）
乾隆鑑賞（白文圓印）
三希堂精鑑璽（朱文長方印）
宜子孫（白文方印）
宣統御覽之寶（朱文橢圓印）

Dong Bangda

Qing dynasty 1699-after1769

Zi Fucun, *hao* Dongshan, native of Fuyang, Zhejiang province. Dong led an outstanding career as a scholar-official at court, ultimately rose to become the President of the Ministry of Rites. He was also a highly respected painter of landscapes. He served as one of the compilers of the imperial collection catalogues, particularly the *Shiqu baoji.*

59. Landscape in the Style of Wang Fu

Handscroll, ink on paper
23.5 × 232 cm

With inscription, signature, 2 seals of the artist, and 10 imperial seals of the Qing emperors Qianlong, Jiaqing and Xuantong.

李世倬

清代　約1690－1770

字漢章，號穀齋。鐵嶺（遼寧）人。高其佩甥，少年隨父宦遊江南，學畫於王翬與馬昂。

60. 烟雨歸舟圖

紙本水墨立軸　100×54厘米

此畫寫秋江殘柳烟雨歸舟江南景色，用筆有乾有濕，風雨中老榦剛實，殘枝搖蕩，烟濛掩映，令人有身入其境之感。

款識：
此圖創諸唐六如，然於風雨之際，偶憶及江南，故頻寫之矣。李世倬。

印章：
世倬私印（白文方印）
穀齋（朱文方印）
芥道人（朱文長方印）

Li Shizhuo

Qing dynasty　ca.1690-1770

Zi Hanzhang, *hao* Guzhai, native of Tieling, Liaoning province and nephew of Gao Qipei. In his youth Li accompained his father on official postings in southern China. His teachers in art included Wang Hui and Ma Ang, in addition to his famous uncle, Gao Qipei.

60. Returning Boat in Rain and Mist

Hanging scroll, ink on paper
100×54 cm

With inscription, signature and 3 seals of the artist.

鄒一桂

清代　1686－1772

字原褒，號小山，江蘇無錫人。官至禮部侍郎。善畫工筆花卉。著《小山畫譜》。

61. 玉堂富貴圖

絹本設色立軸　159.5×94厘米

此畫寫玉蘭及牡丹，象徵玉堂富貴。畫法效惲壽平，不及惲之秀逸清雅。

款識：
倣北宋徐熙賦色。鄒一桂。

印章：
鄒一桂印（白文方印）
小山（朱文方印）

Zou Yigui

Qing dynasty　1686-1772

Zi Yuanbao, *hao* Xiaoshan, native of Wuxi, Jiangsu province. Zou was an official of the Ministry of Rites. He was most famous for painting flowers in the detailed and coloured manner (*gongbi*). He wrote a painting treatise entitled *Xiaoshan huapu*.

61. Magnolias and Peonies

Hanging scroll, ink and colour on silk
159.5×94 cm

With inscription, signature and 2 seals of the artist.

依北宋徐熙賦色 郎一桂

崔 鏴

清代　十八世紀

字象州，三韓（遼寧）人。雍正、乾隆間人。工畫人物、花鳥、學焦秉貞、鄒一桂法，略近清代宮廷畫風。

62. 百雀圖

1740年作
絹本設色立軸　161.5×96厘米

此圖畫羣雀棲聚梅竹，用雙鈎法，筆致清勁，唯肖唯妙。

款識：
伯爵圖。庚申（1740年）立春前三日橅宋人筆，寫於槐雲堂。襄平崔鏴。

印章：
崔鏴（白文方印）
象州（朱文方印）

Cui Sui

Qing dynasty　18th century

Zi Xiangzhou, native of Sanhan, Liaoning province. Cui was known to be active during the Yongzheng and Qianlong periods as a painter of figures, flowers and birds. His style was reminiscent of court painting following the manner of Zhao Bingzhen (fl. ca. 1689-1726) and Zou Yigui.

62. A Hundred Sparrows

Hanging scroll, ink and colour on silk
161.5 × 96 cm

With inscription, signature and 2 seals of the artist.

伯爵圖

張 經

清代 十八世紀

字研夫，生平不詳。

63. 載鶴圖

紙本設色立軸 133×104.5厘米

此圖畫溪流中，小舟載鶴，上空一鶴飛翔相隨，畫法略近張路。

款識：
載鶴圖。奉祝怡翁老道翁六秩華誕，研夫張經。

印章：
張經圖書（白文方印）
研夫（朱文方印）

Zhang Jing

Qing dynasty 18th century

Zi Yanfu. Little is known of this artist.

63. Boat Carrying Crane

Hanging scroll, ink and colour on paper
133×104.5 cm

With inscription, signature and 2 seals of the artist.

王　雲

清代　1652－1735後

字漢藻，號清癡，江蘇高郵人。工畫人物樓閣近似仇英，康熙時馳名江淮。

64. 山水册

絹本設色册頁十一開　各28×24厘米

此册畫四季山水，筆致清腴工整，設色鮮艷明麗，極具生活氣息。原十二頁，散失一頁。曾爲廣東清代鑑藏家吳榮光（1773－1843）收藏。

(1)至(8)、(10)

印章：
漢藻（朱文方印）

(9)

印章：
漢藻（朱文方印）

鑑藏印章：
劍齋珍賞（朱文方印）

(11)

款識：
長安寓齋，應芝山太史先生命。邗上王雲。

印章：
王雲之印（白文方印）
竹里（朱文方印）
塵外（白文長方印）

鑑藏印章：
吳氏筠清館所藏書畫（朱文方印）
景氏珍藏（朱文方印）

Wang Yun

Qing dynasty　1652-after 1735

Zi Hanzao, *hao* Qingchi, native of Gaoyou, Jiangsu province. A well-known painter in the Jiangsu-Zhejiang region during the Kangxi period. Wang was particularly noted for painting landscapes with figures and buildings in a style deriving from Qiu Ying.

64. Landscape Album

Album of eleven leaves, ink and colour on silk
each leaf 28×24 cm

(1)-(8), (10)
Each with 1 seal of the artist.

(9)
With 1 seal of the artist and 1 collector's seal.

(11)
With inscription, signature, 3 seals of the artist and 2 collectors' seals.

64.1

64.2

64.3

64.4

64.5

64.6

64.7

64.8

64.9

64.10

64.11

顏　嶧

清代　1666－1749尚在

字青來，江都（江蘇揚州）人。曾隨李寅（十七世紀晚期至十八世紀早期）學畫，善畫工筆山水，學北宋人風格。

65. 江樓對奕圖

1740年作
絹本設色立軸　115.5×62.5厘米

此圖爲設色界畫，江樓主客對奕，江中漁舟撒網，對岸村舍數間，遠山浮煙迷濛。用筆工致，功力極深。

款識：
乾隆庚申歲（1740年）春二月，江都顏嶧時年七十又五。

印章：
顏嶧印（白文方印）

Yan Yi

Qing dynasty　1666-after 1749

Zi Qinglai, native of Jiangdu (present-day Yangzhou, Jiangsu province). Yan studied painting under Li Yin. He was noted for painting landscapes in a detailed manner after the Northern Song masters.

65. Playing Chess in a Pavilion by the River

Dated 1740
Hanging scroll, ink and colour on silk
115.5 × 62.5 cm

With inscription, signature and 1 seal of the artist.

乾隆庚申歲春二月

華　嵒

清代　1682－1756

字秋岳，號新羅山人、東園生。臨汀（福建）人，後寓杭州。善書、工畫人物、山水、花鳥。以花鳥畫最具特色，爲清代傑出大家。

66. 山水花鳥册

絹本設色册頁十二開　各30×25.5厘米

⑴ **秋枝白鳳**

款識：
瑤崖便有千尋樹，靈鳥飛來占好枝。

印章：
華嵒（白文方印）

鑑藏印章：
梁柏如印（朱文長方印）

⑵ **枯枝鳥鳴**

款識：
東風蘇鳴條，修羽一以暘。

印章：
華嵒（白文方印）

鑑藏印章：
傳語平安（朱文長方印）

⑶ **畫眉刷羽**

款識：
刷羽申寒條，薄閒憩幽唱。

印章：
華嵒（白文方印）

⑷ **雙鳥飛低**

款識：
錦翎飄草去。

印章：
華嵒（白文方印）

⑸ **山澗桃花**

款識：
玉莎瑤草連谿碧，流水桃花滿澗香。

印章：
華嵒（白文方印）

鑑藏印章：
梁柏如印（朱文長方印）

⑹ **溪山雲嶺**

款識：
樵路細盤雲外嶺。

印章：
華嵒（白文方印）

鑑藏印章：
眞率齋（朱文方印）

⑺ **僧歸雲寺**

款識：
細逕僧歸雲外寺，疎燈人語酒家樓。

印章：
華嵒（白文方印）

鑑藏印章：
柏如（朱文方印）
永康（朱文方印）

⑻ **竹舍賞雨**

款識：
玉壺買春，賞雨茅屋，座中佳士，左右修竹。

印章：
華嵒（白文方印）

鑑藏印章：
柏如珍玩（朱文長方印）

⑼ **飲馬**

款識：
鐵喙騧連錦驄，何年影墜水中。蒲梢西來八尺龍，天間十二爲爾空，五花雲錦吹東風。

印章：
華嵒（白文方印）

鑑藏印章：
梁柏如（朱文方印）
眞率齋（朱文方印）
柏如珍玩（朱文長方印）

⑽ **人物踏雪買魚**

款識：
就船買得魚偏美，踏雪沽來酒更佳。

印章：
華嵒（白文方印）

⑾ **人物遠歸**

款識：
雞聲茅店月，人跡板橋霜。

印章：
華喦（白文方印）

⑿ **高樓夜思**

款識：
誰知獨夜高樓上，對此秋光思不勝。新羅山人寫研幽書舍。

印章：
華喦（白文方印）

鑑藏印章：
梁柏如印（朱文長方印）
柏如珍玩（朱文長方印）

Hua Yan

Qing dyasty 1682-1756

Zi Qiuyue, *hao* Xinluo Shanren, Dongyuansheng, native of Linding, Fujian province. Hua left his native city and settled at Hangzhou. He was an accomplished calligrapher and a versatile painter of figures, landscapes, flowers, and birds. His major contribution lies in the flower and bird category and his innovative representations gained him recognition as a creative master of the Qing period.

66. Album of Miscellaneous Subjects

Album of twelve leaves, ink and colour on silk
each leaf 30×25.5 cm

(1) Perching Bird
With inscription, 1 seal of the artist and 1 collector's seal.

(2) Perching Bird
With inscription, 1 seal of the artist and 1 collector's seal.

(3) Thrush Brushing Feathers
With inscription and 1 seal of the artist.

(4) Two Birds in Flight
With inscription and 1 seal of the artist.

(5) Peach Tree by the Stream
With inscription, 1 seal of the artist and 1 collector's seal.

(6) Streams and Mountains in Clouds
With inscription, 1 seal of the artist and 1 collector's seal.

(7) Monk Returning to Monastery in Clouds
With inscription, 1 seal of the artist and 2 collectors' seals.

(8) Rainy Landscape with Figures
With inscription, 1 seal of the artist and 1 collector's seal.

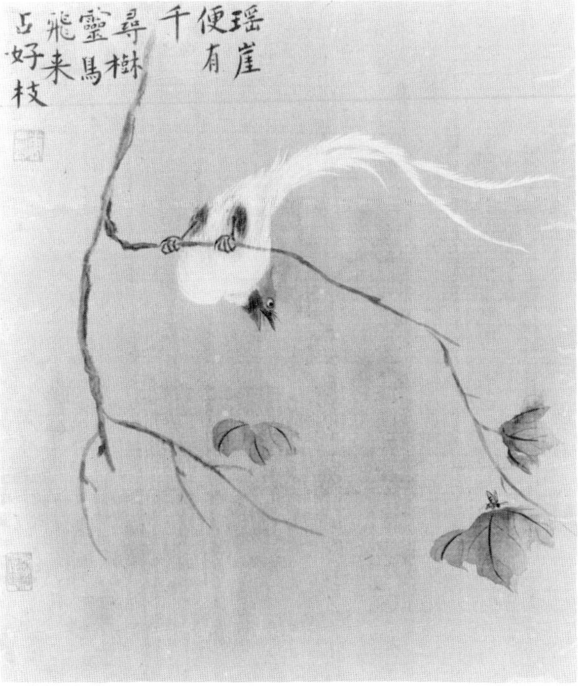

66.1

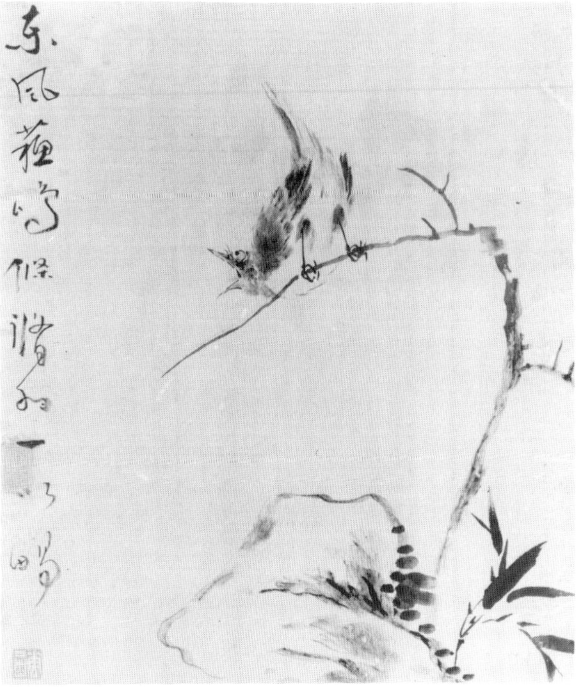

66.2

(9) Drinking Horse
With inscription, 1 seal of the artist and 3 collectors' seals.

(10) Return from the Market in the Snow
With inscription and 1 seal of the artist.

(11) Landscape with Figures
With inscription and 1 seal of the artist.

(12) Lady in Pavilion
With inscription, 1 seal of the artist and 2 collectors' seals.

66.3

66.4

66.5

66.6

66.9

66.7

66.8

66.10

66.11

66.12

高鳳翰

清代　1683－約1748

字西園，號南村，晚號南阜。膠州（山東）人。曾官徽州績溪縣知縣。工書畫篆刻，作山水花卉不拘於法度。晚年病臂，以左手作書畫，號尚左生。嗜硯，收藏千餘，著有《硯史》。

67．指畫綠天清蔭圖

絹本水墨立軸　130×61.5厘米

此畫寫芭蕉下湖石竹菊，筆法略近徐渭，沒署年款，是病臂中年之作。

款識：
綠天清蔭圖。用指頭墨法，寫奉方翁老父臺鑒正之，□□高鳳翰拜之。

印章：
鳳翰（白文聯珠印）
翰墨之曰閒作（白文方印）
□而荅草（白文方印）

Gao Fenghan

Qing dynasty　1683-ca. 1748

Zi Xiyuan, *hao* Nancun, Nanfu in later years, native of Jiaozhou, Shandong province. Gao took up residence in Yangzhou following his dismissal from the post of magistrate of Shexian, Anhui province. Skilled in calligraphy, painting and seal carving, he painted landscapes and flowers in a free and spontaneous style. His right arm became crippled in his old age. Thereafter he painted with his left hand and assumed a *hao*: shangzuosheng. He had a passion for ink-stones, accumulating a collection of over one thousand pieces and tracing their history in a book entitled *Yanshi.*

67. Finger Painting of Banana and Rock

Hanging scroll, ink on silk
130×61.5 cm

With inscription, signature and 3 seals of the artist.

綠天清
蔭圖

汪士慎

清代　1686－約1759

字近人，號巢林。安徽歙縣人。流寓揚州，淸貧窮窘。工詩、篆刻，善畫梅竹，與金農友善，世稱〝揚州八怪〞之一。

68. 松柏圖

1730年作
紙本水墨立軸　144.5×57厘米

此畫寫松柏於雲烟中，筆勢雄勁，雲烟繚繞，未見高山，彷彿於高山頂，爲汪氏中年力作。

款識：
庚戌（1730年）冬十月爲天翁先生教之。近人汪士愼。

印章：
士愼（白文方印）
七峯草堂（朱文方印）
甘泉山人（白文方印）

Wang Shishen

Qing dynasty　1686-ca.1759

Zi Jinren, *hao* Chaolin, native of Shexian, Anhui province. Wang lived in Yangzhou where he earned a meagre living from painting. He excelled in poetry, seal carving and painting of prunus and bamboo. He befriended Jin Nong, both of whom wre included among the ''Eight Eccentrics of Yangzhou''.

68. Pine and Cypress

Dated 1730
Hanging scroll, ink on paper
144.5×57 cm

With inscription, signature and 3 seals of the artist.

庚戌冬十月為
天翁先生壽之
近人汪士慎

李　鱓

清代　1686－1760後

字宗揚，號復堂。興化（江蘇）人。曾官山東滕縣知縣，善畫花鳥。早歲從蔣廷錫（1669－1732）、高其佩學，多作工筆，後受石濤影響，並繼承和發揚了陳淳、徐渭（1521－1593）的傳統。"揚州八怪"之一。

69. 竹蕉圖

紙本水墨立軸　126×62厘米

此畫寫暴雨中竹蕉，水墨淋漓，筆勢縱橫，墨色變化得自然天趣，有徐渭氣格。

款識：
祈雨聽風聽不得，道人何苦畫芭蕉。復堂李鱓醉後寫於竹窗寓齋。

印章：
木頭老子（朱文不規則形印）
知我貴希（朱文長方印）

Li Shan

Qing dynasty　1686-after 1760

Zi Zongyang, *hao* Futang, native of Xinghua, Jiangsu province. Li served as the magistrate of Tengxian, Shandong province. He studied painting under Jiang Tingxi (1669-1732) and Gao Qipei in his early years and painted mostly in the detailed *gongbi* style. Later on, he came under the influence of Yuanji and followed the tradition of Chen Chun and Xu Wei (1521-1593). He was also labelled as one of the "Eight Eccentrics of Yangzhou"

69. Bamboo and Banana

Hanging scroll, ink on paper
126×62 cm

With inscription, signature and 2 seals of the artist.

蔡　嘉

清代　1687前－1756後

字松原，號朱方老民。江蘇丹陽人。善山水、人物，與高翔（1688－1753）、汪士愼詩畫友。

70. 馮虛閣秋爽圖

1752年作
紙本設色立軸　132.5×73厘米

此畫描寫秋晨江邊之馮虛閣景色，人物凭欄遠眺，紅葉紛飛，遠山沒骨設色，近處山石樓閣，筆墨厚拙，清氣浮動，別具新意。

款識：
朝爽馮虛閣，天高秋氣清。江山眞可愛，草木有餘情。萬象從心會，纖毫入眼明。乾坤留粉本，筆底任縱橫。壬申（1752年）初夏，孝思先生正之。蔡嘉並題。

印章：
蔡嘉之印（白文方印）
朱方老民（朱文方印）
朱方（朱文長方印）

Cai Jia

Qing dynasty　before 1687-after 1756

Zi Songyuan, *hao* Zhufang Laomin, native of Danyang, Jiangsu province. Cai was proficient in landscape and figure painting. He shared a common interest in painting and poetry with Gao Xiang (1688-1753) and Wang Shishen.

70. The *Fengxuge* in Autumn

Dated 1752
Hanging scroll, ink and colour on paper
132.5 × 73 cm

With inscription, signature and 3 seals of the artist.

金　農

清代　1687－1764

字壽門，自號冬心先生。浙江杭州人。流寓揚州。精鑑賞，工詩古文詞，又工八分書。五十歲後始作畫，別具風格。被稱爲“揚州八怪”之一。

71. 梅花圖

1750年作
紙本水墨立軸　132×31厘米

此畫寫湖石間老梅盛開，筆致流暢，點苔拙重。

款識：

古來畫梅誰最好，僧中獨數華光老。花光衣缽付吾人，信手寫來得其眞。曾聞花光能畫影，墨暈含苞偏耐冷。石門畫梅兼畫月，比校烘雲尤幻絕。只圈花瓣不安鬚，看去朧朧月如潑。畫月之外更畫烟，烟籠玉質難爲傳。斜陽一抹忽中斷，似倚孤山向晚船。流落南屏定幾時，君今幸得收藏之。寫作春風十分態，擧似湘西江瘦阿師（此句疑衍一字），箇是浪子無聲詩。小玲瓏山館隙地，高高下下多種梅。主人性癖愛奇古，更令遠訪江之隈。蔣陵氣暖首靈谷，花匠家多住鳳臺。根蟠數世仍護墢，蕚點十月先含肧。殷勤揀取六七本，乘濤東下將春回。江神豈是妬花者，魚龍鼓鬣揚其頦。封姨拗怒得無恙，園丁上番工移栽。南枝記取解束縛，凡卉見之皆輿儓。清泉百道足生意，微陽潛伏扶新荄。西疇居士稱好事，行厨招客御深杯。酒闌客散寒月上，疎影一一堪疑猜。挨石鬅鬙鎮水怪，循墻屈曲藏凍虺。預想他時雪滿眼，彷彿此際香橫苔。不須健步煩杜老，芳心更用狂吟催。姑射仙神鍊玉砂，丹光晴貫洞中霞。無端夜半東風起，吹作江南第一花。漫天風雪正交加，三徑泥融酒懶賒。閒殺老夫無箇事，炙開冰硯畫梅花。乾隆庚午（1750年）冬十一月上浣。稽留山民金農拜題。

印章：

金吉金（朱文長方印）
冬心先生（朱文方印）

鑑藏印章：

賀天健（白文方印）
王賢印信（白文方印）
稚柳居士（朱文方印）

Jin Nong

Qing dynasty　1687-1764

Zi Shoumen, *hao* Dongxin Xianshen, native of Hangzhou, Zhejiang province. Jin took up residence in Yangzhou. He was a learned scholar, connoisseur and calligrapher. He began painting after the age of fifty in a highly individualistic manner that qualified him as one of the "Eight Eccentrics of Yangzhou".

71. Prunus Blossoms

Dated 1750
Hanging scroll, ink on paper
132×31 cm

With inscription, signature, 2 seals of the artist and 3 collectors' seals.

古來畫梅誰最好僧中獨數華光老華光衣缽付吾人信手
寫來得其真曾閱華光能畫影墨暈含苞偏耐冷石門畫
夫無箇事多閒冰硯畫梅卷
乾隆庚午冬十一月上浣 稽留山民金農畫并題

黃　慎

清代　1687－1768後

字恭懋，號癭瓢子。寧化（福建）人。僑寓揚州。工詩、草書。善畫人物、花卉、山水，格調放縱。世稱"揚州八怪"之一。

72. 五湖夜雨圖

紙本水墨立軸　183×55.3厘米

此畫寫狂雨猛瀉，漁人在歸途中。用筆豪縱，水墨淋漓，夜雨景象逼眞。

款識：
夜雨寒潮憶敝廬，人生只合老樵漁。五湖收拾看花眼，歸去青山好著書。

印章：
黃愼（朱文方印）
恭壽（白文方印）

Huang Shen

Qing dynasty　1687-after 1768

Zi Gongmu, *hao* Yingpiaozi, native of Ninghua, Fujian province. Huang resided in Yangzhou and was one of the ''Eight Eccentrics of Yangzhou''. A poet and calligrapher, he was equally proficient in painting landscapes, figures and flowers in a bold and expressive style.

72. Night Rain

Hanging scroll, ink on paper
183×55.3 cm

With inscription and 2 seals of the artist.

鄭　燮

清代　1693－1765

字克柔，號板橋。興化（江蘇）人。官任山東範縣、濰縣知縣。工詩文、書法。折衷行、隸書，自稱“六分半書”。專長蘭竹石。以詩意入畫，以畫寫詩境，落筆縱橫錯落，飄灑有致。

73. 竹石圖

紙本水墨立軸　193×108厘米

此圖水墨畫竹石，濃淡層次分明。

款識：
畫舫停橈倚汴河，揚鞭走馬竹窗過。春雷昨夜抽新笋，新竹高於舊竹多。板橋老人鄭燮寫。

印章：
鄭燮之印（白文方印）
爽鳩氏之官（朱白文方印）
橄欖軒（朱文長方印）

鑑藏印章：
吳璧城鑒定印（朱文長方印）
馬公愚印（朱文方印）
大年經眼（白文方印）
唐雲審定（白文方印）
嘯梅過目（白文方印）
曾在江右饒嘯梅家（朱文方印）
霍丘裴氏珍藏書畫（朱文長方印）

Zheng Xie

Qing dynasty　1693-1765

Zi Kerou, *hao* Banqiao, native of Xinghua, Jiangsu province. Zheng followed an official career which included serving as the magistrate of Fanxian and Weixian in Shandong. A literatus and a calligrapher, he was known for his poems and essays as well as a distinctive calligrahic style combining the running and clerical scripts. As a painter he specialized in orchid and bamboo.

73. Bamboo and Rock

Hanging scroll, ink on paper
193×108 cm

With inscription, signature, 3 seals of the artist and 7 collectors' seals.

李方膺

清代　1695－1754

字虬仲，號晴江，又號秋池。南通州（江蘇）人。曾官安徽合肥知縣，後寓南京。善松竹蘭菊，墨氣淋漓，不守矩矱。世稱"揚州八怪"之一。

74. 蒼松怪石圖

1752年作
絹本設色立軸　140×74厘米

此畫寫石上蒼松，下筆縱橫，水墨交融，沉著痛快。

款識：

君不見歲之寒，何處求芳草，又不見松之喬，青青復矯矯。天地本無心，萬物貴其真。直幹壯川岳，秀色無等倫，飽歷冰與霜，千年方未已。擁護天闕高且堅，迴幹春風碧雲裏。乾隆十八年（1752）三月寫於合肥五柳軒，晴江李方膺。

印章：
自食其力（白文方印）
松鄰穌尚（朱文方印）
僕本恨人（白文方印）
竹石居（白文長方印）

鑑藏印章：
多子印（白文方印）
天上無人天下有（白文方印）
物之儻來寄心寄之其來不可禦其去不可止（朱文方印）
斬（朱文圓印）
漢天下大明室（白文方印）
另一朱文印待考。

Li Fangying

Qing dynasty　1695-1754

Zi Qiuzhong, *hao* Qingjiang and Qiuchi, native of Nantong, Jiangsu province. Li served as magistrate in Hefei in Anhui and finally settled in Nanjing. As one of the ''Eight Eccentrics of Yangzhou'', he was best known for his paintings of pine, bamboo, orchid and chrysanthemum in an individual style that is both powerful and spontaneous.

74. Pine and Rock

Dated 1752
Hanging scroll, ink and colour on silk
140×74 cm

With inscription, signature, 4 seals of the artist and 5 collectors' seals. 1 collector's seal unidentified.

羅　聘

清代　1733－1799

字遯夫，號兩峯，又號花之寺僧，揚州人。曾漫遊越、楚、齊、豫、燕、趙各地，三次進京，廣爲交遊。金農弟子，"揚州八怪"之一。工畫人物、山水、花卉，工力深穩，筆墨樸厚，自成風格。

75. 水仙圖

紙本水墨立軸　71.5×26厘米

此畫寫水仙根生草地，水墨沒骨畫石襯托，使水仙玉質淸香，體態高潔動人。在羅氏作品中，別具氣格。

款識：
羅聘。

印章：
花之寺僧（朱文方印）

題跋(一)
碧玉釵搖欲近人，曉寒吹粉不成春。月波未動簾波冷，一剪空雲鎖洛神。風流可許澹相期，翠袖天寒有所思。紙帳銀屏請到我，五湖天遠夢西施。劍潭汪端光題。

題跋印章：
臣光（白文方印）
劍潭（朱文方印）

題跋(二)
生成弱質不知春，銀海飛來逈絕塵。水態雲容還自賞，梅兄礬弟鎮相親。一叢綠玉枝逾淨，幾朶瑤華韻更眞。坐對恰宜殘雪後，美人香草認全身。梁夢善。

題跋印章：
午樓（朱文方印）

題跋(三)
抱月飄煙百恨成，凌波猶怯步盈盈。亂香弱水情難定，寒色冰天韻自淸。離合神光三素遠，飛揚巾帔五銖輕。春魂別夢無人見，只有驚潮午夜生。蕙圃熊。

題跋印章：
夢、熊（朱白文聯珠印）

鑑藏印章：
長樂柯寅家藏之寶（朱文長方印）
寅所好（朱文方印）
篋齋珍藏（白文長方印）

Luo Pin

Qing dynasty　1733-1799

Zi Tunfu, *hao* Liangfeng, Huazhisiseng, native of Yangzhou. As a disciple of Jin Nong, Luo was also known as one of the ''Eight Eccentrics of Yangzhou''. He was a versatile artist, equally proficient in figures, landscapes and flowers. He was technically accomplished, though his style was marked by simplicity and strength.

75. Narcissus

Hanging scroll, ink on paper
71.5×26 cm

With signature, 1 seal of the artist, 3 colophons and 3 collectors' seals.

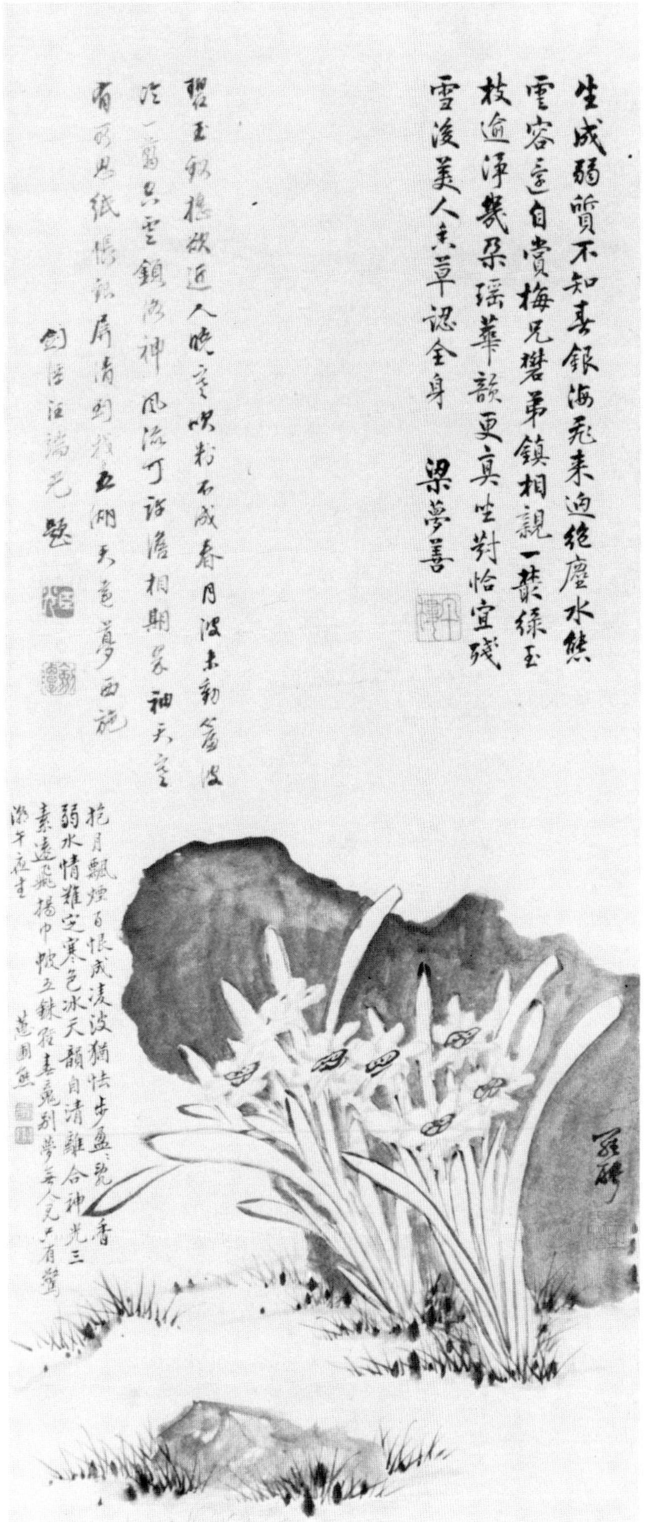

閔　貞

清代　1730－1788後

字正齋。江西人，僑寓漢口、揚州。工寫意人物，兼精寫眞。

76. 調琴圖

紙本水墨立軸　62.5×27厘米

此畫寫二仕女坐石上，一調琴，一靜聽。下筆隨意轉折，意態自然，墨色濃淡有致，格調清新。

款識：
正齋閔貞畫。

印章：
閔貞之印（白文方印）
正齋（朱文方印）

Min Zhen

Qing dynasty　1730-after 1788

Zi Zhengzhai, native of Jiangxi province. Min took up residence in Hankou and Yangzhou. He specialized in figures in the spontaneous *xieyi* style. At the same time he gained recognition as a portrait painter who was capable of capturing the physical features as well as the spirit of his sitters.

76. Ladies Playing *Qin*

Hanging scroll, ink on paper
62.5×27 cm

With signature and 2 seals of the artist.

正齋閔貞畫

王　宸

清代　1720－1797

字子凝，號蓬心，晚號柳東居士，太倉人。王原祁曾孫，是所謂〝小四王〞之一。畫山水承家傳，以元四家爲宗，喜用枯毫重筆。

77. 仿各家山水册

1782年作
紙本設色册頁十二開　各24×32厘米

此册自識仿各家法，筆法出自一家，只面貌略有所變而已。

⑴ 擬吳鎮山水

款識：
溪山無盡。法梅花菴主。蓬心宸。

印章：
子冰（朱文方印）

⑵ 擬倪瓚山水

款識：
隔江春色。師迂翁眞跡。宸。

印章：
蓬心（朱文長方印）

⑶ 擬王蒙山水

款識：
橅王叔明鐵網珊瑚眞本。王宸。

印章：
柳東居士（白文方印）

⑷ 擬倪瓚山水

款識：
摹雲林子疎林遠岫。柳東王宸。

印章：
王宸印、柳東居士（朱白文聯珠印）

鑑藏印章：
吳雲平齋過眼金石文字書畫印（白文方印）

⑸ 擬吳鎮山水

款識：
秋山行旅。此圖始於北苑，元季諸家俱有之，此特仿梅花翁者。王宸。

印章：
蓬心（朱文長方印）

⑹ 擬荊關山水

款識：
江濤石壁。橅荊關法。蓬心宸。

印章：
王宸印、柳東居士（朱白文聯珠印）

⑺ 擬米芾山水

款識：
山川出雲爲天下雨。擬米襄陽。子凝宸。

印章：
王宸印、柳東居　（朱白文聯珠印）

鑑藏印章：
壺公心賞（朱文方印）

⑻ 擬黃公望山水

款識：
仿大癡道人楚山秋曉圖一曲。蓬心宸。

印章：
蓬心（朱文長方印）

⑼ 擬王蒙山水

款識：
橅王黃鶴松山蕭寺。柳東居士。
王宸印、柳東居士（朱白文聯珠印）

⑽ 擬趙孟頫山水

款識：
吳興清遠圖。壬寅（1782年）秋八月，橅趙鷗波。蓬心宸。

印章：
王宸印、柳東居士（朱白文聯珠印）

鑑藏印章：
蔭北鑑藏（朱文方印）

⑾ 擬黃公望山水

款識：
摹大癡道人姚山雨霽。子凝宸。

印章：
王宸之印（白文方印）

⑿ 擬李安忠山水

款識：
雪溪待渡。仿宋人李安忠眞跡。

印章：
蓬心（朱文長方印）

再識：
此册余作於壬寅（1782年）秋日，時官於鄂城，終日游眺，頗領江山之助。修白三兄愛之，以此爲贈。弟王宸。

印章：
王宸印、柳東居士（朱白文聯珠印）

鑑藏印章：
壺中墨緣（朱文方印）
平齋審定眞跡（朱文長方印）

Wang Chen

Qing dynasty 1720-1797

Zi Zining, *hao* Pengxin, later *hao* Liudong Jushi, native of Taicang, Jiangsu province. Wang was the great-grandson of Wang Yuanqi and was known as one of the "Lesser Four Wangs" of the mid-Qing period. His painting style continued the family tradition of modelling after the four Yuan masters but showed his personal preference for dry and heavy brushwork.

77. Landscapes after Various Masters

Dated 1782
Album of twelve leaves, ink and colour on paper.
each leaf 24 × 32 cm

(1) Landscape after Wu Zhen
With inscription, signature and 1 seal of the artist.

(2) Landscape after Ni Zan
Same as leaf (1).

(3) Landscape after Wang Meng
Same as leaf (1).

(4) Landscape after Ni Zan
With inscription, signature, 2 seals of the artist and 1 collector's seal.

(5) Landscape after Wu Zhen
Same as leaf (1).

(6) Landscape after Jin Hao and Guan Tong
With inscription, signature and 2 seals of the artist.

(7) Landscape after Mi Fu
Same as leaf (4).

(8) Landscape after Huang Gongwang
Same as leaf (1).

(9) Landscape after Wang Meng
Same as leaf (6).

(10) Landscape after Zhao Mengfu
Same as leaf (4).

(11) Landscape after Huang Gongwang
Same as leaf (1).

(12) Landsape after Li Di
With inscription, signature, 3 seals of the artist and 2 collectors' seals.

77.1

77.2

77.3

77.4

77.5

77.6

77.7

77.8

77.9

77.10

77.11

77.12

王宸、閔貞合作

作者小傳分別見(76)及(77)。

78. 青柯坪圖

1777年作
紙本設色手卷　35×295厘米

此圖爲柯坪以閔貞爲其寫眞，交王宸以華山之青柯坪景爲之補景。王宸未游其地，讀陳以忠《華山遊記》所述，以意補景。

引首：
柯坪青柯坪圖。陽湖楊瑞蓮。

引首印章：
楊恒夫氏（朱文方印）
瑞蓮（白文方印）

款識(一)
廣濟閔貞寫照。

印章：
閔正之印（白文方印）

款識(二)
乾隆丁酉（1777年）長夏，柳東居士王宸爲柯坪先生補青柯坪圖。

印章：
王宸之印（白文方印）
子冰（朱文方印）

後幅題跋：
平生苦奔走，少小辭鄉關。迄今數十載，未得賦居閒。頭童兼齒豁，百體俱疲頑。先生騁驥足，萬里力不殫。所至著能績，聲名滿仕班。吾來分郡篆，幸識荊州韓。昔作夔陵守，仰止如高山。薦章達九閽，即日蒙殊恩。雄疆待君治，竹馬兒童欣。高碑立峴巔，望之何嶙嶙。行旌會當發，有客來傳神。命余繪一景，結念華山垠。石尋卧仙迹，方峯石罅門。四山高臨澗，青柯路由分。奇秀勞應接，絕壁留斧痕。橫松龍吸水，飛藤虬攫雲。此境非身歷，毋乃言無倫。偶讀華山記，即爲神所親。昔賢重遊目，往往難其羣。我材老而禿，枯研常自捫。今君有同趣，圖留王宰眞。青山同碧水，執卷求前因。丁酉（1777年）夏秋之交，柯坪先生將發襄陽，出照索圖，且謂字青子，命作華山之青柯坪。余未歷其地，因讀明陳君以忠遊記，略布其意。昔孫興公天台山賦云，遙想存之者，又何必泥其迹耶，並余以詩以誌數年相命之雅，幸明教之。柳東居士王宸拜草。

題跋印章：
王宸之印（白文方印）
子冰（朱文方印）
另有儲秘、羅暹春、紀淑曾、姚念曾、洪樸、蔣業晋、聞鏞等人題跋，不錄。姚念曾末跋題於乾隆甲辰（1784年）。

鑑藏印章：
歐陽竹平（朱文方印）
渤海後人（朱文方印）

Wang Chen and Min Zhen

For biographies see cat. nos. 76 and 77.

78. Portrait of Keping

Dated 1777
Handscroll, ink and colour on paper
35 × 295 cm

With inscription, signature and 1 seal of Min Zhen, inscription, signature and 2 seals of Wang Chen and 2 collectors' seals. With frontispiece by Yang Ruilian and 8 colophons, including one by Wang Chen, on paper separate from the painting.

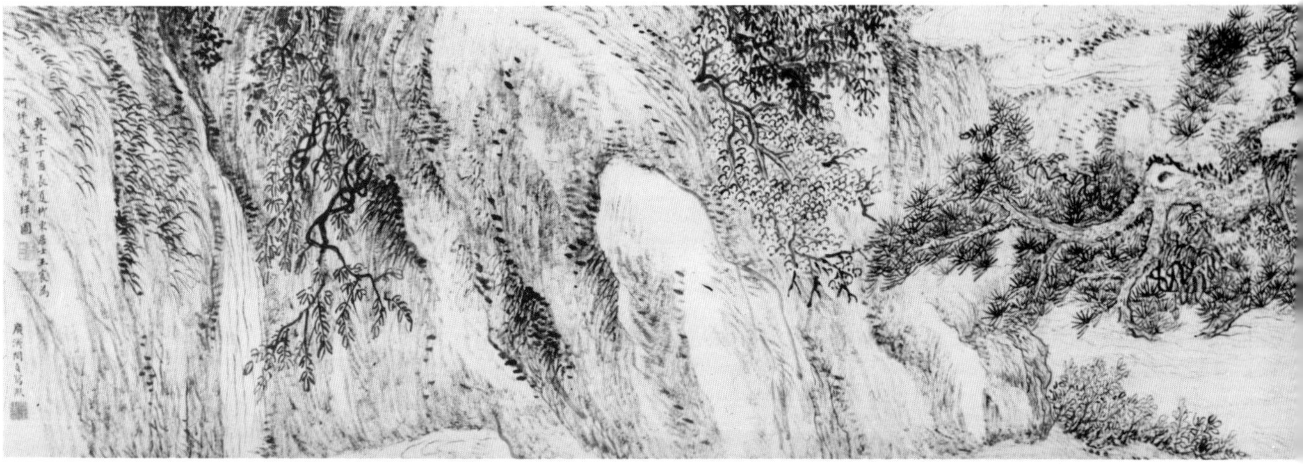

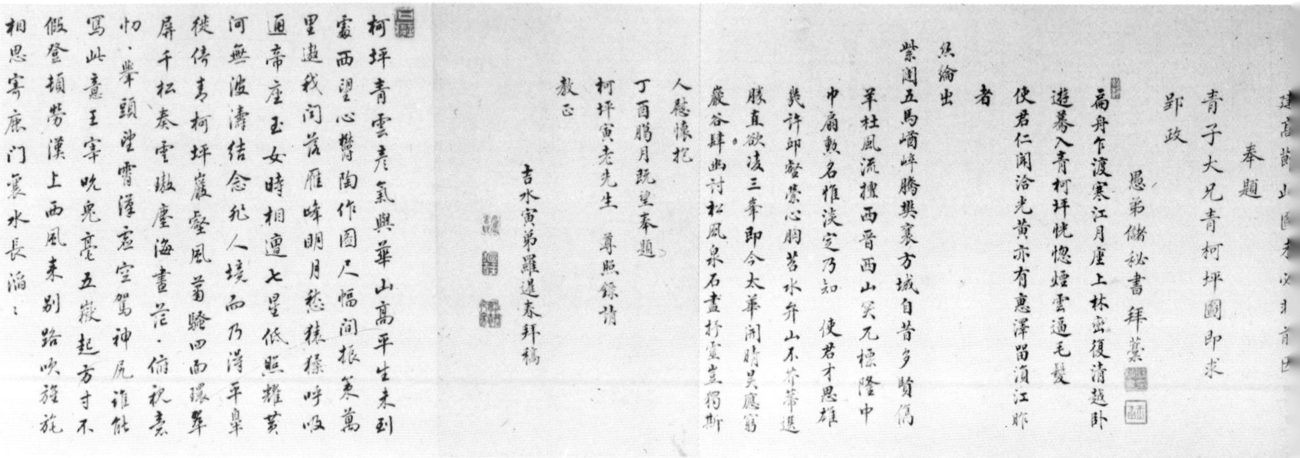

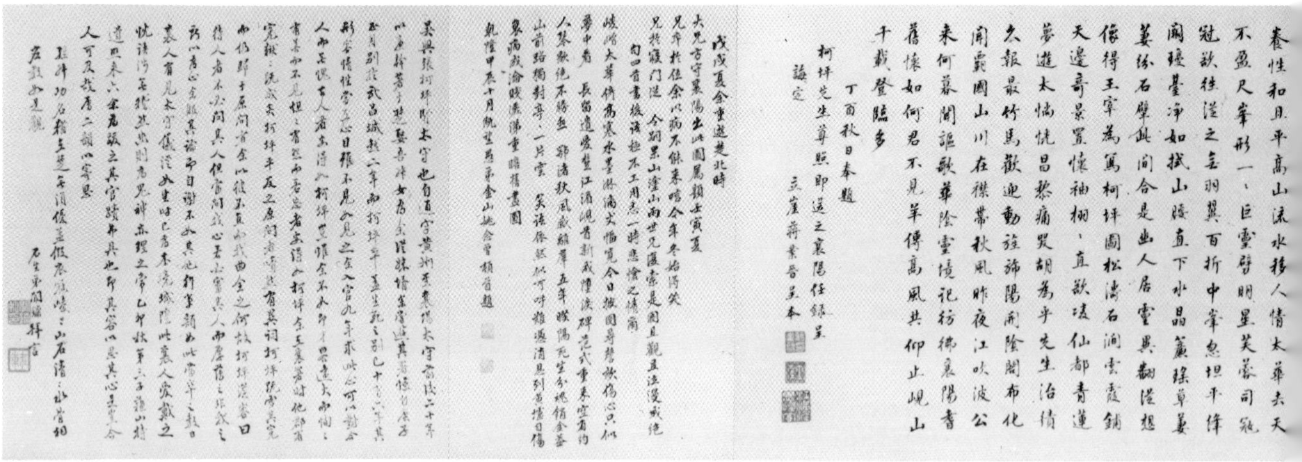

平生苦奇走少小靜鄉闈追今數十載未
得賦居澗頭童真豈豁百體俱疲頑
先生踽躂直萬里力不殫研玉茗餘績聲
名滿仕籍東南郡篆章濟荊以韓苦
作吳陵守仰止如高山萬章達
九閩即日家
殊恩羅躔待　君治竹馬兒童欣高碑立峴山巔
望之何峰之行篋會當薦有家奉傳神
命余繪一景語余華山根石尋卧仙迹
方峰石礴門四山高莊澗青　柯致曲分奇
秀芳應搞絶壑西斧痕橫松蒞吸水
飛蘿北攫雲片淺非身歷安乃言無偏
偶讀嘉山記知為神所藏昔賢重摽目
往往難其群我材去而充指研常自嗣
今君有同趣幽而王寧真青山同璩不
執筆求前因
丁酉夏秋之交
柯坪先生將發家陽出此索圖且詩容青子為
作嘉山之青柯坪並未曆覽地因讀明陳右以
未遊記略布其意書於奧於天台山路之道也
右之衣又何必泥其迹耶　合余以詩以誌歲
年相知之雅幸以教之
柳東居士王宸并草

巨靈仙掌勢壓泰蓮峰岸嶙凌高
吳青柯之坪更窈窕樹石斑駁披
虬鱗二十八潭滙其下懸流飛瀑
成奔淪希夷毛女古窟宅靈境往
往棲仙真吳興公子淡宕人翰墨
揮洒工無倫壯懷經濟歷楚甸遇
事剖決明如神上官交章薦循
卓姓氏特達標
楓宸朱轓領郡來峴首襄樊萬户歌
[illegible]

奉題
柯坪大兄　尊照即送之任錄請
教定
愚弟紀洲曾拜稿

太華削成不計里三吾芙蓉拔地起峯回嶂
合十八盤斗絶直上丹霄峙勢極嶔寄地勢
平每到青柯嶺觀止峯勝匹練縈復行散落
懸崖激飛矢長松掛壁積鐵蒼老鶴啄苔古
雪紫鼎山下望爭獻奇奇趣不敢匿厥美古來
靈蹟閟幽深時有飛儛霞節拜
使君履齒未曾經又非夢遊天姥比胡為置身
在其間嵐翠濕衣雲滾蹊　君品峭削絶攀援
君心坦夷無嶮巇喜峻而不孤高不危截於此坪
有取爾輞川巨手繪成圖磴道盤迴了可指長風
颯颯卷歸來雲光蕩漾草樹靡天雞恍叫呀賓
中桃花細落空岩裏錦鷺絶境在眼前雨脫崖
巍風還耳他年果作虞擢遊客我追陪既泥濘
里句奉題
柯坪大兄大人尊照即呈
教正
愚弟姚令聲頓首稿

漢江春漲鴨頭波硯峴首秋容瀅蜊游羅側著
襴衫笑襄陽太守興如何張侯即今羊叔子坐
嘯江山入妙理政成人愛魚鳥親心間夢恬濟游
美空堂哭首見蒼山高丹崖翠壁紛周遭白帝
坐精凝元氣衝風萬壑生濤濤青柯坪上結
茅屋萬株松映鬢眉綠張侯手持九節杖
仰摘芙蓉騎白鹿前身將是術叔卿不然
不死丹邱生山人抱冬夜珠異真靜脈脈朝
玉京平生切與一邱壑人事紛紛空六鑿何
似張侯天機精萬嶽峰頭恣磅礴我家住
近天都峰十年夢想杵轅它今來亦我
秋坪畫倏忽雲海摸心胸前年曾陟羊公
峴愛絶秋山小平遠淙山大澤豈偶然福地
致身豈緣淺君家留侯赤松游我亦洪崖
羨隱淪三千年後玉漿飲会看羊公

沈宗騫

清代　活躍於1757－1815年間

字熙遠，號芥舟。烏程（浙江吳興）人。工畫山水、人物。所著《芥舟學畫編》爲清代中期重要畫學論著。

79. 城南山色圖

1779年作
紙本水墨立軸　145.5×63厘米

此畫山石多作乾筆點擦，有蒼老氣格。

款識：
道場山頂何山麓，上徹雲峯下幽谷。我從山水窟中來，尙愛此山看不足。陂湖行盡白漫漫，青山忽作龍蛇盤。山高無風松自響，誤認石齒號驚湍。山僧不放山泉出，屋底淸池照瑤席。堦前合抱香入雲，月裏仙人親手植。出山回望翠雲鬟，碧瓦朱欄縹緲間。白水田頭問行路，小溪深處是何山。高人讀書夜達旦，至今山鶴鳴夜半。我今廢學不歸山，山中對酒空三歎。己亥（1779年）夏五作城南山色，並錄坡公遊道場何山詩。吳興沈宗騫。

印章：
沈宗騫印（白文方印）
芥舟（朱文方印）
開心寫意君所知（白文方印）
我生不可一日無山水友朋（白文方印）
另一印待考。

Shen Zongqian

Qing dynasty　fl. 1757-1815

Zi Xiyuan, *hao* Jiezhou, native of Wucheng (present-day Wuxing, Zhejiang province). Shen was an accomplished landscape and figure painter, as well as a theorist. His major work, *Jiezhou xuehua pian*, was a significant study on painting theory in the mid-Qing period.

79. Mountains at South of the City

Dated 1779
Hanging scroll, ink on paper
145.5×63 cm

With inscription, signature and 5 seals of the artist.

童　鈺

清代　1721－1782

字璞巖，號二樹，又號借庵子，山陰（浙江紹興）人。擅長畫梅花，工詩。

80. 墨梅圖

1777年作
紙本水墨立軸　153.5×85.5厘米

此圖畫一樹橫出寒梅，密蕾初開，雪骨冰魂，有〝昨夜雪夜晴，寒梅破蕾新〞意。

款識：
半山殘雪半山陰，忽地香來冷不禁。青漠漠連苔點點，白濛濛映竹深深。風情莫比秋娘老，鐵口先爲閔統心。記得上皇於畔路，幾人相約得重尋。丁酉（1777年）冬仲寫於洛下之雪香齋中。二樹山人。

印章：
童鈺之印（白文方印）
字二樹（白文方印）
萬幅梅花萬首詩（白文方印）

Tong Yu

Qing dynasty　1721-1782

Zi Puyan, *hao* Ershu, Jie'anzi, native of Shanyin (present-day Shaoxing, Zhejiang province). A poet and a painter, Tong was best known for his painting of prunus blossoms.

80. Prunus Blossoms

Dated 1777
Hanging scroll, ink on paper
153.5×85.5 cm

With inscription, signature and 3 seals of the artist.

王學浩

清代　1754－1832

字孟養，號椒畦。江蘇昆山人。工畫山水，學王原祁筆法，屬婁東派。中年兼重寫生，賦色澹雅，著有《南山論畫》。

81. 萍跡山水圖

1800年作
紙本設色手卷　25.5×131厘米

此畫寫江南景色，墨色清潤，筆法蒼秀。

款識：
無數兼葭一葉舟，天涯萍跡自悠悠。富春山色青如許，飛去人間幾白鷗。余既爲箬村先生題萍跡圖詩，暇日又爲作圖，又係以詩，盖拳拳於圖意，而不自知其畫與詩之拙也。庚申（1800年）五月望前二日記。椒畦浩。

印章：
王學浩（朱文方印）
畫中詩（白文方印）

鑑藏印章：
忠浩心賞（白文長方印）
曾在吳縣俞鐐英家（朱文長方印）
陳湘濤家珍藏（朱文長方印）
張晋審定（朱文方印）

Wang Xuehao

Qing dynasty　1754-1832

Zi Mengyang, *hao* Jiaoqi, native of Kunshan, Jiangsu province. Wang was a landscape painter and followed Wang Yuanqi. Therefore, he was grouped with the Loudong school. In his middle years, he emphasized painting from nature, and the use of light and elegant colours.

81. Landscape

Dated 1800
Handscroll, ink and colour on paper
25.5×131 cm

With inscription, signature, 2 seals of the artist and 4 collectors' seals.

張　崟

清代　1761－1829

字寶巖，號夕庵。丹徒（江蘇鎮江）人。工畫山水，遠宗沈周而得其蒼秀，爲丹徒派名家之一。

82. 桂蔭涼適圖

1819年作
紙本設色立軸　111×54厘米

此畫寫桂蔭下人物乘涼，筆墨渾厚，乃張氏五十九歲之作。

款識：
己卯（1819年）仲秋寫於安蕺草堂。張崟。

印章：
夕菴（白文方印）
張崟之印（朱白文方印）

Zhang Yin

Qing dynasty　1761-1829

Zi Baoyan, *hao* Xi'an, native of Dantu, Jiangsu province. He was skilled in landscape painting in the tradition of Shen Zhou and was considered to be one of the masters of the Dantu school.

82. Cooling in the Shade of Cassia Trees

Dated 1819
Hanging scroll, ink and colour on paper
111×54 cm

With inscription, signature and 2 seals of the artist.

奚 岡

清代　1764－1803

字鐵生，號蒙泉外史、冬花庵主。錢塘（浙江杭州）人。工詩書、善畫山水花卉，亦善篆刻，與丁敬（1695－1765）、蔣仁（1743－1795）、黃易（1744－1802），稱爲"西泠四家"。

83. 西湖放舟圖

1797年作
紙本水墨手卷　15×57厘米

此畫寫西湖景色，用筆着墨簡略，清逸秀雅，乃奚氏三十四歲時作。

引首：
蒙泉高寄。爲夢華三兄題。山舟寫。

引首印章：
山舟（白文方印）
梁同書印（白文方印）
曰毋齋（朱文長方印）

款識：
丁巳（1797年）十月三日同慈柏壽、石雲伯放舟西湖，時寒雨空濛，雲山如畫，篷窗進茗，逸思霞飛。即訪夢華三兄於葛林園，小酌數尊，適蘭坨綠飲來會，欣暢非常，乘興作此。苦紙澀拒筆，聊寫其大略，不足言畫也。在夢華自有空中邱壑，眼底湖山，又何必如倪迂大痴者，方能動其精鑒耶。醉後書此，以發夢華一笑。鐵生奚岡記。

印章：
奚九（朱文方印）
鐵生（白文方印）

後幅題跋：
阮元、查揆、嚴元照三人題跋，均爲夢華題記。

鑑藏印章：
世珩珍藏（白文方印）
之泗嗣守（朱文方印）
韻初審定（朱文方印）
曾經貴池南山邨鐂氏聚學軒所藏（白文方印）
鐂蔥石藏（朱文方印）
聚卿長樂（白文方印）
韻初心賞（朱文長方印）
聚學軒物（白文方印）
鐂氏審貨（朱文方印）

Xi Gang

Qing dynasty 1764-1803

Zi Tiesheng, *hao* Mengquan Waishi, Donghua Anzhu, native of Hangzhou, Zhejiang province. Xi was proficient in poetry, calligraphy and the painting of landscapes, flowers and birds. He also excelled in seal carving and was known as one of the "Four Masters of Xiling" with Ding Jing (1695-1765), Jiang Ren (1743-1795) and Huang Yi (1744-1802).

83. Boating on West Lake

Dated 1797
Handscroll, ink on paper
15 × 57 cm

With 1 collector's seal on painting, inscription, signature and 2 seals of the artist on paper separate from painting. Frontispiece by Liang Shanzhou, 3 colophons and 8 additonal collectors' seals on paper separate from painting.

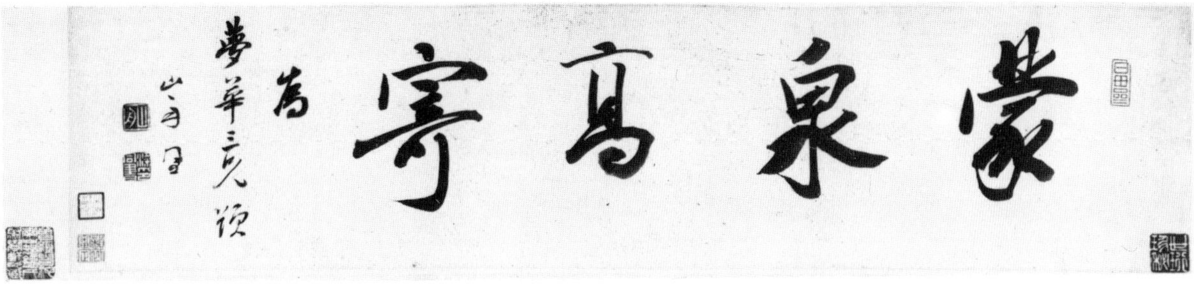

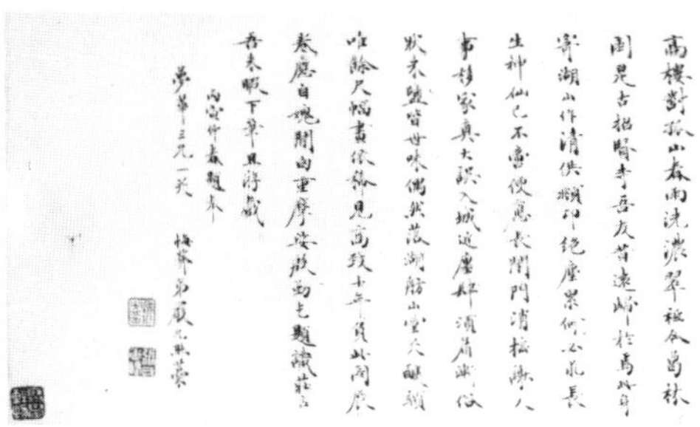

陳　墫

清代　十八世紀後期至十九世紀前期

字仲尊，號葦汀，又號白隄花隱。工畫山水，學畫翟大坤（1804年歿）。

Chen Zun

Qing dynasty　late 18th to early 19th centuries

Zi Zhongzun, *hao* Weiding, Baiti huayin. Chen was a landscape painter who had studied under Zhai Dakun (?-1804).

84. 松亭授讀圖

紙本設色立軸　120.5×35.3厘米

此畫寫松蔭下屋舍，老人坐對童子授讀，橋上老人挾杖來訪，另小童院中掃地，一派山居景色，屋後山巒重疊，筆勢蜷曲繁密，布墨蒼潤有致。

款識：
松亭授讀。白堤花隱陳墫。

印章：
白堤花隱（白文方印）

84. Lecturing in Pavilion among Pine Trees

Hanging scroll, ink and colour on paper
120.5×35.3 cm

With inscription, signature and 1 seal of the artist.

松亭夜讀
白堤花隱陳

童　衡

清代　十八世紀後期

號僊潭。籍貫待考。

85. 雙鹿圖

1786年作
紙本設色立軸　209.5×106.5厘米

此圖以細筆畫兩鹿於山澗飲水，筆法略近沈銓（1682－1761）。傳世童氏畫蹟中另有年款之《松鶴圖》，爲乾隆五十九年（1794）所作。

款識：
乾隆丙午（1786年）春日，僊潭童衡寫。

印章：
童衡（白文方印）
聘式（朱文方印）
家住苕南餘不溪（白文方印）
不碍雲山（朱文長方印）

Tong Heng

Qing dynasty　late 18th century

Hao Xiantan. Little is known of his biography.

85. Two Deer

Dated 1786
Hanging scroll, ink and colour on paper
209.5 × 106.5 cm

With inscription, signature and 4 seals of the artist.

乾隆丙午春日

上官蕙

清代

汀州（福建）人。工畫山水。

86. 山水

紙本水墨立軸　168×79.5厘米

此圖畫羣山環抱，雲烟繚繞，樹木蓊蔚，石縫中流泉潺潺，淡墨皴擦，濃墨點苔，別具氣格。

款識：
辛未秋八月寫，天翁老年兄大人正之。上官蕙。

印章：
上官蕙印（白文方印）

Shangguan Hui

Qing dynasty

Native of Tingzhou, Fujian province. Shangguan was known as a landscape painter.

86. Landscape

Hanging scroll, ink on paper
168×79.5 cm

With inscription, signature and 1 seal of the artist.

辛未秋八月寫
天翁老年兄大人政之
上官蕙

黎 簡

清代 1747－1799

字簡民，自號二樵。廣東順德人。工詩書，畫山水得石濤畫意。筆疏澹遠，淋漓蒼潤，各盡其趣。

87. 爲虛舟作山水圖

1795年作
紙本水墨立軸 93×32.5厘米

此圖略近倪雲林畫法，清逸雅淨，前景開闊，後景高聳，別具氣勢。虛舟即黃丹書，乾隆六十年（1795）舉人，二樵同縣好友。

款識：
十餘年不數爲虛舟作畫，作亦少當意者。今年同處所最久，多病之餘，又苦應酬。今夕微雨微寒，賤軀頗適，始一鼓，卒□鼓而畢，頗不俗。乙卯（1795年）十月十日，二樵簡記。

印章：
黎簡之印（白文方印）
二樵（白文方印）
是眞畫者也（白文方印）

Li Jian

Qing dynasty 1747-1799

Zi Jianmin, *hao* Erqiao, native of Shunde, Guangdong province. Li was a poet, calligrapher and painter. His landscape style, displaying an influence from Yuanji, ranges from arid simplicity to exuberant vitality.

87. Landscape Dedicated to Xuzhou

Dated 1795
Hanging scroll, ink on paper
93×32.5 cm

With inscription, signature and 3 seals of the artist.

謝蘭生

清代　1760－1831

字佩士，號里甫。廣東南海人，寓廣州。嘉慶七年（1802）進士。父亡，絕意進取，主粵秀、越華、羊城等書院掌教。善詩文、書法及書畫鑑定。工畫山水，用筆雄峻，自成一家，與黎簡齊名。

88. 山水册

紙本設色册頁十二開　各30.5×40.5厘米

本册共十二開，雖自題倣各家法，實爲自家法，且極具南方景色。傳里甫晚年多作畫册留傳親族後人，此册爲晚年筆致，想爲其留傳家人之作。

⑴ 紅棉溪閣

款識：
二樵先生碧嶂紅棉圖。里道人作。

印章：
謝蘭生印（白文方印）

⑵ 秋江漁笛

款識：
里甫。

印章：
蘭、生（朱白文聯珠印）

⑶ 松閣聽瀑

款識：
里甫。

印章：
蘭、生（朱白文聯珠印）

⑷ 臨溪屋舍

款識：
里甫。

印章：
理圃（白文方印）

⑸ 秋樹竹石

款識：
仿倪高士法。里甫畫。

印章：
謝蘭生印（白文方印）

⑹ 秋山觀瀑

款識：
里道人作。

印章：
理圃（白文方印）

⑺ 古木村屋

款識：
小池兼鶴靜，古木帶蟬聲。里道人畫。

印章：
謝蘭生印（白文方印）

鑑藏印章：
頌齋（朱文方印）

⑻ 寒江歸艇

款識：
仿李將軍法。里甫。

印章：
澧浦（白文方印）

⑼ 夏山聽流

款識：
法高房山意。里甫。

印章：
蘭、生（朱白文聯珠印）

⑽ 溪屋停舟

款識：
仿石田老人法。里甫。

印章：
謝蘭生印（白文方印）

⑾ 古木秋亭

款識：
古木秋亭。仿雲林筆。里甫畫。有竹山房。

印章：
蘭、生（朱白文聯珠印）

⑿ 桐陰書屋

款識：
桐陰書屋。里甫。

印章：
蘭、生（朱白文聯珠印）

Xie Lansheng

Qing dynasty 1760-1831

Zi Peishi, *hao* Lifu, native of Nanhai, Guangdong province. Xie was awarded the *jinshi* degree in 1802, but instead of entering government service he served as a lecturer at several colleges, including Yuexiu, Yuehua and Yangcheng. A learned scholar, poet and calligrapher, he also gained recognition as a connoisseur of old calligraphy and paintings. As a painter he specialized in landscapes and enjoyed equal prominence with Li Jian.

88. Landscape Album

Album of twelve leaves, ink and colour on paper
each leaf 30.5 × 40.5 cm

(1) Water Pavilion by the Kapok Trees
With inscription, signature and 1 seal of the artist.

(2) Fishing in Autumn River
With signature and 1 seal of the artist.

(3) Listening to the Sound of Waterfall
Same as leaf (2).

(4) Waterside Pavilions
Same as leaf (2).

(5) Autumn Trees with Bamboo and Rock
Same as leaf (1).

(6) Watching Waterfall in Autumn Mountains
Same as leaf (2).

(7) Cottage by Old Trees
Same as leaf (1). 1 additional collector's seal.

(8) Boat on Wintry River
Same as leaf (1).

(9) Summer Mountains
Same as leaf (1).

(10) Riverside Village
Same as leaf (1).

(11) Pavilion by Autumn Trees
Same as leaf (1).

(12) Study under Paulownia Trees
Same as leaf (1).

88.1

88.2

88.3

88.4

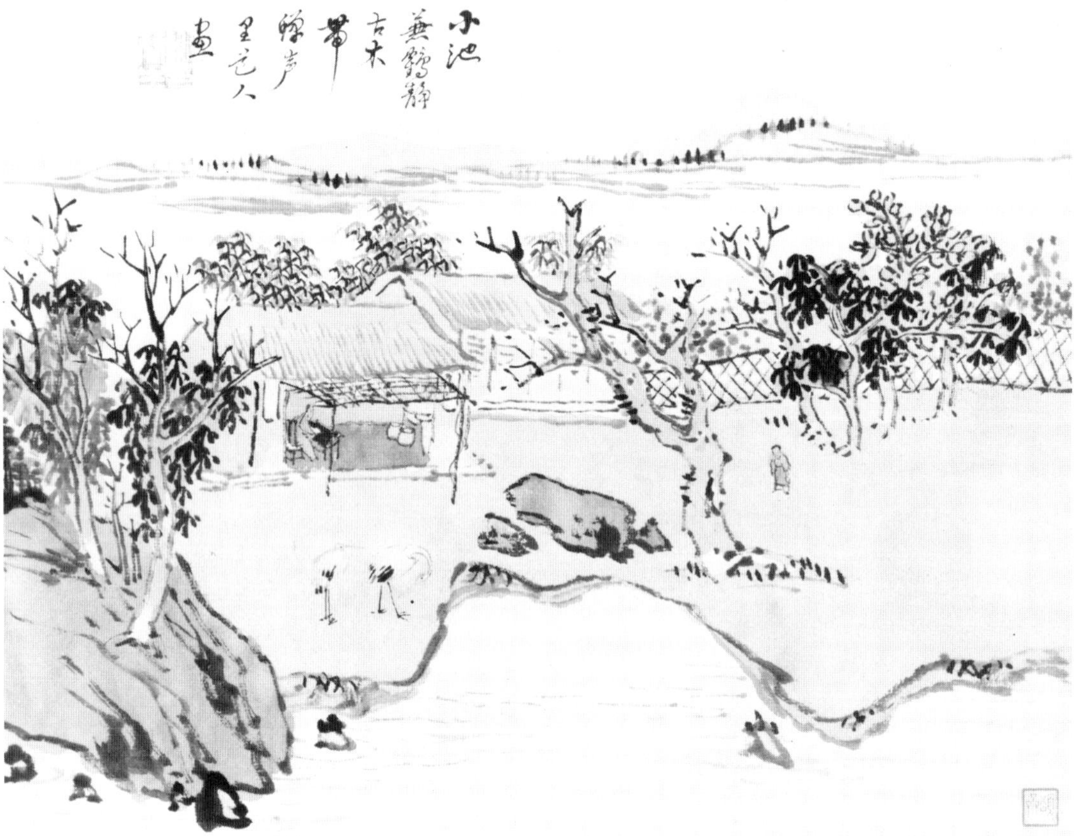

88.7

88.8

88.5

88.6

88.9

88.10

88.11

88.12

改　琦

清代　1773－1828

字伯蘊，號七薌，又號玉壺外史。其先祖西域人，後居松江（江蘇）。工畫仕女，稱妙一時，亦能蘭竹。

89. 竹下仕女圖

絹本設色立軸　129×41.5厘米

此圖畫仕女二人坐竹下停簫對話，設色清妍，筆調潔淨。

款識：
憮六如居士粉本，泖東七薌改琦。

印章：
改琦（白文方印）
伯韞（朱文方印）

鑑藏印章：
種石軒（朱文方印）
狄曼農鑑藏書畫印（朱文方印）

Gai Qi

Qing dynasty　1773-1828

Zi Boyun, *hao* Qixiang, Yuhu Waishi, native of Songjiang (present-day Shanghai). Gai's ancestry could be traced to Xinjiang in northwest China. He was best known for his paintings of ladies, though he was equally proficient in orchid and bamboo.

89. Ladies under Bamboo

Hanging scroll, ink and colour on silk
129×41.5 cm

With inscription, signature, 2 seals of the artist and 2 collectors' seals.

撫〻如居士粉本
七薌改琦

湯貽汾

清代　1778－1853

字雨生。武進（江蘇常州）人。曾歷官江、浙、粵東，後寓居南京。咸豐癸丑（1853年）太平天國克攻南京，投池而死。工詩文，善畫山水、松梅。

90. 臨青藤書屋八景册

1850年作
紙本設色册頁十一開　各41.2×30.5厘米

此册臨明徐渭（1521－1593）青藤書屋八景。八景分別爲漱籐阿、天池、自在巖、孕山樓、渾如舟、柿葉居、櫻桃館、酬字堂。

⑴ 臨徐渭自畫像

款識：
吾年十歲植青藤，吾今稀年花甲藤。寫圖壽藤壽吾壽，他年吾去不朽藤。壽藤道士七十歲小像，徐渭自作並題。正德（疑爲嘉靖之誤）辛卯（1531年），吾年十歲，手植青藤一本於天池之傍，迄今萬曆庚寅（1590年）吾年正七十矣，此藤亦六十年之物。流光荏苒，兩鬢如霜，是藤大若虬松，綠陰如蓋，今作此圖壽藤亦壽吾也。田水月又題。道光庚戌（1850年）之秋，臨徐文長先生壽藤圖。湯貽汾。

印章：
雨生（朱文方印）
貽汾印信（朱文方印）
湯（朱文圓印）
雨翁（白文方印）
老雨（朱文方印）
毘陵湯貽汾雨生氏章（白文方印）

鑑藏印章：
鶴舫眼福（朱文方印）

⑵

款識：
漱籐阿。

印章：
雨生（朱文方印）

鑑藏印章：
容庚（朱文方印）

⑶

款識：
天池。

印章：
雨生（朱文方印）

鑑藏印章：
鶴舫眼福（朱文方印）

⑷

款識：
自在巖。

印章：
雨生（朱文方印）

⑸

款識：
孕山樓。

印章：
老雨（朱文方印）

⑹

款識：
渾如舟。

印章：
雨翁（白文方印）

⑺

款識：
柿葉居。

印章：
雨生（朱文方印）

⑻

款識：
櫻桃館。

印章：
雨翁（白文方印）

⑼

款識：
酬字堂。

印章：
老雨（朱文方印）

⑽、⑾
抄錄徐渭原跋，略述八景由來。

印章：
湯（朱文圓印）
毘陵湯貽汾雨生氏章（白文方印）

鑑藏印章：
鶴舫所藏（朱文方印）
趙大（朱文長方印）

Tang Yifeng

Qing dynasty 1778-1853

Zi Yusheng, native of Wujin, Jiangsu province. Tang settled in Nanjing after a long official career which took him to the provinces of Jiangsu, Zhejiang and Guangdong. However, when the city fell to the Taiping rebels, Tang drowned himself. A literatus noted for poetry and prose, he was also proficient in painting landscape, pine and prunus blossoms.

90. The Eight Views of Qingteng Studio

Dated 1850
Album of eleven leaves, ink and colour on paper
each leaf 41.2 × 30.5 cm

(1) Portrait of Xu Wei
With copy of 2 inscriptions originally by Xu Wei (1521-1593), inscription, signature, 6 seals of the artist and 1 collector's seal.

(2) Old Vine
With inscription, 1 seal of the artist and 1 collector's seal.

(3) Pool of Heaven
Same as leaf (2).

(4) *Zizai* Rock
With inscription and 1 seal of the artist.

(5) *Yunshan* Tower
Same as leaf (4).

(6) *Hunruzhou* Pavilion
Same as leaf (4).

(7) Residence of Persimmon Leaves
Same as leaf (4).

(8) Cherries Lodge
Same as leaf (4).

(9) Hall of Award for Writing
Same as leaf (4).

(10), (11)
With copy of 1 colophon originally by Xu Wei, 2 seals of the artist and 2 collectors' seals.

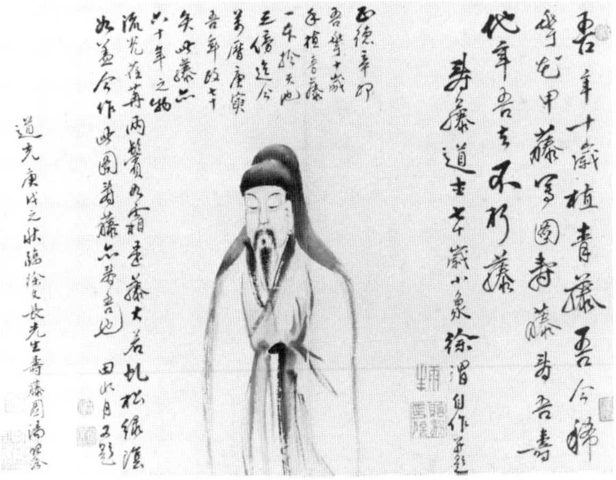

90.1

90.2

90.3

90.5

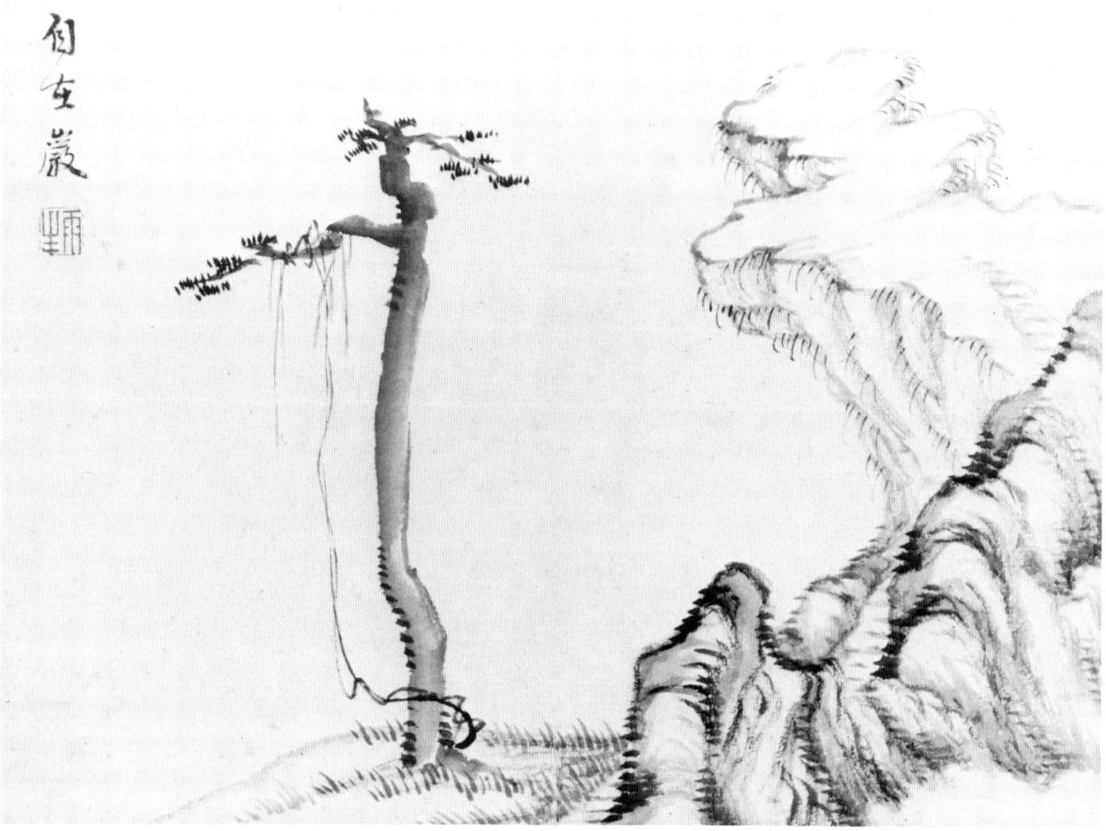

90.4

90.10

90.6

90.7

90.8

90.9

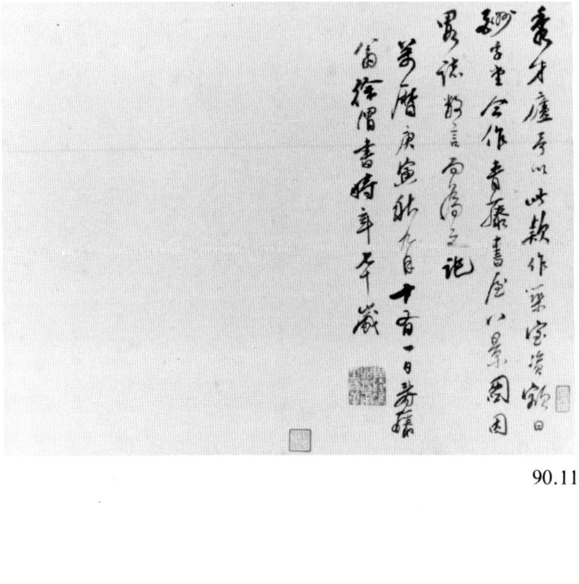

90.11

戴　熙

清代　1801－1860

字醇士，號榆庵，又號井東居士，鹿床居士。錢塘（浙江杭州）人。道光間進士，官至兵部侍郎。咸豐十年（1860）太平天國攻克杭州時自盡。工畫山水，法王時敏、王翬，小品停勻妥貼，自有意境。著有《習苦齋畫絮》。

91．海天霞唱圖

1846年作
絹本設色手卷　36.5×137.7厘米

此圖乃戴氏於廣東任官時爲張維屏作。

款識(一)
海天霞唱圖。丙午（1846年）九月爲南山先生畫。醇士戴熙作於淸遠舟中。

印章：
戴熙（白文方印）

款識(二)
釣鰲歸去正長空，吹起晴霞一片。傑閣高寒烟霧杪，小試紫鸞仙管。萬木無聲，衆山皆響，咳唾從天半。元龍豪氣，怒濤飛上歌版。曾記烏帽靑衫，銅琶鐵綽，正斜陽秋晚。猛拍闌干翻變徵，不怕海風吹斷。孤鶴盤雲，瘦蛟掀浪，聽我紅牙按。數聲終徹，月輪空際圓滿。畫後復題壺中天一闋，即求拍正。醇士翊日又書。

印章：
習苦齋（白文方印）
鹿床（朱文方印）

鑑藏印章：
程（朱文圓印）
淸遺鑑藏（朱文方印）
容庚秘匧（白文方印）

Dai Xi

Qing dynasty 1801-1860

Zi Chunshi, *hao* Yu'an, Jingdong Jushi, Luchuang Jushi, native of Hangzhou, Zhejiang province. Dai was awarded the *jinshi* degree in the Daoguang era, and subsequently entered officialdom, rising to the rank of junior Vice-President of the Ministry of War. He retired to Hangzhou where he committed suicide in 1860 when the city was captured by the Taiping rebels. As a painter he specialized in landscapes, following the traditions of Wang Shimin and Wang Hui. He wrote a commentary on art entitled *Xikuzhai huaxu*.

91. Landscape

Dated 1846
Handscroll, ink and colour on silk
36.5 × 137.7 cm

With inscription, signature, 3 seals of the artist and 3 collectors' seals.

張之萬

清代　1811－1897

字子清。直隸南皮（河北天津）人。道光丁未（1847年）狀元，官至大學士。工畫山水，清秀蒼潤，近王石谷畫派，與戴熙並稱為"南戴北張"。

92. 今雨樓卷

絹本設色手卷　33.5×102厘米

引首：
今雨廔圖。紹香賢弟屬題。馮譽驥。

引首印章：
譽驥私印（白文方印）
仲艮（朱文方印）

款識：
舊雨軒圖，錢叔美先生為湘山觀察作也。兵火之後，遺址蕩然。少湘賢弟構軒，額曰："今雨"，繼述之思，有足稱者，屬余為圖，惜拙筆不足步叔美後塵耳。亦系一詩，即用叔美原韻：當日同岑緊異苔，於今堂構喜重開。故交漫感晨星沒，新詠都成今雨來。名墨尚存堪什襲，拈毫學步幾低徊。千霄更看龍孫長，預賀庭前進一杯。子青張之萬未定草。

印章：
張之萬（白文方印）

後幅題跋：
于紹湘自題（1875年），萬基、陳寶、于嗇之、于實之、馮譽驥、劉溎年、王棻、黃錫禧、顧雲臣等人題跋。

Zhang Zhiwan

Qing dynasty　1811-1897

Zi Ziqing, native of Nanpi, Hebei province. Zhang won the *zhuangyuan* (Principal Graduate) honour and his official career included the post of Grand Secretary in 1847. He was skilled in landscape painting, achievig an elegant style which is close to that of Wang Hui. Together with Dai Xi, the two were acclaimed as ''Dai of the South and Zhang of the North''.

92. *Jinyulou*

Handscroll, ink and colour on silk
33.5 × 102 cm

With inscription, signature and 1 seal of the artist. Frontispiece by Feng Yuji and 10 colophons on paper separate from painting.

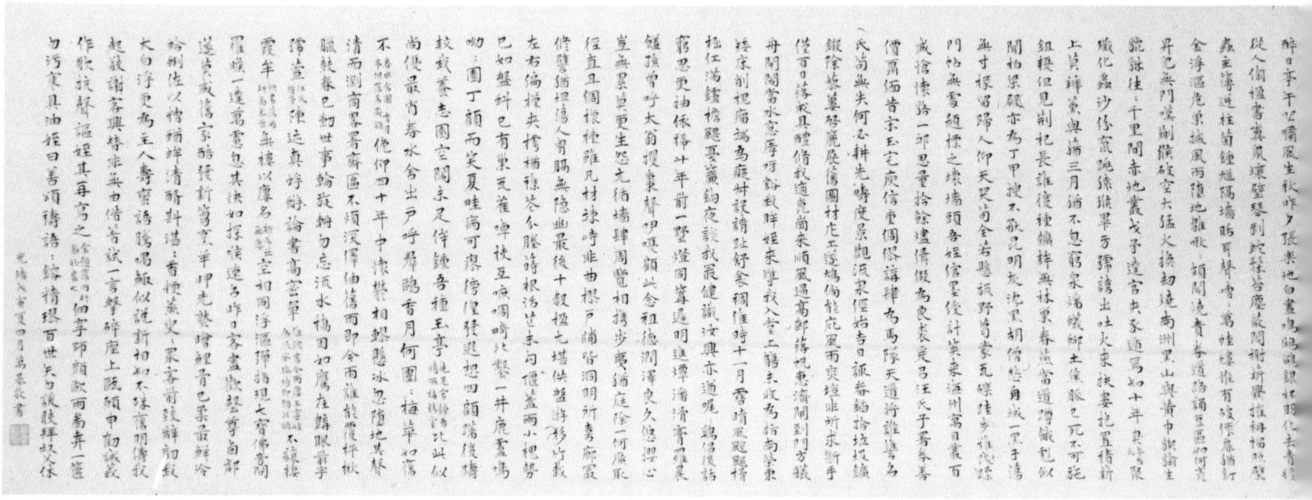

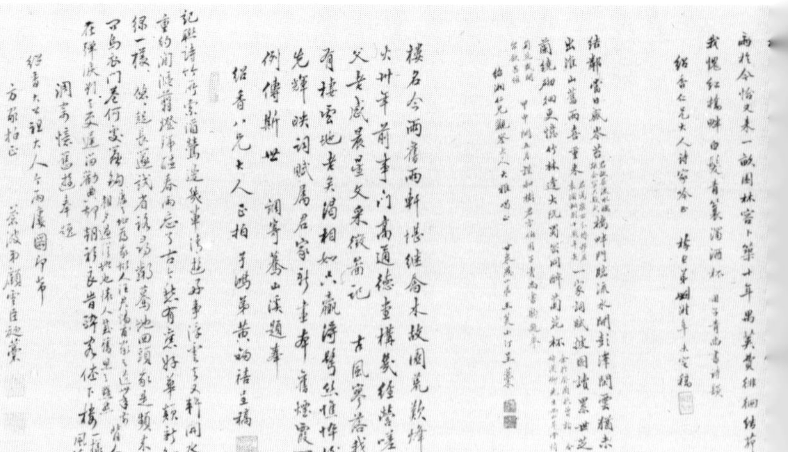

令雨廔圖
紹香賢弟屬題

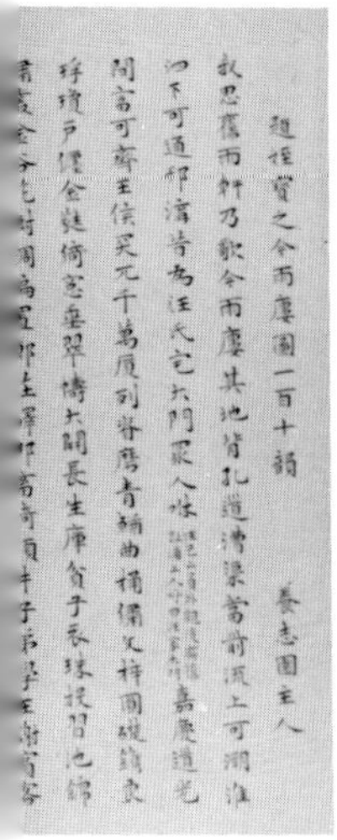

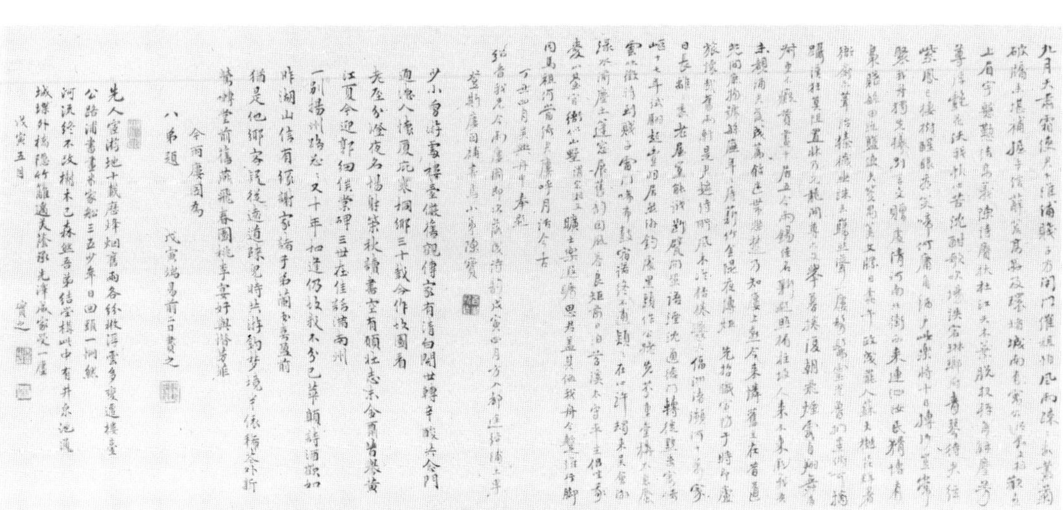

蘇六朋

清代　？－約1860

字枕琴，號怎道人。廣東順德南水人。工人物、山水、花鳥。早年學畫於羅浮山德堃和尚，長寓廣州賣畫。

93. 清平調圖

1833年作
紙本設色立軸　236×101.5厘米

此畫寫唐天寶年間，唐玄宗召李白作《清平調》之故事。屬蘇六朋早年作品。

款識：
癸巳（1833年）上元節，枕琴蘇六朋畫於麗春館。

印章：
蘇子朋（白文方印）
浮山樵子（白文方印）

Su Liupeng

Qing dynasty　?-ca.1860

Zi Zhenqin, *hao* Zendaoren, native of Shunde, Guangdong province. Su was a versatile painter of figures, landscapes, flowers and birds. In his early years he studied painting with Monk Dekun of Luofu Mountain. He subsequently took up residence in Guangzhou where he earned his living from the sale of his paintings.

93. Li Bai Composing the *Qingpingdiao*

Dated 1833
Hanging scroll, ink and colour on paper
236×101.5 cm

With inscription, signature and 2 seals of the artist.

蘇仁山

清代　1814－1849？

字靜甫，號長春，又號壽莊等。廣東順德杏壇人。少年才華過人，個性孤僻，作畫不受拘束，隨意揮毫，獨具一格。

94. 香積圖

紙本水墨立軸　166×58.3厘米

此圖白描羅漢仙女一羣，雲上地下共聚。左角石洞中一光頭少年石枱上作畫。香積本佛家故事，云維摩詰化作菩薩到衆香國化食，飯香熏毗耶離城，及三千大千世界。仁山此畫及所題識待考。此畫爲香港李凡夫先生捐贈。

款識(一)
香積圖。唐岱嘗作萬壑秋風起山水，故添其像於羅漢傍。又盧元素亦嘗作下人已乘黃鶴去句，作畫菊，故併繪之，以同拈花微笑意云爾。仁山附十九觀音於後。

印章：
長春（白文方印）
仁山（朱文方印）

款識(二)
沱江。仁山擬古。

印章：
靜甫（朱文長方印）

鑑藏印章：
李凡夫藏（朱文長方印）

Su Renshan

Qing dynasty　1814-1849?

Zi Jingfu, *hao* Changchun, Shouzhuang, native of Shunde, Guangdong province. Su was an artist whose talent was apparent at an early age. An ecentric in both personality and art, Su paid little attention to rules. His paintings demonstrate extraordinary originality and expressive power.

94. The *Xiangji* Story

Hanging scroll, ink on paper
166×58.3 cm

With inscription, signature, 3 seals of the artist and 1 collector's seal.

香積圖

趙之謙

清代　1829－1884

字撝叔，號悲盦。會稽（浙江紹興）人。咸豐己未（1859年）舉人，官江西鄱陽奉新縣。工詩文、篆刻、書法。畫以花卉木石見長，秉承徐渭、石濤、李鱓而獨具面目，開清末寫意花卉之風貌。

95. 五色牡丹圖

1870年作
紙本設色立軸　147×77.5厘米

此圖畫湖石後五色牡丹盛開。墨氣厚重，設色艷麗，色墨交融，自成一脉。爲畫家四十二歲時所作。

款識：
毓陔公祖大人法鑒。同治九年（1870）十月，趙之謙。

印章：
趙之謙印（白文方印）

Zhao Zhiqian

Qing dynasty　1829-1884

Zi Huishu, *hao* Bei'an, native of Kuaiqi (Shaoxing, Zhejiang province). Zhao was awarded the *juren* degree in 1859 and was appointed the magistrate of Fengxin and Poyang in Jiangxi. He was a renowned poet, calligrapher and seal engraver. In painting he was acclaimed to be the foremost painter of flowers in the late Qing period, fusing the traditions of Xu Wei, Yuanji and Li Shan with his study of calligraphy on *jinshi* (calligraphy engraved on bronze and stone).

95. Peonies in Five Colours

Dated 1870
Hanging scroll, ink and colour on paper
147×77.5 cm

With inscription, signature and 1 seal of the artist.

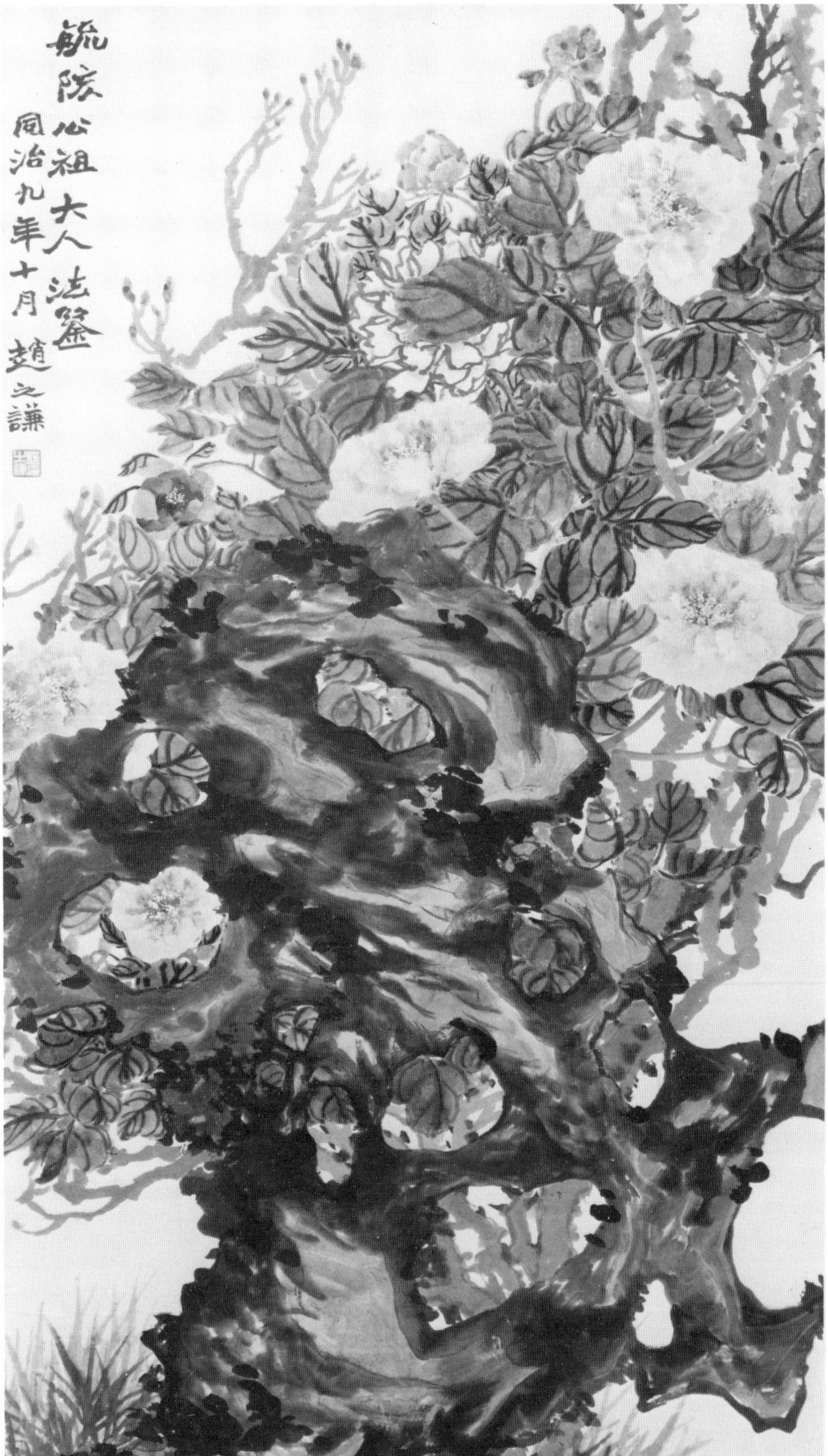
毓陔心祖大人法鋻
同治九年十月 趙之謙

任　熊

清代　1823－1857

字渭長。浙江蕭山人，居上海賣畫。工人物、山水、花鳥，學陳洪綬而有所變化。

96. 人物册

絹本設色册頁八開　各21.5×26.5厘米

(1) 管夫人像

款識：
陳無名有此管夫人象。

印章：
渭長（朱文方印）

(2) 老子像

款識：
永興任熊。

印章：
渭長（朱文方印）

(3) 養馬圖

款識：
曾見宋時院本，背臨之。

印章：
熊（朱文方印）

(4) 顧愷之像

款識：
何年顧虎頭。渭長法章矦畫。

印章：
渭長（朱文方印）

(5) 徐渭像

款識：
背摹青藤先生自寫照。渭長。

印章：
渭長（朱文長方印）

(6) 張芝像

款識：
陳章矦畫草聖。任熊背臨。

印章：
熊（朱文方印）

(7) 樂毅像

款識：
王鹿公搨樂毅像。任渭長臨畫並書。

印章：
熊（朱文方印）

(8) 仕女

款識：
渭長。

印章：
熊（朱文方印）

Ren Xiong

Qing dynasty　1823-1857

Zi Weichang, native of Xiaoshan, Zhejiang province. Ren lived in Shanghai as a professional painter. He was equally proficient in painting figures, landscapes, flowers and birds, in a personal style which was evolved from that of Chen Hongshou.

96. Album of Figure Painting

Album of eight leaves, ink and colour on silk
each leaf 21.5×26.5 cm

(1) Portrait of Madam Guan
With inscription and 1 seal of the artist.

(2) Portrait of Laozi
With inscription, signature and 1 seal of the artist.

(3) Horse and Groom
Same as leaf (1).

(4) Portrait of Gu Kaizhi
Same as leaf (2).

(5) Portrait of Xu Wei
Same as leaf (2).

(6) Portrait of Zhang Zhi
Same as leaf (2).

(7) Portrait of Le Yi
Same as leaf (2).

(8) Lady
With signature and 1 seal of the artist.

96.1

96.2

96.4

96.5

96.3

96.6

96.7

96.8

任 薰

清代　1835－1893

字阜長。浙江蕭山人。任熊弟，善畫人物、花鳥，學陳洪綬法。

97. 花鳥四屏

紙本設色立軸　各140×37.5厘米

(1) **孔雀牡丹**
款識：
阜長任薰寫。
印章：
任薰（白文方印）

(2) **雄鷄雁來紅竹石**
款識：
阜長任薰寫。
印章：
任薰（白文方印）

(3) **荷花鴛鴦**
款識：
阜長任薰。
印章：
任薰（白文方印）

(4) **白鷺蘆葦葵花**
款識：
任薰寫。

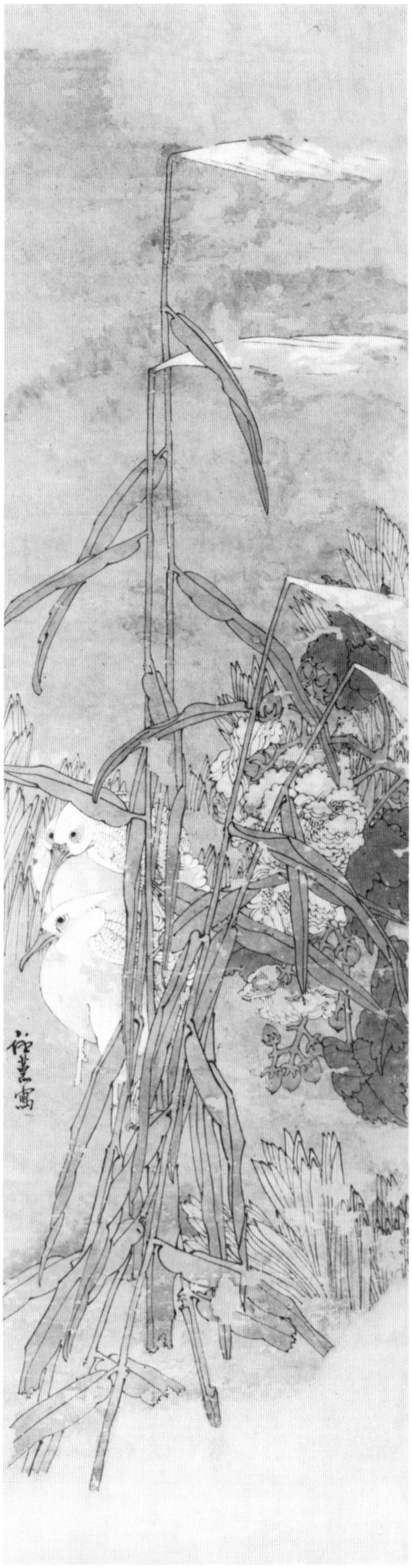

Ren Xun

Qing dynasty　1835-1893

Zi Fuchang, native of Xiaoshan, Zhejiang province. Ren was the younger brother of Ren Xiong who also based his figural style on that of Chen Hongshou. He was equally at ease with flower and bird painting.

97. Flowers and Birds

Set of four hanging scrolls,
ink and colour on paper
each scroll 140×37.5 cm

(1) Peacock and Peonies
With signature and 1 seal of the artist.
(2) Cock and Tricolour Amaranth
Same as scroll (1).
(3) Mandarin Ducks in Lotus Pond
Same as scroll (1).
(4) Herons by the Reeds
With signature of the artist.

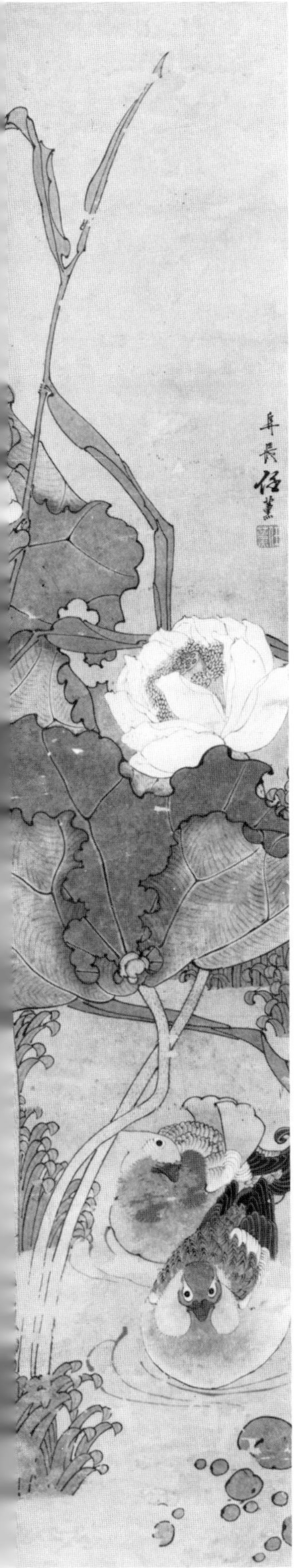
阜長任薰
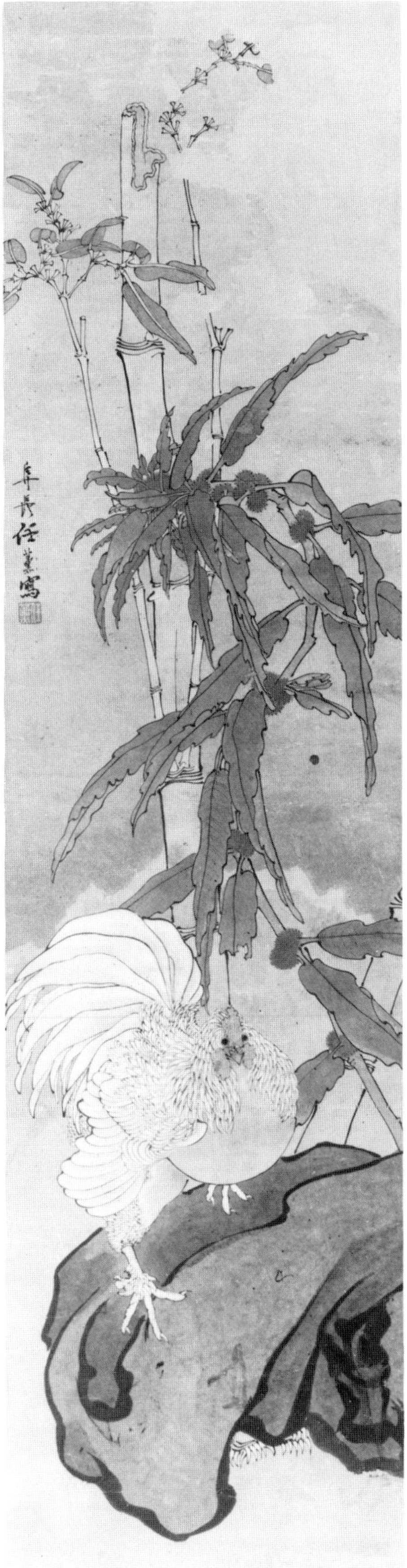
阜長任薰寫

阜長任薰寫

任　頤

清代　1840－1896

初名潤，字小樓，後改字伯年。山陰（浙江紹興）人。工畫人物、肖像、花鳥。任熊弟子，風格豪邁縱放。居上海賣畫，後人稱爲"上海派"。

98. 湔裙仕女圖

紙本設色立軸　145×35厘米

此圖畫仕女河邊湔裙，設色清雅，筆墨秀逸。爲仕女四屏之一。

款識：
伯年。

印章：
任頤長壽（白文方印）

鑑藏印章：
半閒廬方珍藏書畫（朱文方印）
方氏梅孫眞賞古今名人書畫之印（朱文方印）

Ren Yi

Qing dynasty　1840-1896

Qriginal name Run, *zi* Xiaolou, later Bonian, native of Shanyin (Shaoxing, Zhejiang province). Ren was a student of Ren Xiong and was skilled in painting figures, portraits, flowers and birds, in a refreshing style that broke away from traditional restraint. He lived in Shanghai as a professional painter. He was generally acclaimed as the most influential figure in the Shanghai School of painting.

98. Lady Laundering

Hanging scroll, ink and colour on paper
145 × 35 cm

With signature, 1 seal of the artist and 2 collectors' seals.

吳昌碩

清代　1844－1927

名俊卿，晚以字行，號缶翁。安吉（浙江湖州）人。工金石、書畫，善畫花卉，落筆豪放渾厚，自成風格。

99. 墨竹圖

1900年作
紙本水墨立軸　180×47.5厘米

此圖水墨畫風竹，挺拔渾重中兼具動感，乃吳氏五十七歲之作。

款識(一)
山頭雪霽雲橫屼，劍門插天衰陽殘。碧烟隨風吹欲墜，卻是抱巖秋竹竿。荒厓寂寞行深，竹氛一碧纏衣襟。吟聲斷續欸聲作，引得天風來和琴。庚子（1900年）長至節並錄舊作。"行"下奪"徑"字。

印章：
俊卿之印（朱文方印）
倉碩（白文方印）

款識(二)
慕川仁兄先生正寫，吳俊卿。

印章：
湖州安吉縣（白文方印）

Wu Changshi

Qing dynasty　1844-1927

Original name Junqing, *zi* Changshi, *hao* Fouweng, native of Anji (Huzhou, Zhejiang province). A renowned calligrapher and painter, Wu was particularly famous for his flower paintings. His powerful personal style owes a great deal to his profound knowledge of archaic scripts and calligraphic styles as found on bronze and stone.

99. Bamboo in Wind

Dated 1900
Hanging scroll, ink on paper
180×47.5 cm

With inscription, signature and 3 seals of the artist.

主要參攷書目（中文）

1. 《上海博物館藏明清摺扇書畫集》。上海人民美術出版社，1983。
2. 《上海博物館藏畫》。上海人民美術出版社，1959。
3. 于安瀾編：《畫史叢書》，全五册。上海人民美術出版社，1963。
4. 于安瀾編：《畫論叢刊》，全二册。北京人民美術出版社，1962。
5. 中國古代書畫鑒定組鑒選：《中國古代書畫精品錄一》。北京文物出版社，1984。
6. 中國書畫研究會：《中國名畫家叢書》，全二册。香港，1970。
7. 《中國歷代繪畫—天津市藝術博物館藏畫一》。天津人民美術出版社，1985。
8. 孔廣陶：《嶽雪樓書畫錄》，陳其錕序於咸豐十一年（1861）。〔廣州〕三十有三萬卷堂，1889。
9. 王伯敏：《中國繪畫史》。上海人民美術出版社，1982。
10. 四川省博物館編：《明清扇面選》。四川人民美術出版社，1983。
11. 《朵雲》。上海書畫出版社，第一集— （1981— ）。
12. 江兆申：《文徵明與蘇州畫壇》。臺北國立故宮博物院，1977。
13. 吳榮光：《辛丑銷夏記》，序於清道光二十一年（1841）。光緒三十一年（1905）刻本。
14. 汪世清：《清初四大畫僧合考》，《香港中文大學·中國文化研究所學報》，第15卷（1984）。
15. 汪世淸、汪聰合編：《漸江資料集》。合肥安徽人民出版社，1984年修訂本。
16. 李佐賢：《書畫鑑影》。淸同治十年（1871）刋本。
17. 《明淸人題跋》，全二册。《藝術叢編》，第一集。臺北世界書局，1968。
18. 《南京博物院藏畫集》。北京文物出版社，1966。
19. 《故宮博物院藏花鳥畫選》。北京文物出版社，1981。
20. 故宮博物院編：《明代宮廷與浙派繪畫選集》。北京文物出版社，1983。
21. 香港中文大學文物館編：《至樂樓藏明遺民書畫》。香港，1975。
22. 香港中文大學文物館編：《故宮博物院藏清代揚州畫家作品》。香港，1984。
23. 香港博物美術館編：《明淸繪畫展覽》。香港市政局，1970。
24. 香港藝術館編：《中國文物集珍——敏求精舍銀禧紀念展覽》。香港市政局，1985。
25. 徐邦達：《歷代書畫家傳記考辨》。上海人民美術出版社，1983。
26. 徐邦達：《古書畫僞訛考辨》，全四册。江蘇古籍出版社，1984。
27. 國立故宮博物院編：《吳派畫九十年展》。臺北，1975。
28. 國立故宮博物院編：《明淸之際名畫特展》。臺北，1970。
29. 國立故宮博物院編：《晚明變形主義畫家作品展》。臺北，1977。
30. 國立故宮博物院及國立中央博物院：《故宮名畫三百種》。臺中，1959。
31. 國立歷史博物館編：《明代沈周唐寅文徵明仇英四大家書畫集》。臺北，1984。
32. 國立歷史博物館：《漸江石濤八大山人書畫集》。臺北，1978。
33. 張大千編：《大風堂名蹟》，四册。京都便利堂，1955－56。
34. 張萬里及胡仁牧合編：《八大山人書畫集》，二册。香港開發公司，1969。
35. 張萬里、胡仁牧合編：《石濤書畫集》，六册。香港開發公司，1969。
36. 張萬里及胡仁牧合編：《揚州八怪書畫集》，八册。香港開發公司，1970。
37. 張萬里及胡仁牧合編：《漸江畫集》。香港開發公司，1969。
38. 《虛白齋藏書畫選》。東京二玄社，1983。
39. 黃賓虹、鄧實編：《美術叢書》。上海神州國光社，1928。
40. 楊新：《程正揆》，《中國畫家叢書》。上海人民美術出版社，1982。
41. 董其昌：《畫禪室隨筆》，楊無輯。上海進步書屋，192－？。
42. 《虞初新志》。上海大連圖書供應社，1934。
43. 劉綱紀：《龔賢》，《中國畫家叢書》。上海人民美術出版社，1981。
44. 《廣州美術館藏書畫選集》，即《藝苑掇英》，第十六期（1982年4月）。
45. 《廣州美術館藏書畫選集》第二集，即《藝苑掇英》，第二十五期（1985年2月）。
46. 鄭拙廬：《石濤研究》。北京人民美術出版社，1961。
47. 鄭德坤、饒宗頤、屈志仁合編：《明遺民書畫研討會記錄》，《香港中文大學·中國文化研究所學報》第八卷第二期（1976年12月）。
48. 鄭錫珍：《弘仁、髡殘》，《中國畫家叢書》。上海人民美術出版社，1979。
49. 穆孝天：《查士標》，《中國畫家叢書》。上海人民美術出版社，1980。
50. 謝蘭生：《常惺惺齋書畫題跋》。澳門文集圖書公司，1974？。
51. 《藝林叢錄》，十册。香港商務印書館，1961－74。
52. 《藝苑掇英》，上海人民美術出版社，第一期—，（1978年8月— ）。

Selected Bibliography (in English)

1. Bush, Susan and Christian Murck, eds. *Theories of the Arts in China*. Princetion: Princeton University Press, 1983.

2. Cahill, James. *The Compelling Image: Nature and Style in Seventeenth-century Chinese Painting*. Cambridge, Mass.: Harvard University Press, 1982.

3. Cahill, James, *Fantastics and Eccentrics in Chinese Painting*. New York: Asia House, 1967.

4. Cahil, James. *Parting at the Shore: Chinese Painting of the Early and Middle Ming Dynasty*. New York and Tokyo: Weatherhill, 1976.

5. Cahill, James, ed. *The Restless Landscape: Chinese Painting of the Late Ming Period*. Berkeley: University Art Museum, 1971.

6. Cahill, James, ed. *Shadows of Mt. Huang: Chinese Painting and Printing of the Anhui School*. Berkeley: University Art Museum, 1981.

7. Capon, Edmund and Mae Anna Pang. *Chinese Paintings of the Ming and Qing Dynasties, 14th-20th Century*. Victoria: International Cultural Corporation of Australia Limited, 1981.

8. Chou, Ju-hsi and Claudia Brown. *The Elegant Brush: Chinese Painting under the Qianlong Emperor 1735-1795*. Phoenix: Phoenix Art Museum, 1985.

9. Contag, Victoria. *Chinese Masters of the 17th Century*. Tr. by Michael Bullock. London: Lund Humphries, 1969.

10. Dubosc, Jean-Pierre. *Great Chinese Painters of the Ming and Ch'ing Dynasties*. New York: Wildenstein galleries, 1949.

11. Ecke, Tseng Yu-ho. *Poetry on the Wind: The Art of Chinese Folding Fans from the Ming and Ch'ing Dynasties*. Hawaii: Honolulu Academy of Arts, 1981.

12. Edwards, Richard, ed. *The Painting of Tao-chi*. Ann Arbor: University of Michigan Museum of Art, 1967.

13. *Eight Dynasties of Chinese Painting: The Collections of the Nelson Gallery-Atkins Museum, Kansas City, and the Cleveland Museum of Art*. Essays by Wai-kam Ho, Sherman E. Lee, Laurence Sickman and Marc F. Wilson. Cleveland: Cleveland Museum of Art, 1980.

14. Fong, Wen C. et al. *Images of the Mind: Selections from the Edward L. Elliott Family and John B. Elliott Collections of Chinese Calligraphy and Painting at the Art Museum, Princeton Univeristy*. Princeton: The Art Museum, Princeton University and Princeton Unviersity Press, 1984.

15. Fu, Marilyn and Fu Shen. *Studies in Connoisseurship: Chinese Paintings from the Arthur M. Sackler Collection in New York and Princeton*. Princeton: Princeton University Art Museum, 1973.

16. Hyland, Alice R.M. *The Literati Vision: Sixteenth Century Wu School Painting and Calligraphy*. Memphis: Memphis Brooks Museum of Art, 1984.

17. Lee, Sherman E. *Chinese Landscape Painting*. Rev. ed. Cleveland: Cleveland Museum of Art, 1962.

18. Lee, Sherman E. "*Some Problems in Ming and Ch'ing Landscape Painting*", *Ars Orientalis* II (1957), 471-85.

19. Li Chu-tsing. *A Thousand Peaks and Myriad Ravines: Chinese Paintings in the Charles A. Drenowatz Collection*. 2 vols. (Artibus Asiae Supplementum, XXX). Ascona, 1974.

20. Loehr, Max. *Chinese Painting after Sung*. New Haven: Yale University, 1976

21. Murck, Christian F., ed. *Artists and Traditons; Uses of the Past in Chinese Culture*. Princeton Unviersity, 1976.

22. Museum of Fine Arts, Boston. *Chinese Paintings in the Museum (Yuan to Ch'ing Periods)*. Boston, 1961.

23. Natonal Palace Museum, Taipei. *Proceedings of the International Symposium on Chinese Painting*. Taipei, 1972.

24. Siren, Osvald. *Chinese Painting: Leading Masters and Principles*. 7 vols. Reprint ed. New York: Hacker Art Books, 1973

25. Sullivan, Michael. *Symbols of Eternity: The Art of Landscape Painting in China.* Stanford: Stanford University Press, 1979.

26. Suzuki Kei, comp. *Comprehensive Illustrated Catalogue of Chinese Paintings.* 5 vols. Tokyo: Unviersity of Tokyo Press, 1982-83.

27. Whitfield, Roderick, ed. *In Pursuit of Antiquity: Chinese Paintings of the Ming and Ch'ing Dynasties from the Collection of Mr. and Mrs. Earl Morse.* Princeton: The Art Museum, Princeton Univeristy, 1969.

28. Wilson, Marc F. and Kwan S. Wong. *Friends of Wen Cheng-ming: A View from the Crawford Colection.* New York: China House Gallery, 1974.

廣州美術館藏明清繪畫

出版：廣州美術館
香港中文大學文物館

承印：香港明愛印刷訓練中心

國際統一書碼：962-7101-07-9

一九八六年十月初版

Paintings of the Ming and Qing Dynasties from the Guangzhou Art Gallery

ISBN 962-7101-07-9

Printed by Caritas Printing Training Centre, Hong Kong.